TiME ZONE J

JULiE DOUCET

DRAWN & QUARTERLY

THIS BOOK WAS DRAWN FROM BOTTOM TO TOP.
PLEASE READ ACCORDINGLY.

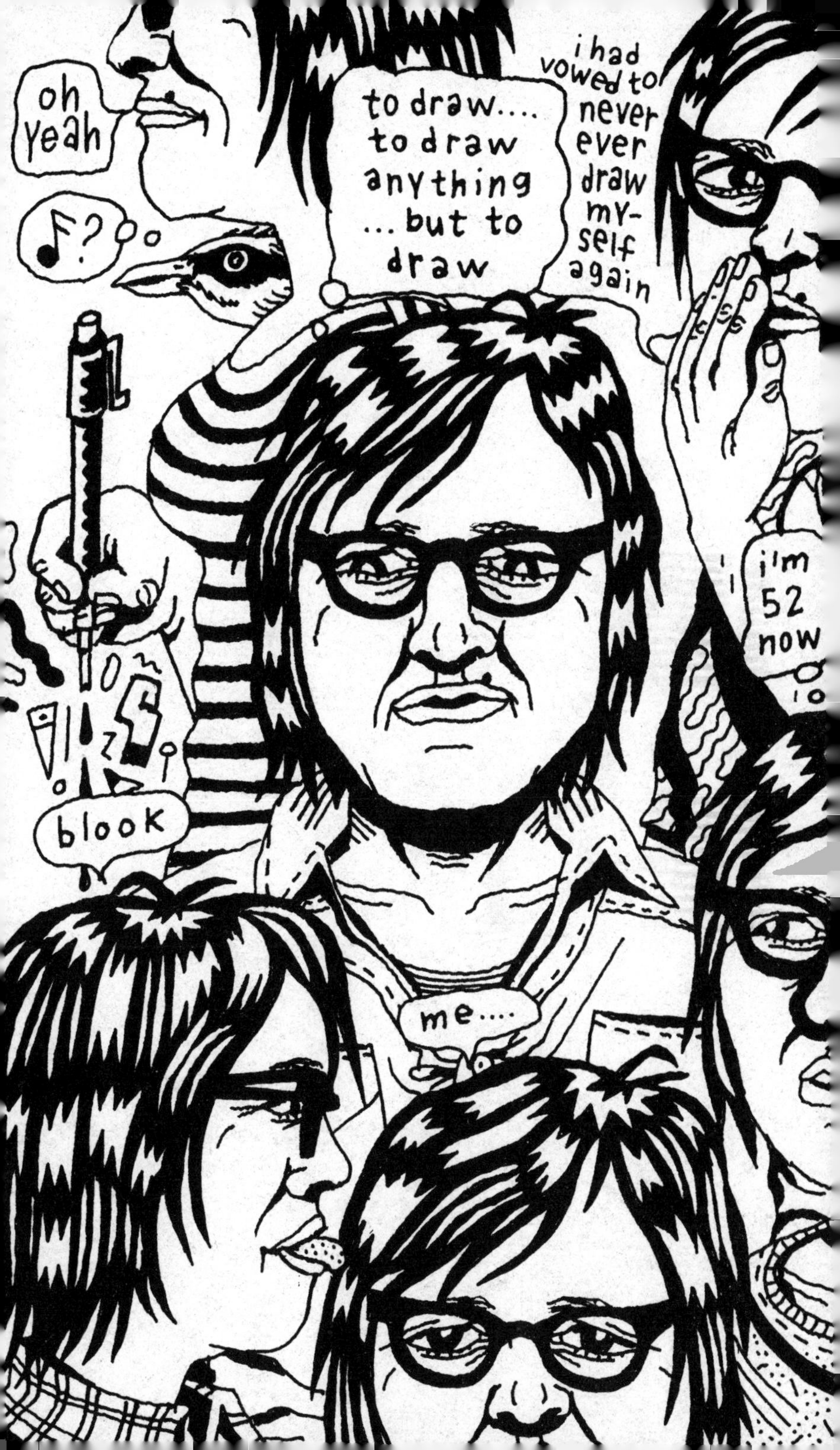
oh yeah
?
to draw.... to draw anything ...but to draw
i had vowed to never ever draw my-self again
i'm 52 now
blook
me....

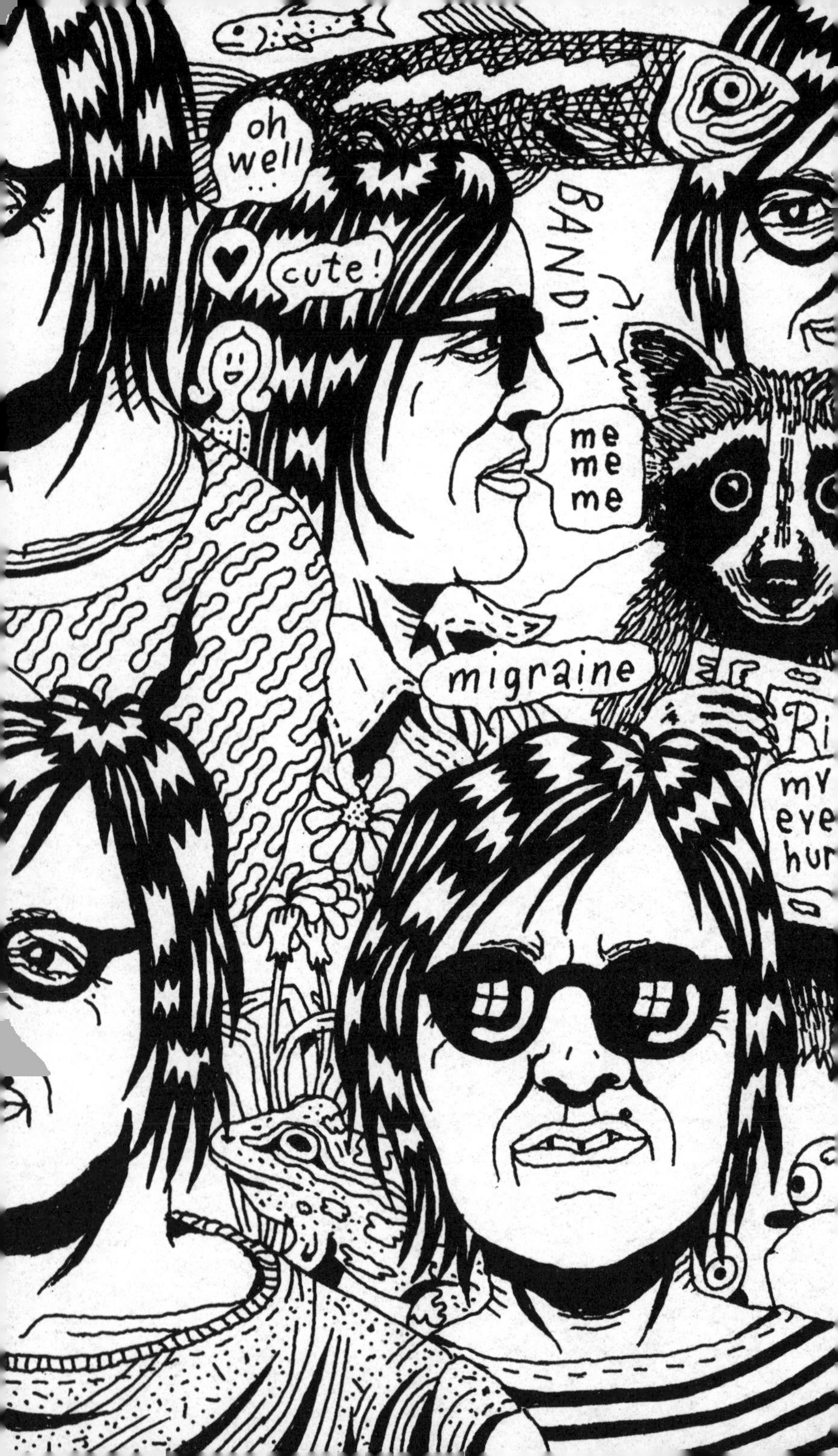
oh well ...
cute!
BANDIT
me me me
migraine
Ri
my eye hur

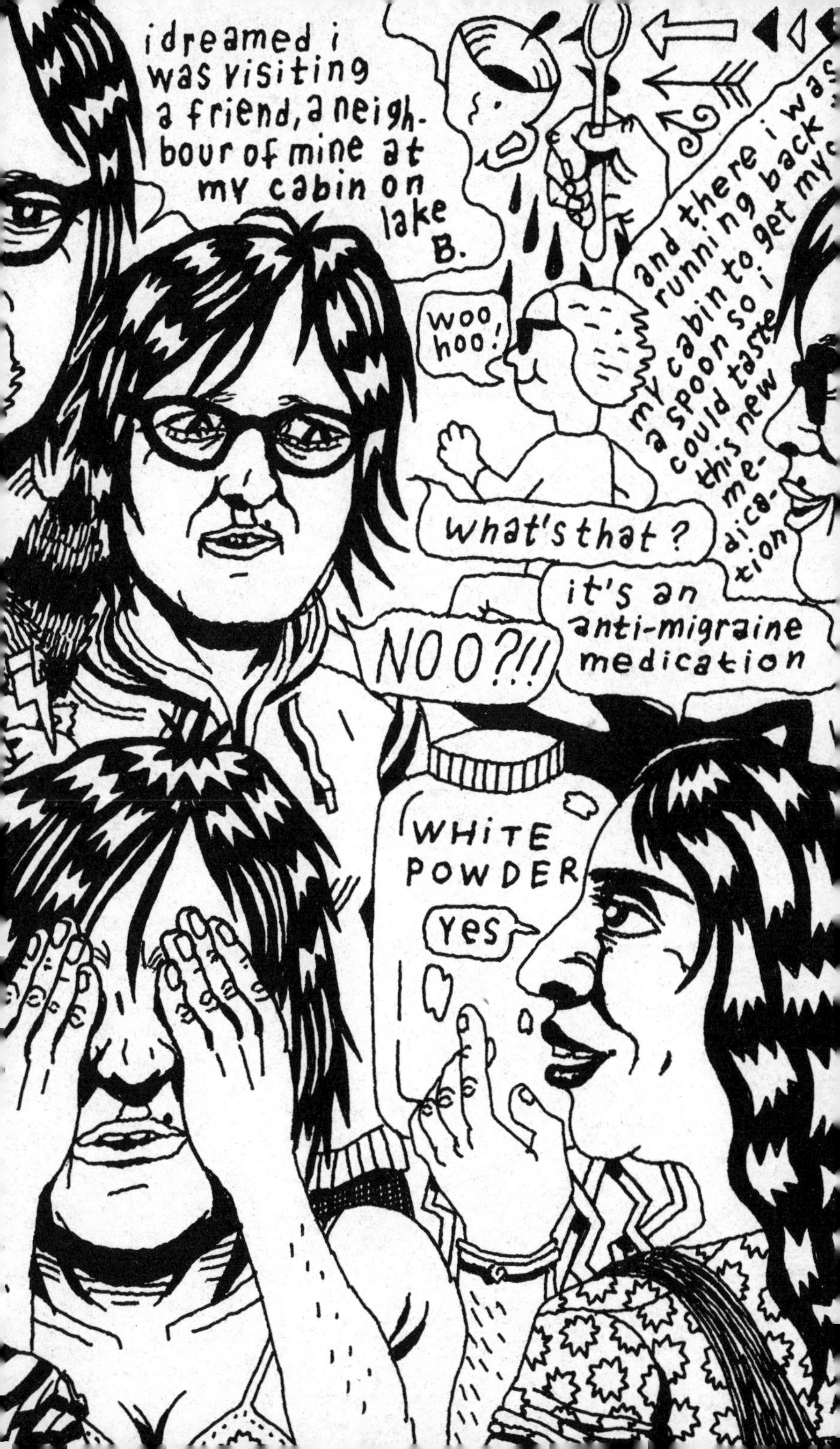

idreamed i was visiting a friend, a neighbour of mine at my cabin on lake B.
and there i was running back to my cabin to get my a spoon so i could taste this new medication
woo hoo!
what's that?
it's an anti-migraine medication
NOO?!!
WHITE POWDER
yes

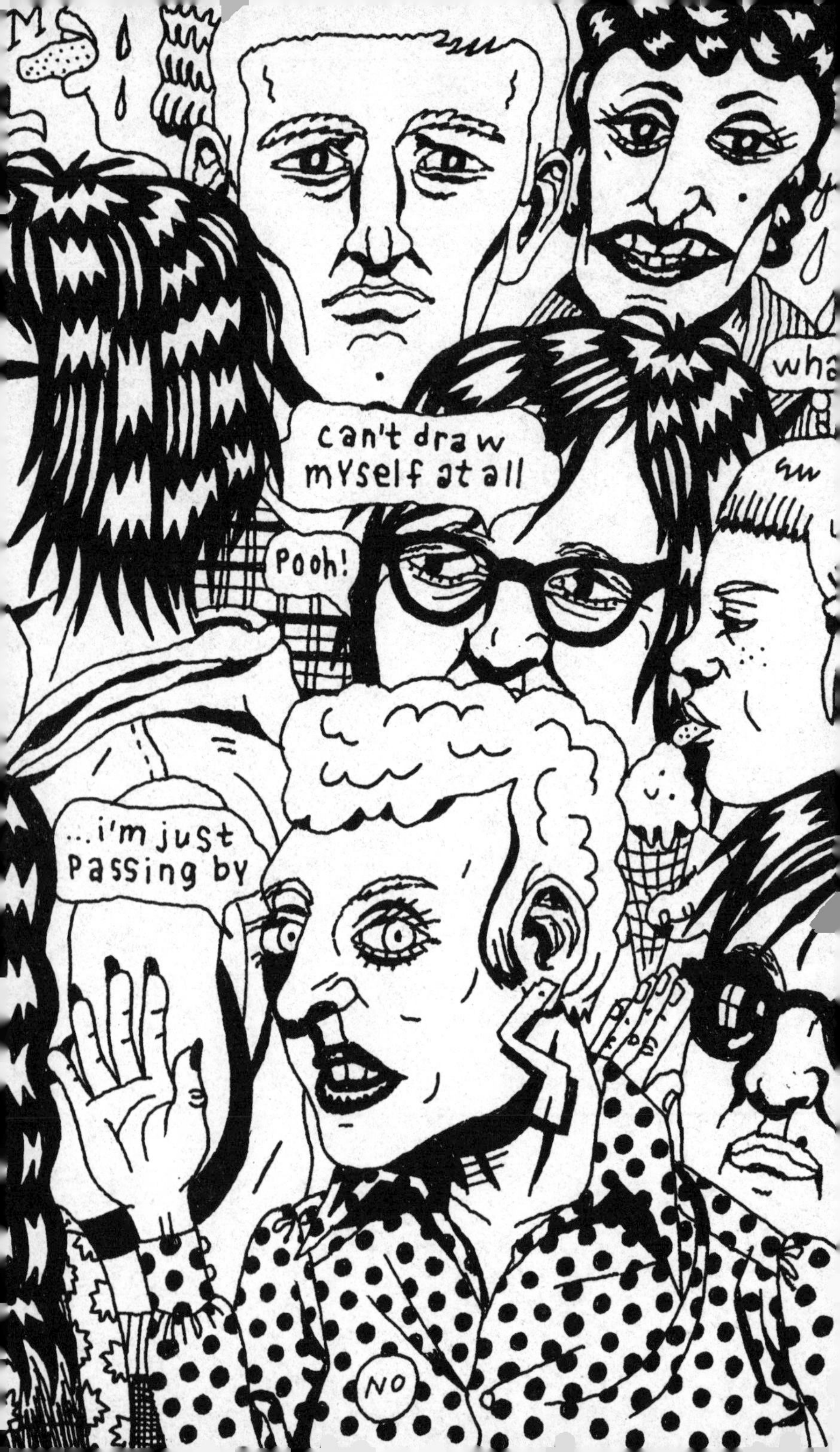
can't draw myself at all
Pooh!
wha
...i'm just passing by
NO

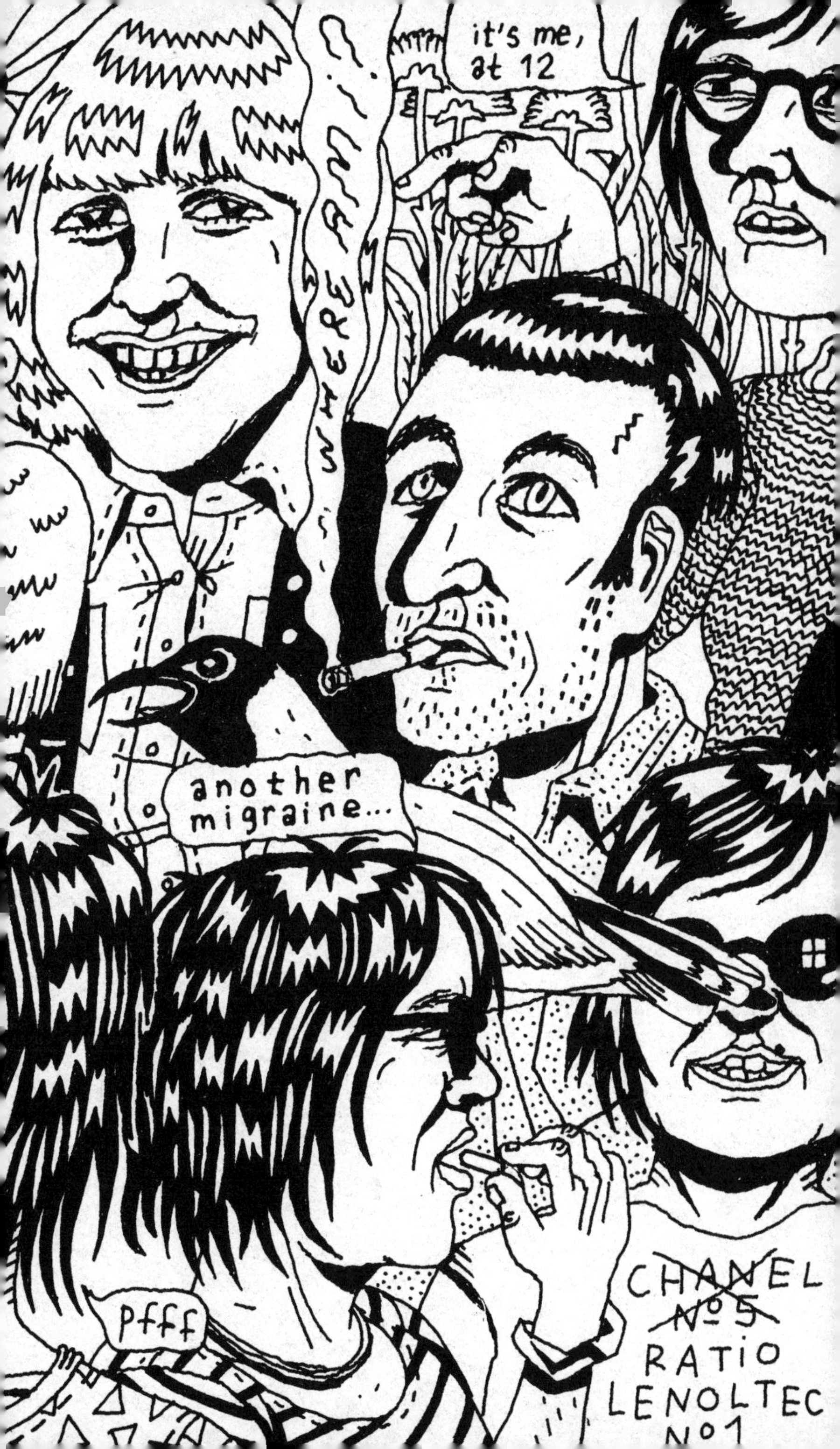
it's me, at 12
another migraine...
pfff
CHANEL
№5
RATIO
LENOLTEC
№1

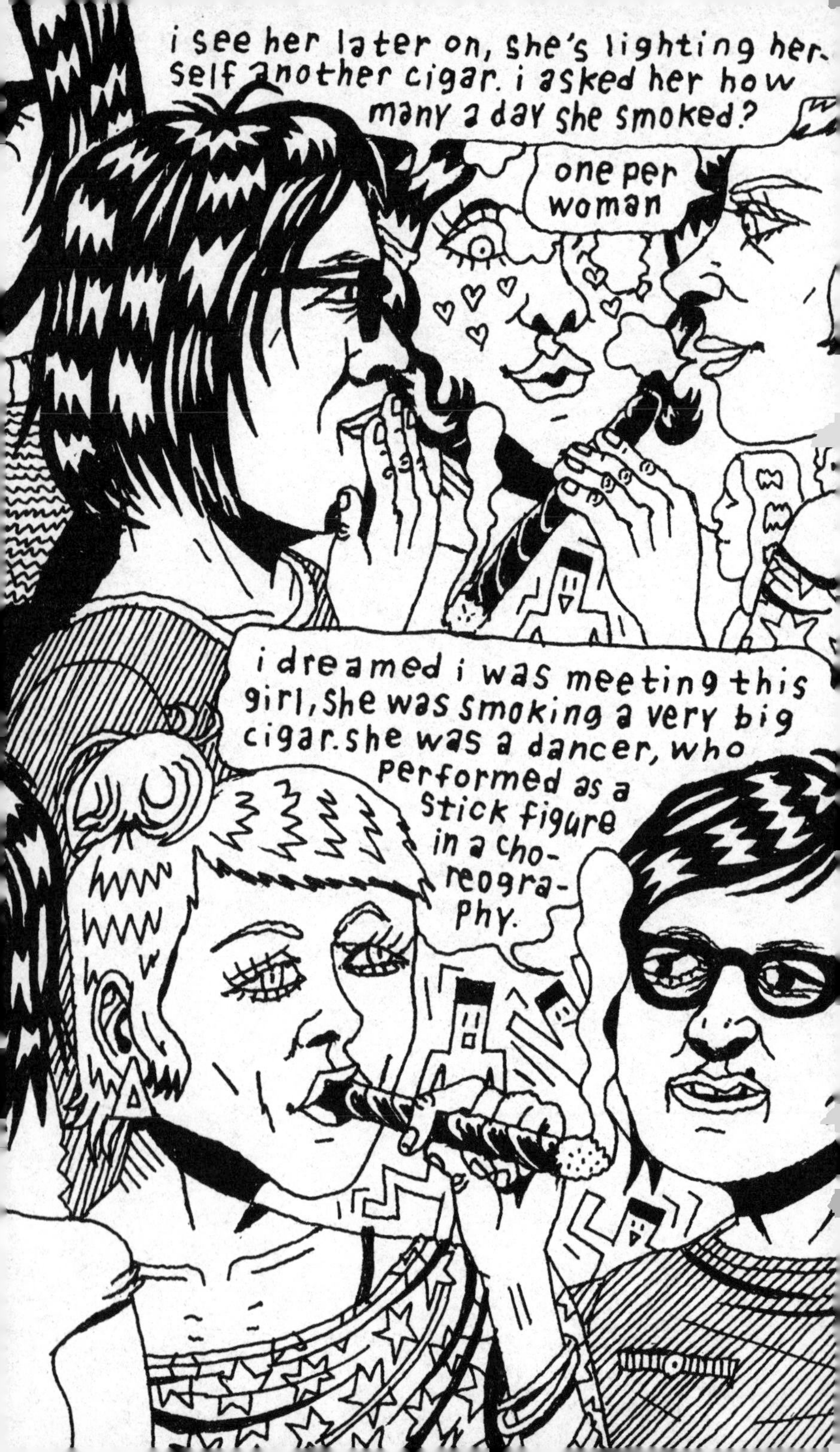
i see her later on, she's lighting herself another cigar. i asked her how many a day she smoked?
one per woman
i dreamed i was meeting this girl, she was smoking a very big cigar. she was a dancer, who performed as a stick figure in a choreography.

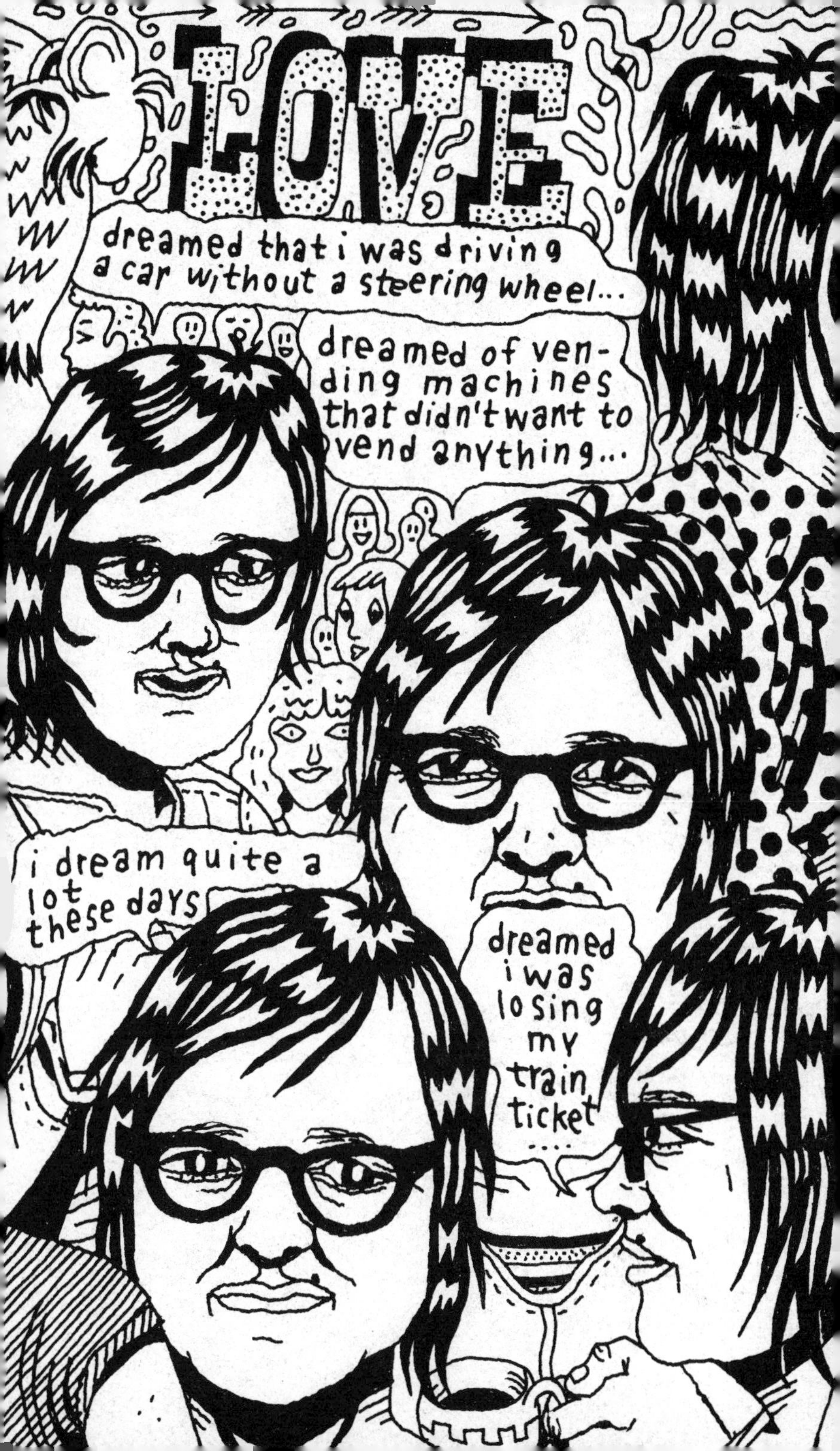
LOVE
dreamed that i was driving a car without a steering wheel...
dreamed of ven-ding machines that didn't want to vend anything...
i dream quite a lot these days
dreamed i was losing my train ticket ...

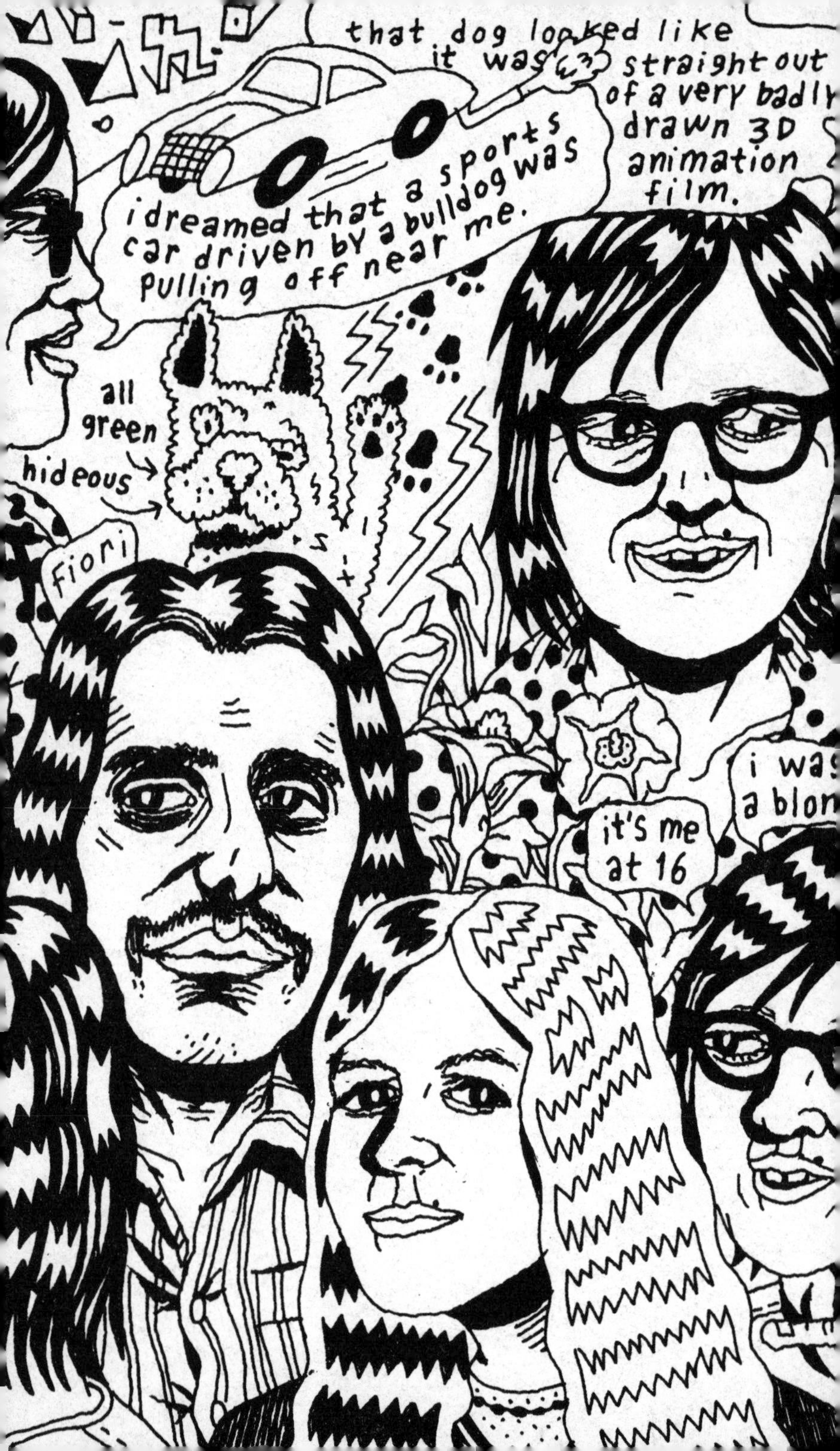
i dreamed that a sports car driven by a bulldog was pulling off near me.
that dog looked like it was straight out of a very badly drawn 3D animation film.
all green
hideous
fiori
it's me at 16
i was a blon

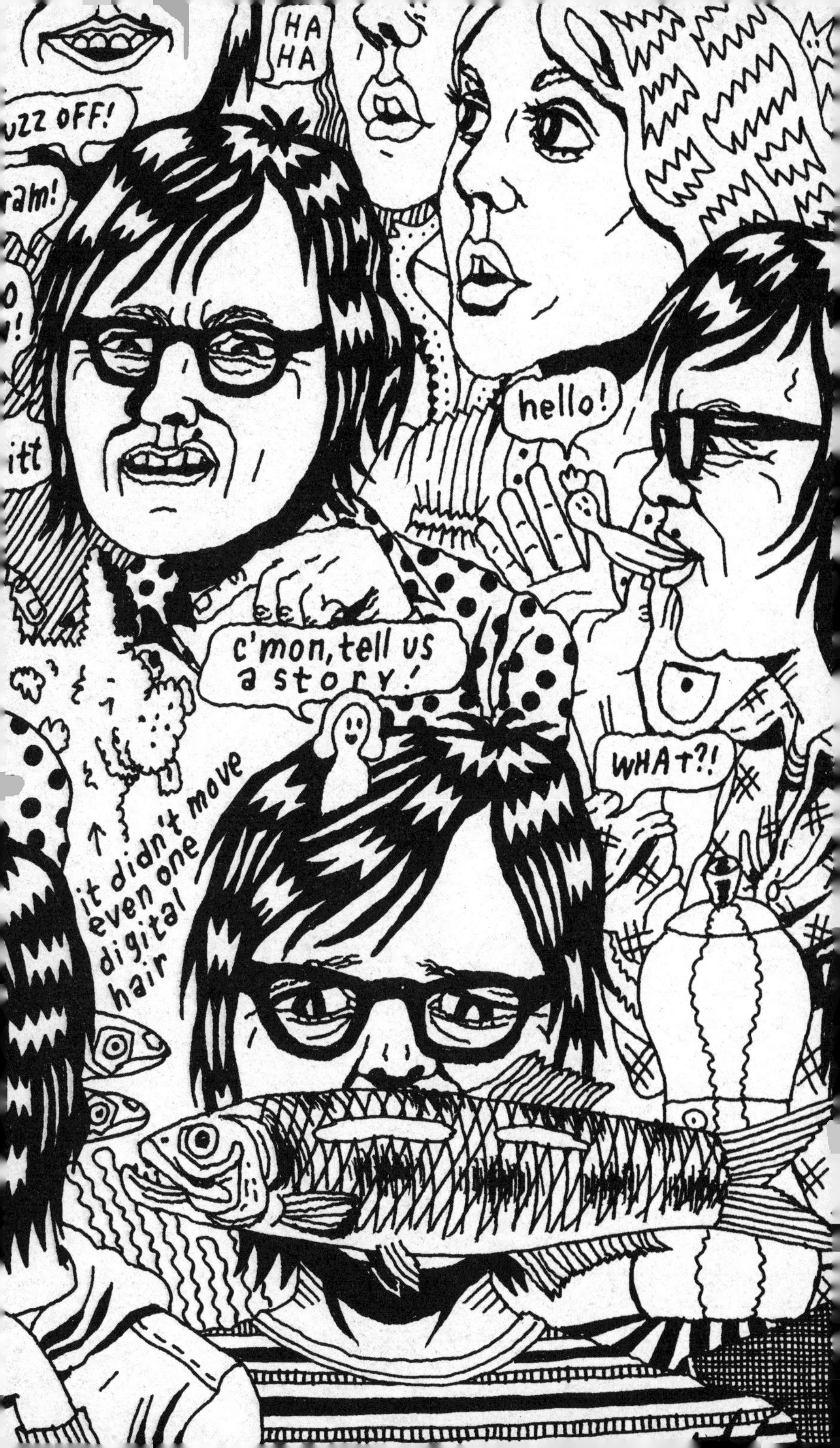
HA HA
uzz OFF!
ram!
itt
hello!
c'mon, tell us a story!
WHAT?!
it didn't move even one digital hair

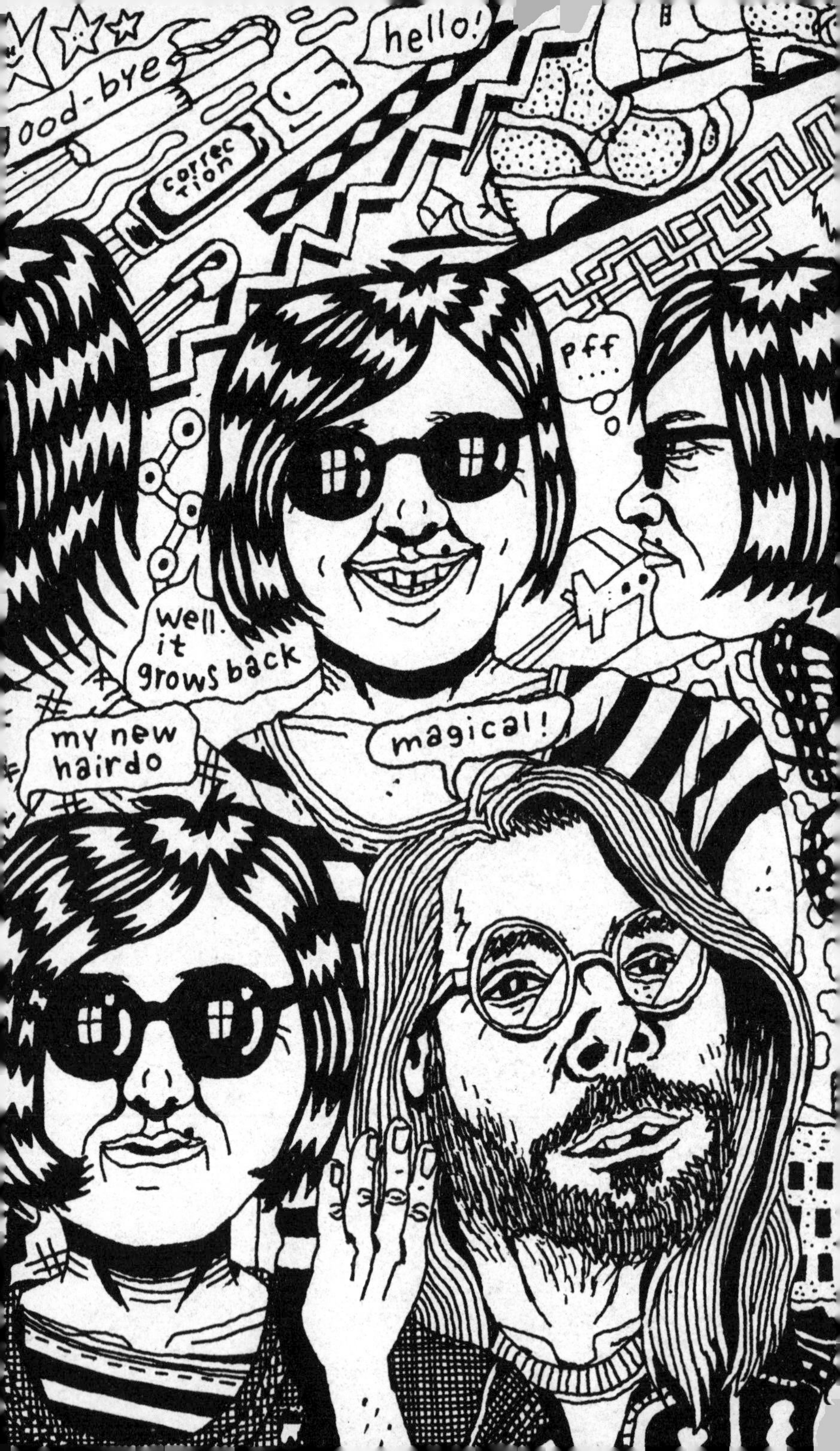

ood-bye
hello!
correc tion
pff ....
well. it grows back
my new hairdo
magical!

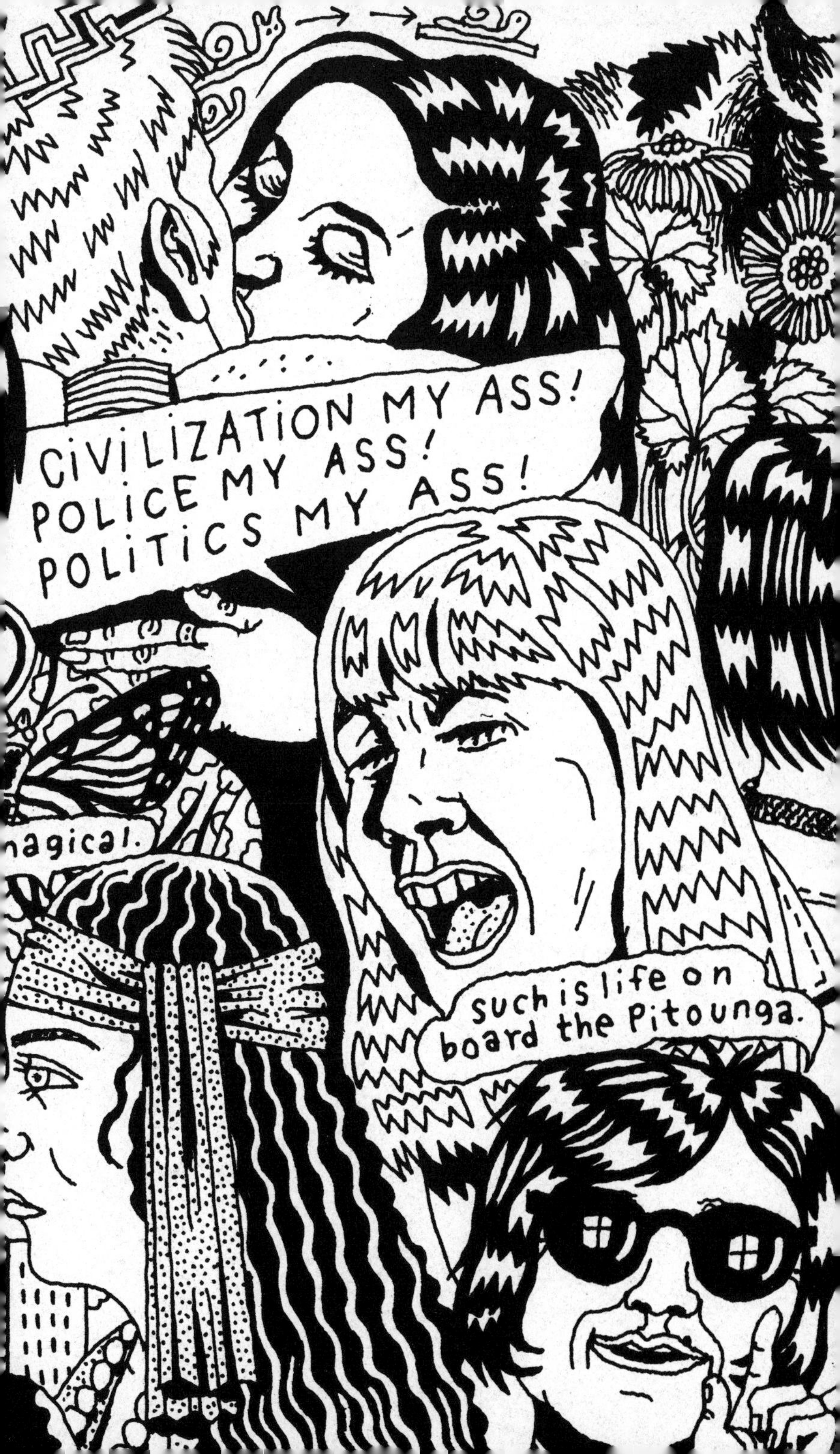
CIVILIZATION MY ASS!
POLICE MY ASS!
POLITICS MY ASS!
nagical.
such is life on board the Pitounga.

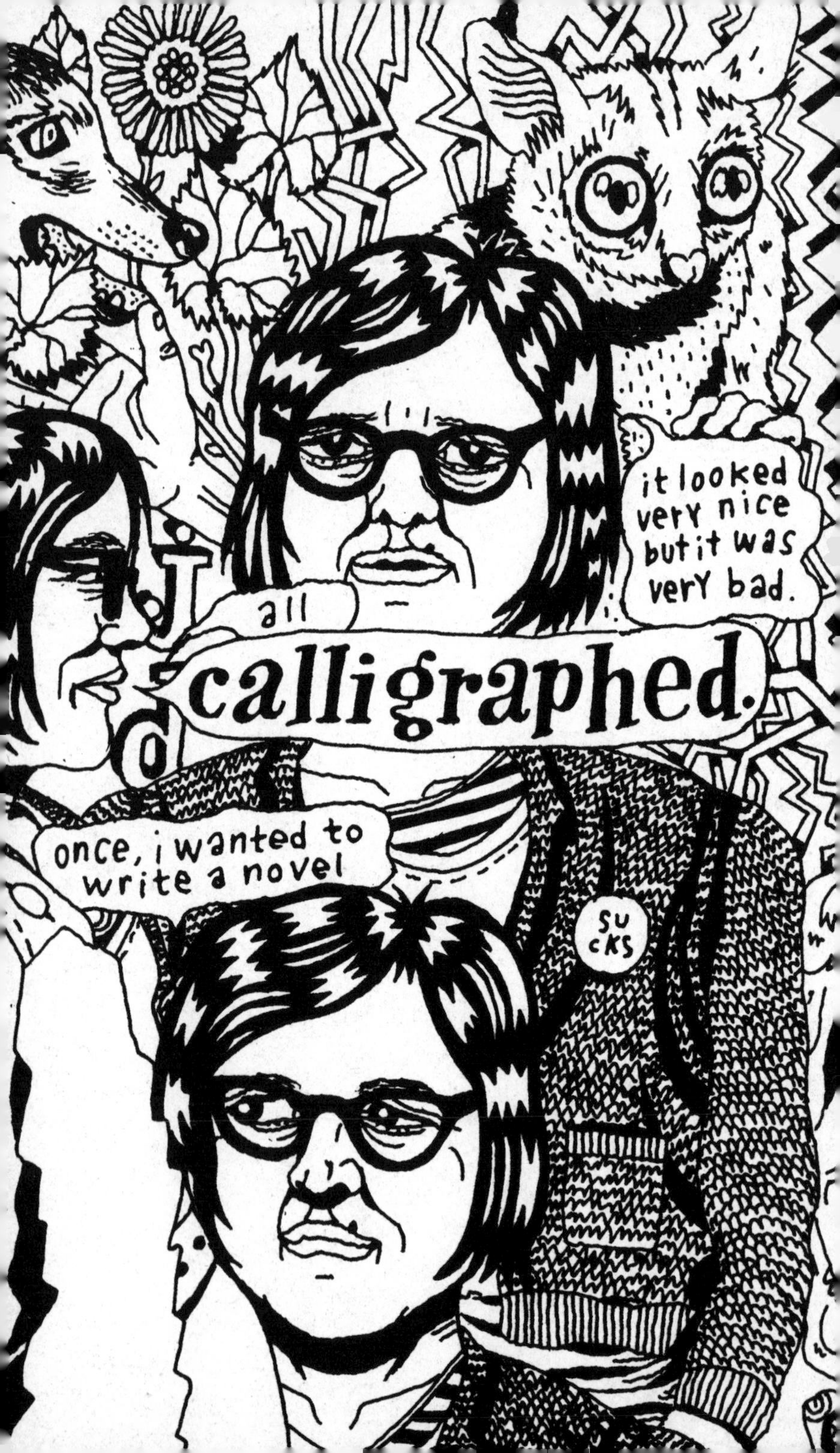

it looked very nice but it was very bad.
all calligraphed.
once, i wanted to write a novel
su cks

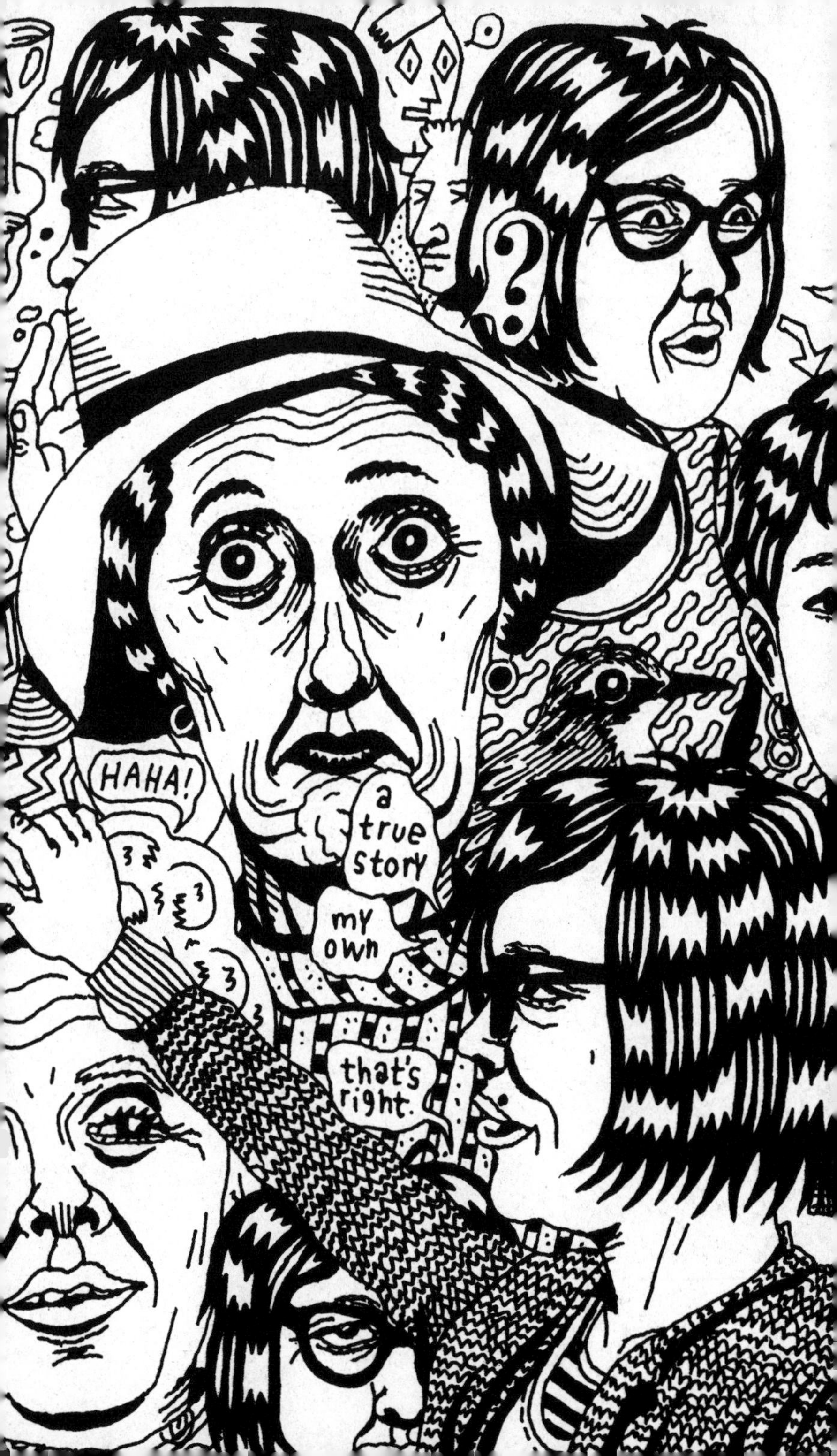
HAHA!
a true story
my own
that's right.

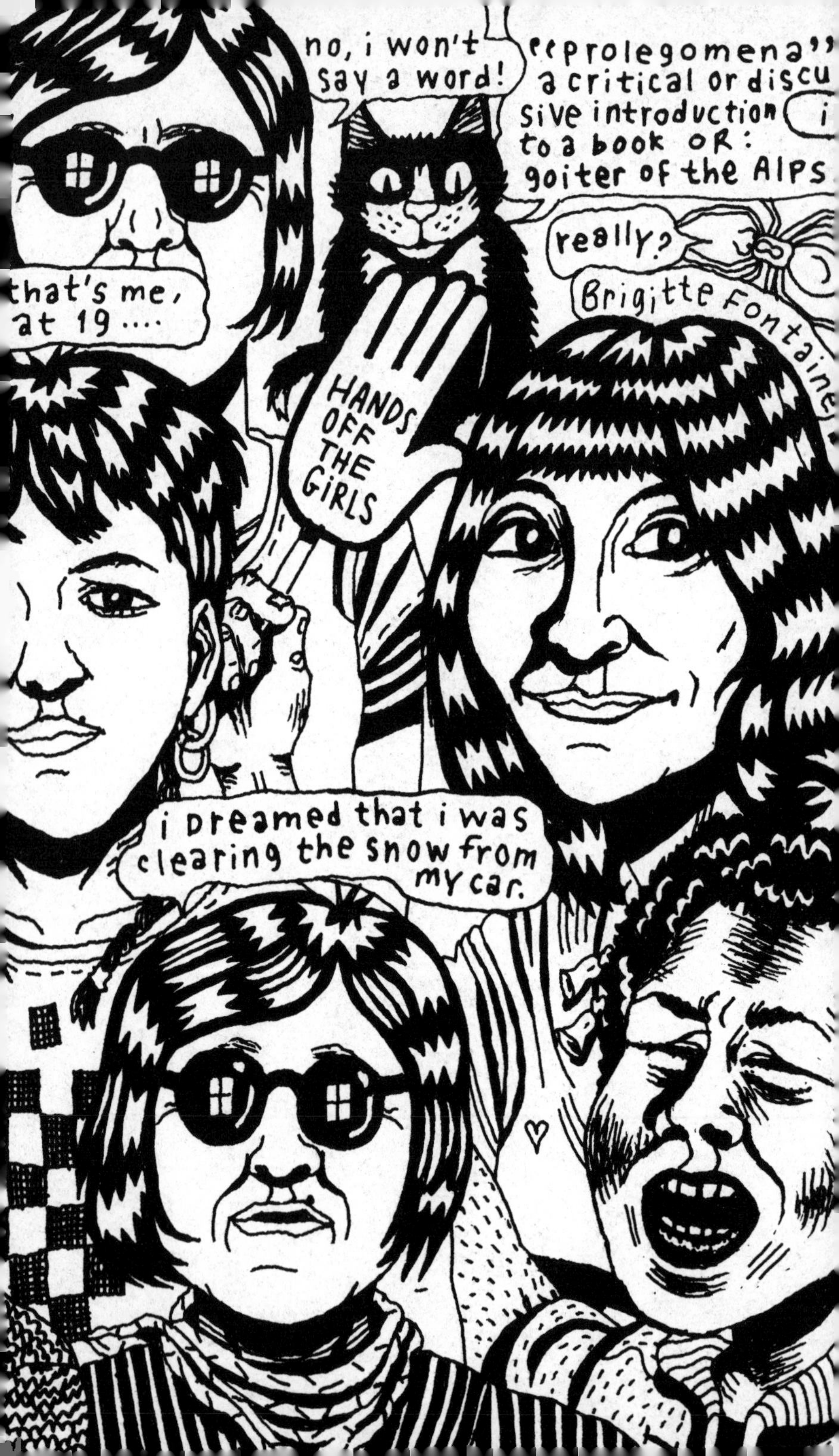
no, i won't say a word!
"prolegomena" a critical or discursive introduction to a book OR: goiter of the Alps
really?
Brigitte Fontaine
that's me, at 19....
HANDS OFF THE GIRLS
i Dreamed that i was clearing the snow from my car.

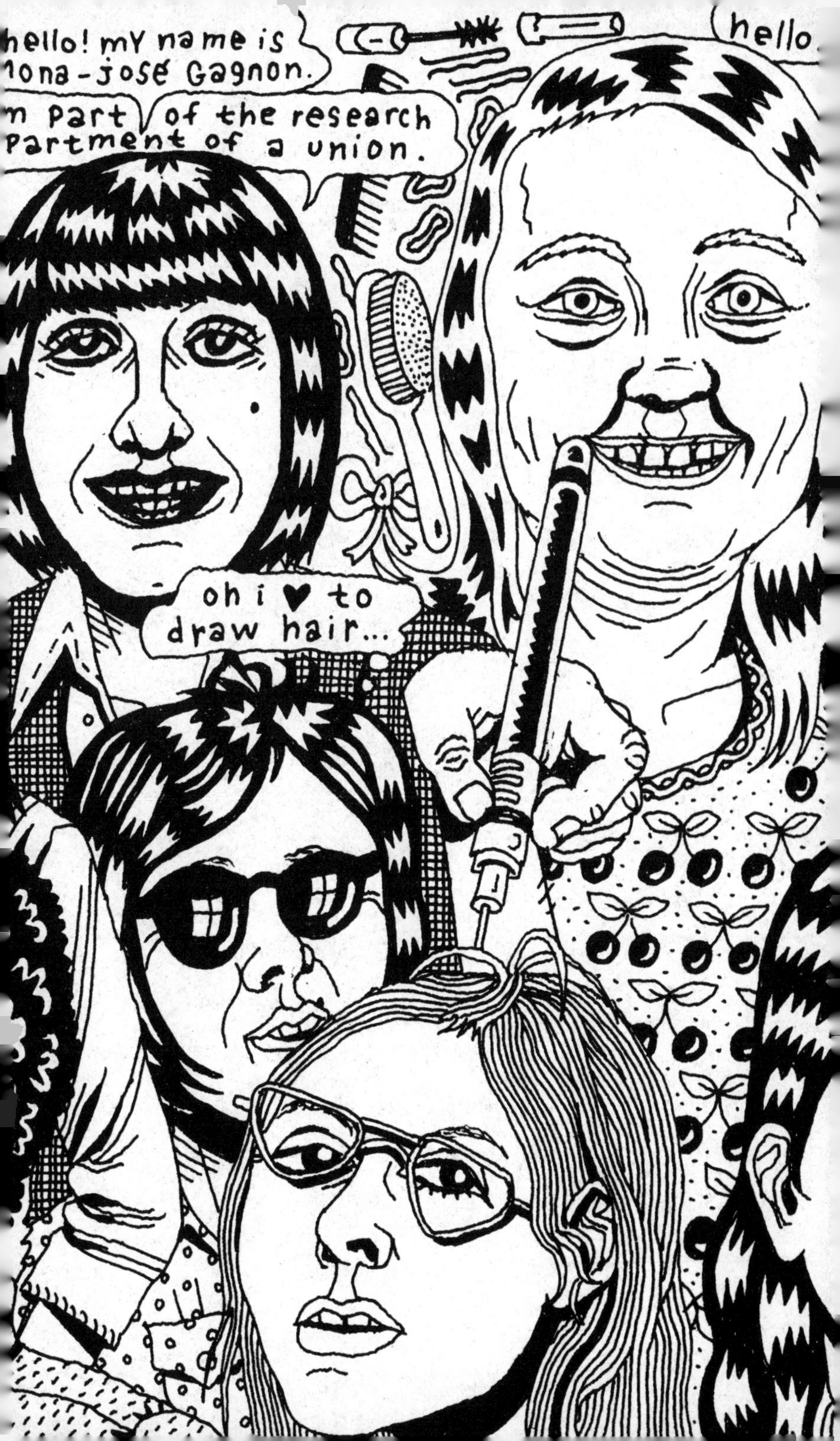
hello! my name is
Mona-José Gagnon.
hello
m part of the research
partment of a union.
oh i ♥ to
draw hair...

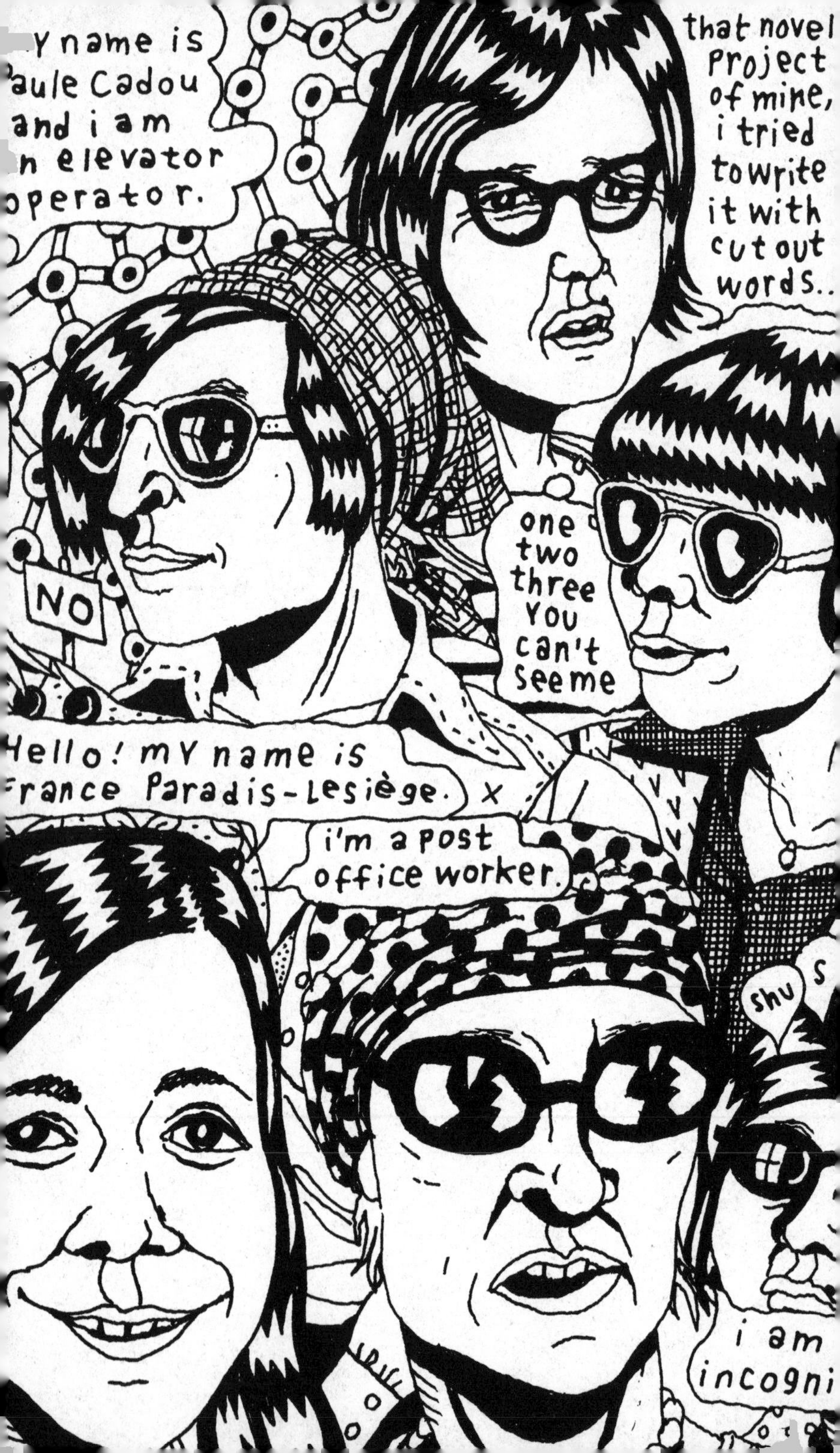

y name is aule Cadou and i am n elevator operator.
that novel project of mine, i tried to write it with cut out words..
one two three you can't see me
Hello! my name is rance Paradis-Lesiège.
i'm a post office worker.
shu
s
i am incogni

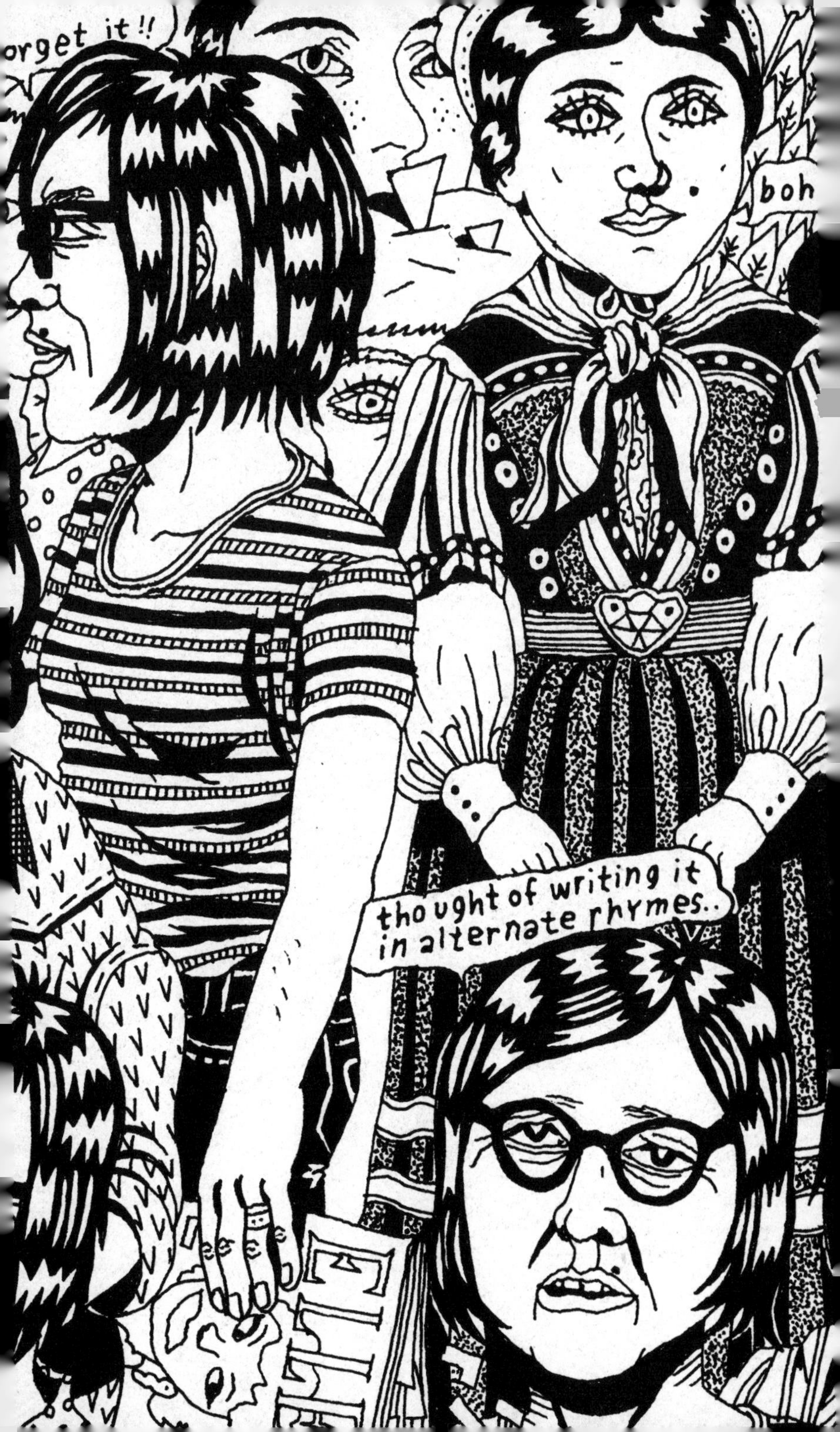
orget it!!
boh
thought of writing it in alternate rhymes..

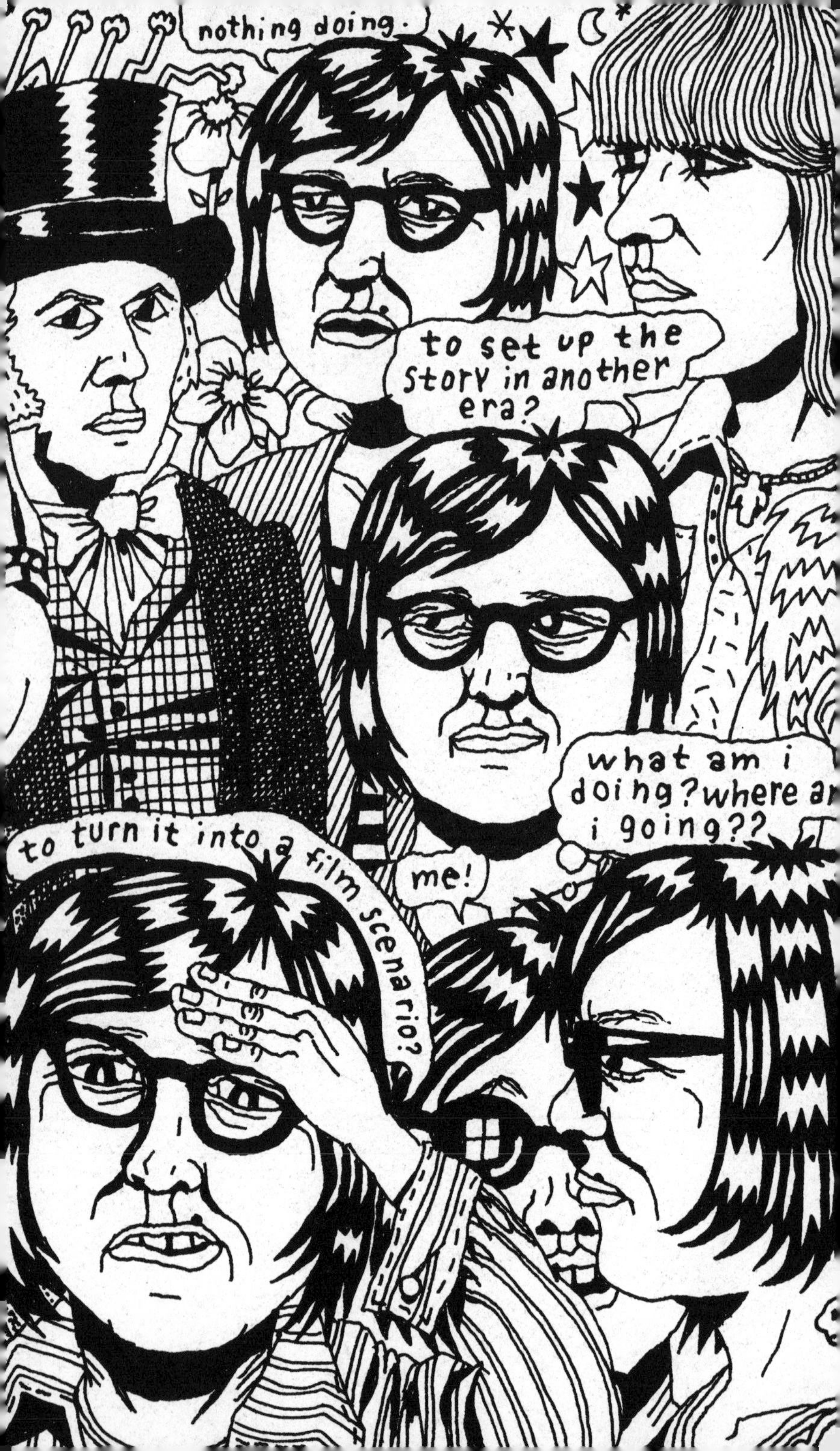
nothing doing.
to set up the story in another era?
what am i doing? where a
i going??
to turn it into a film scenario?
me!

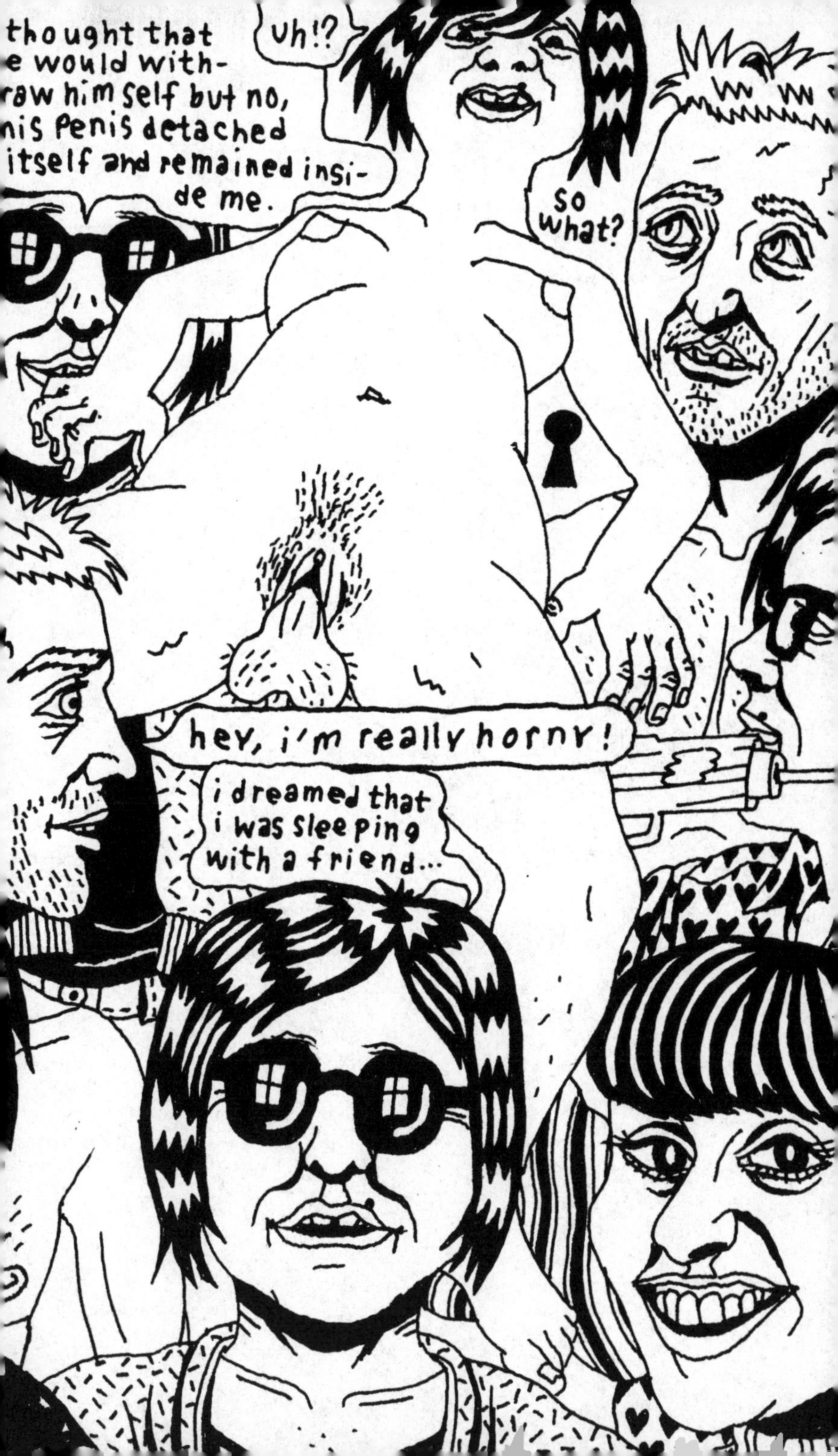
thought that
e would with-
raw himself but no,
nis penis detached
itself and remained insi-
de me.
uh!?
so
what?
hey, i'm really horny!
i dreamed that
i was sleeping
with a friend...

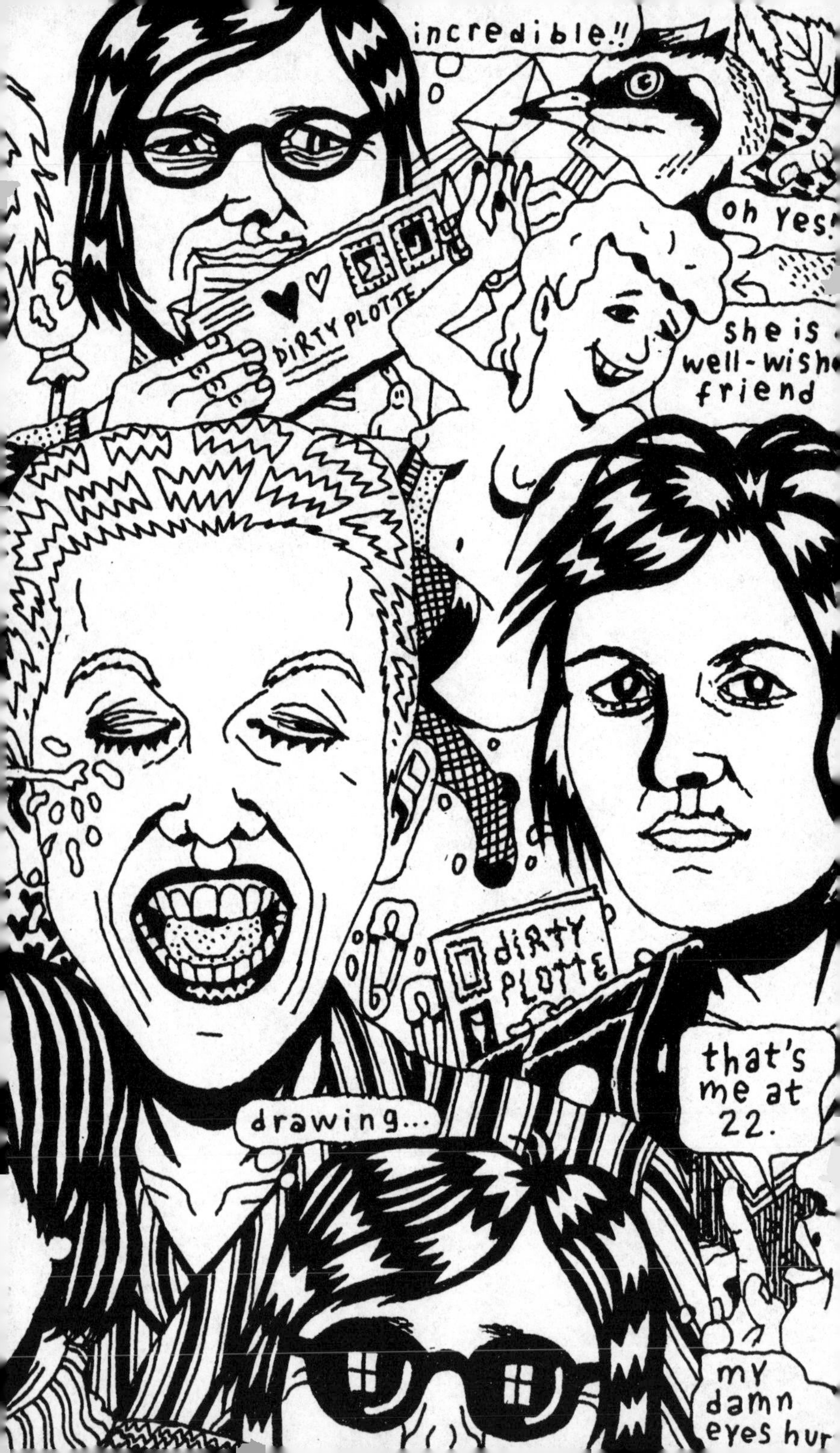
incredible!!
oh yes!
she is
well-wish
friend
DIRTY PLOTTE
DIRTY PLOTTE
drawing...
that's
me at
22.
my
damn
eyes hur

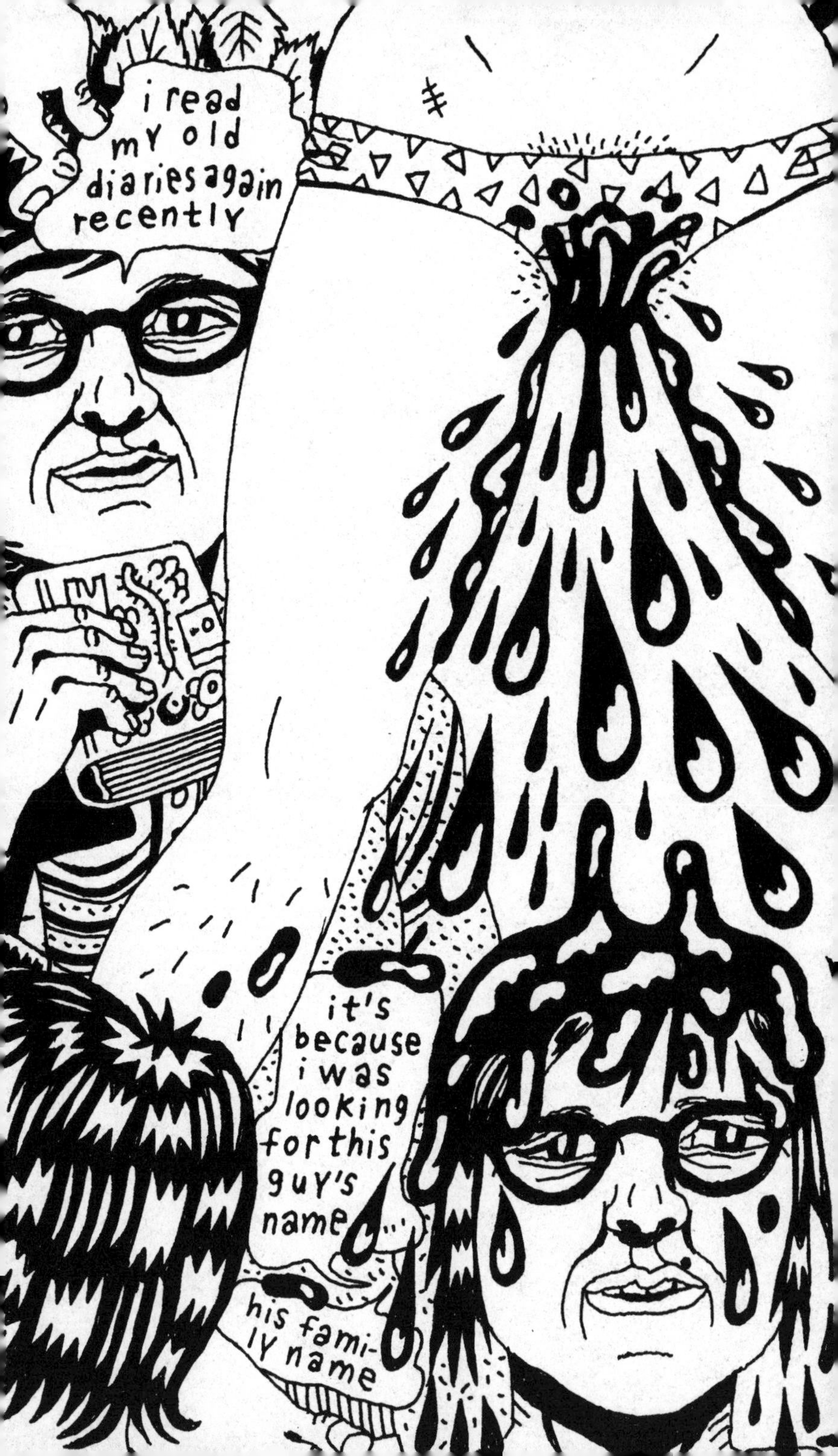
i read my old diaries again recently
it's because i was looking for this guy's name...
his family name

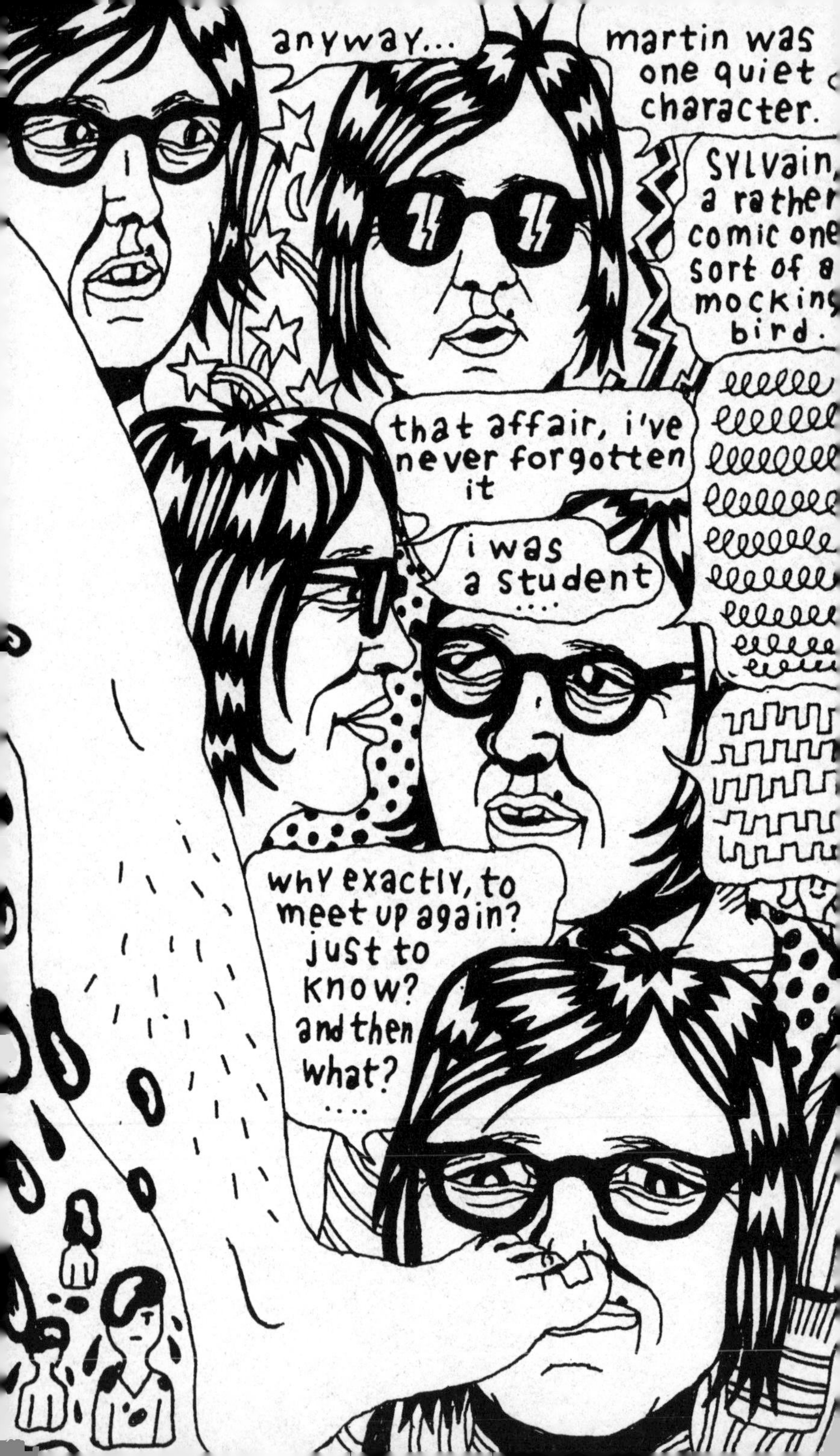
anyway...
martin was one quiet character.
SYLVAIN, a rather comic one sort of a mockingbird.
that affair, i've never forgotten it
i was a student ....
why exactly, to meet up again? just to know? and then what? ....

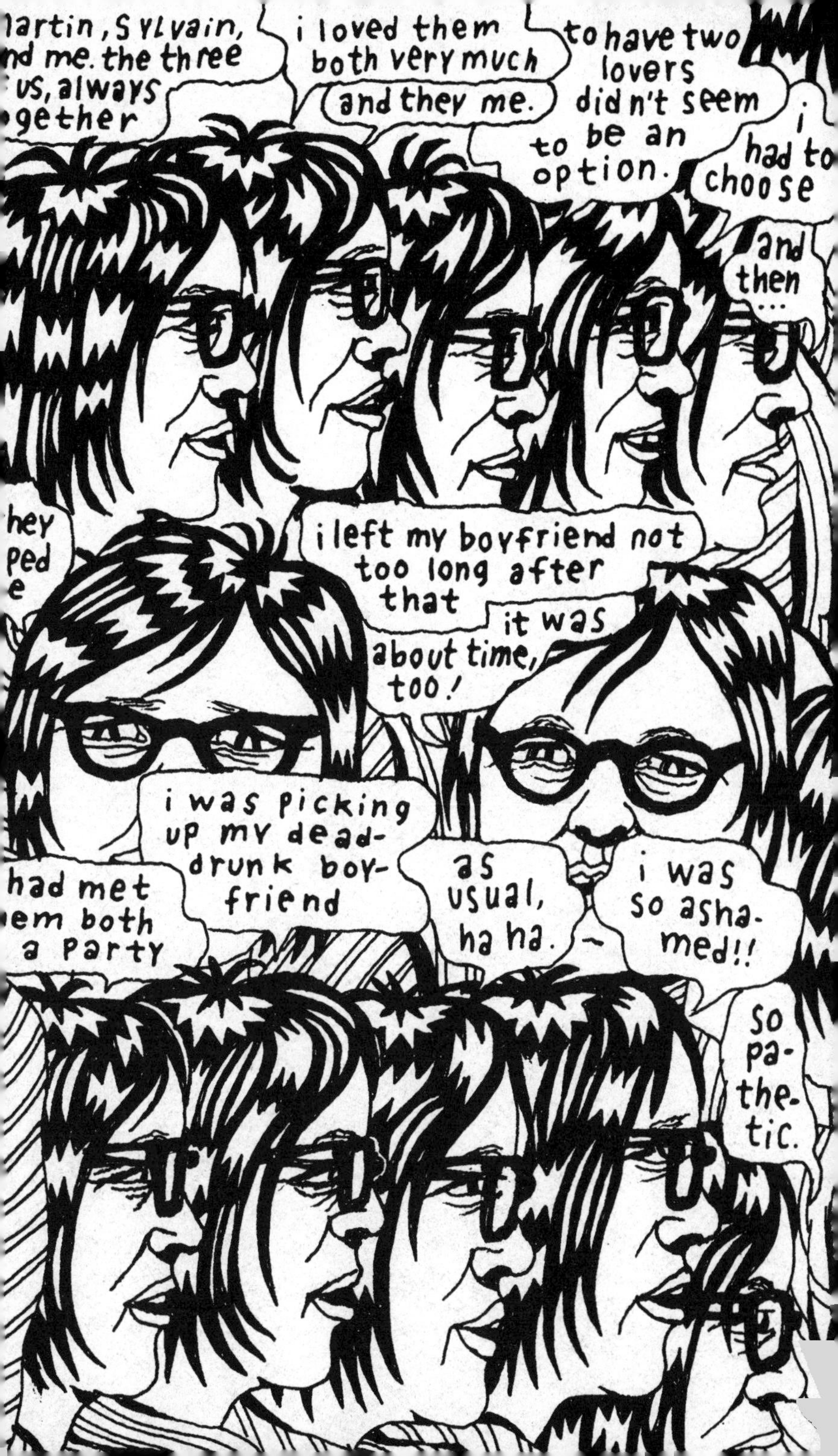

artin, sylvain, nd me. the three us, always gether
i loved them both very much
and they me.
to have two lovers didn't seem to be an option.
i had to choose
and then...
hey ped e
i left my boyfriend not too long after that
it was about time, too!
i was picking up my dead-drunk boy-friend
as usual, ha ha.
i was so asha-med!!
had met em both a party
so pa-the-tic.

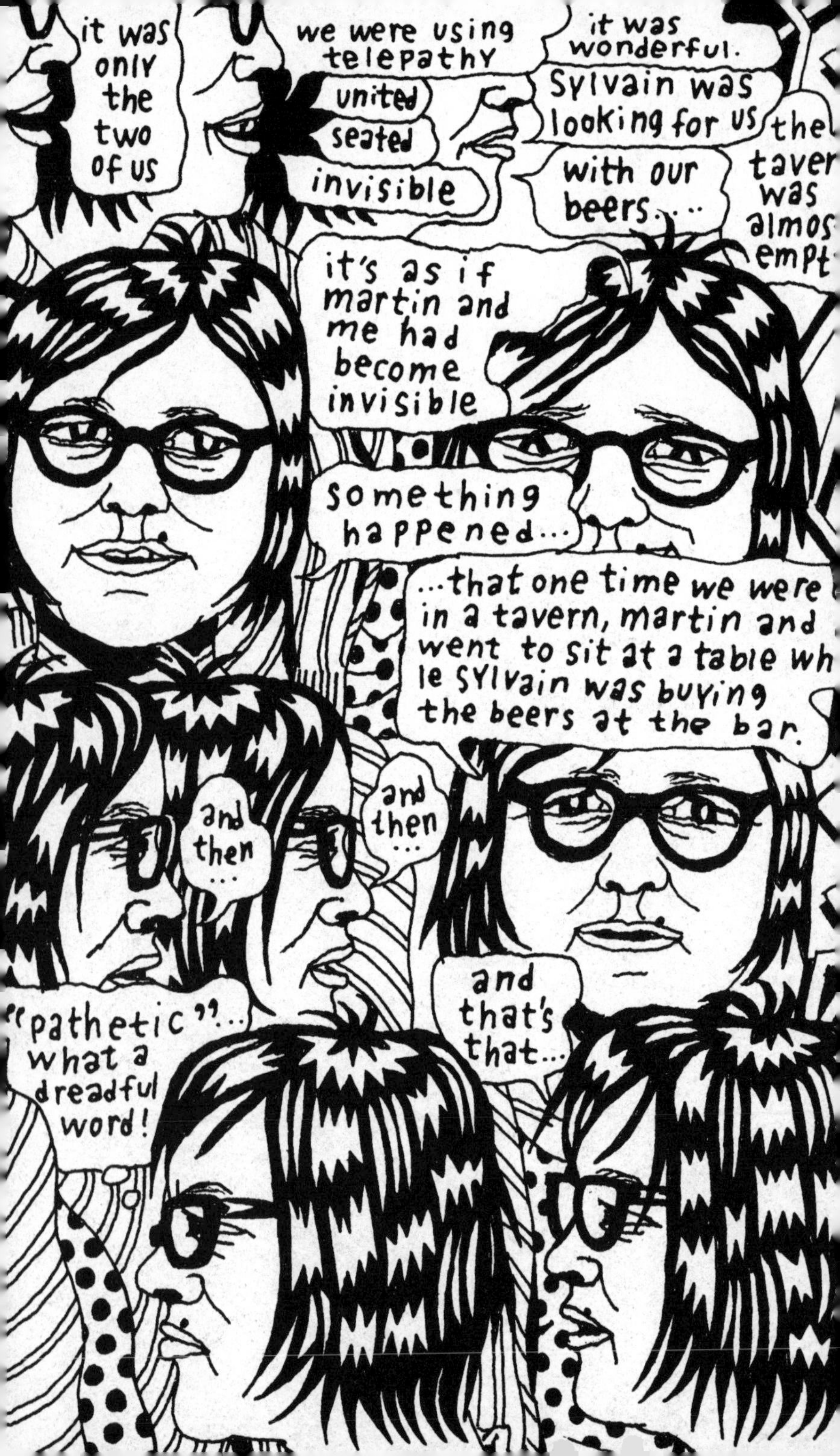
it was only the two of us
we were using telepathy
united
seated
invisible
it was wonderful.
Sylvain was looking for us
with our beers...
the taver was almos empt
it's as if martin and me had become invisible
something happened...
...that one time we were in a tavern, martin and went to sit at a table whle Sylvain was buying the beers at the bar.
and then ...
and then ...
and that's that...
"pathetic"... what a dreadful word!

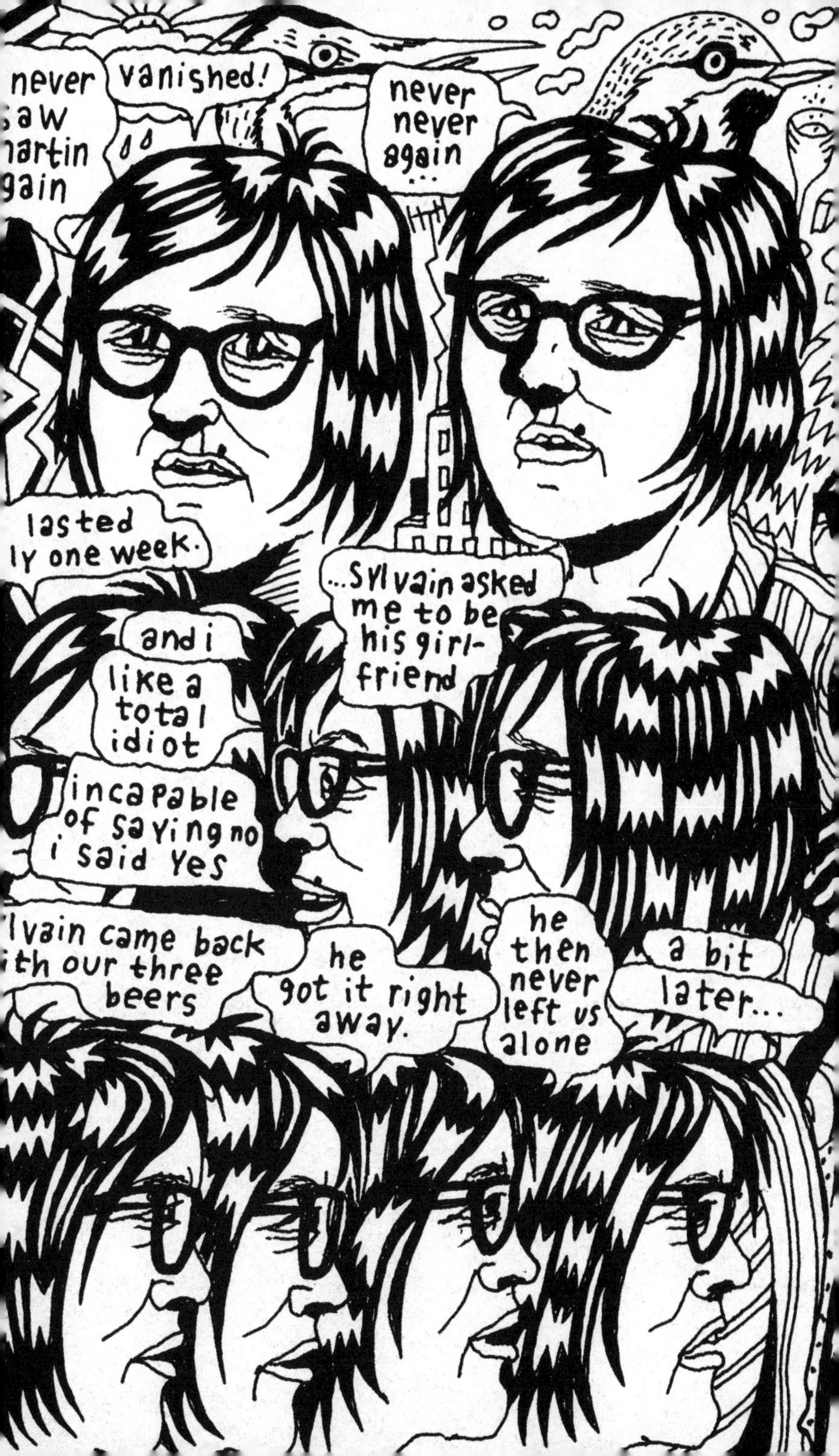
never aw artin gain
vanished!
never never again ...
lasted ly one week.
...Sylvain asked me to be his girlfriend
and i
like a total idiot
incapable of saying no i said yes
lvain came back ith our three beers
he got it right away.
he then never left us alone
a bit later...

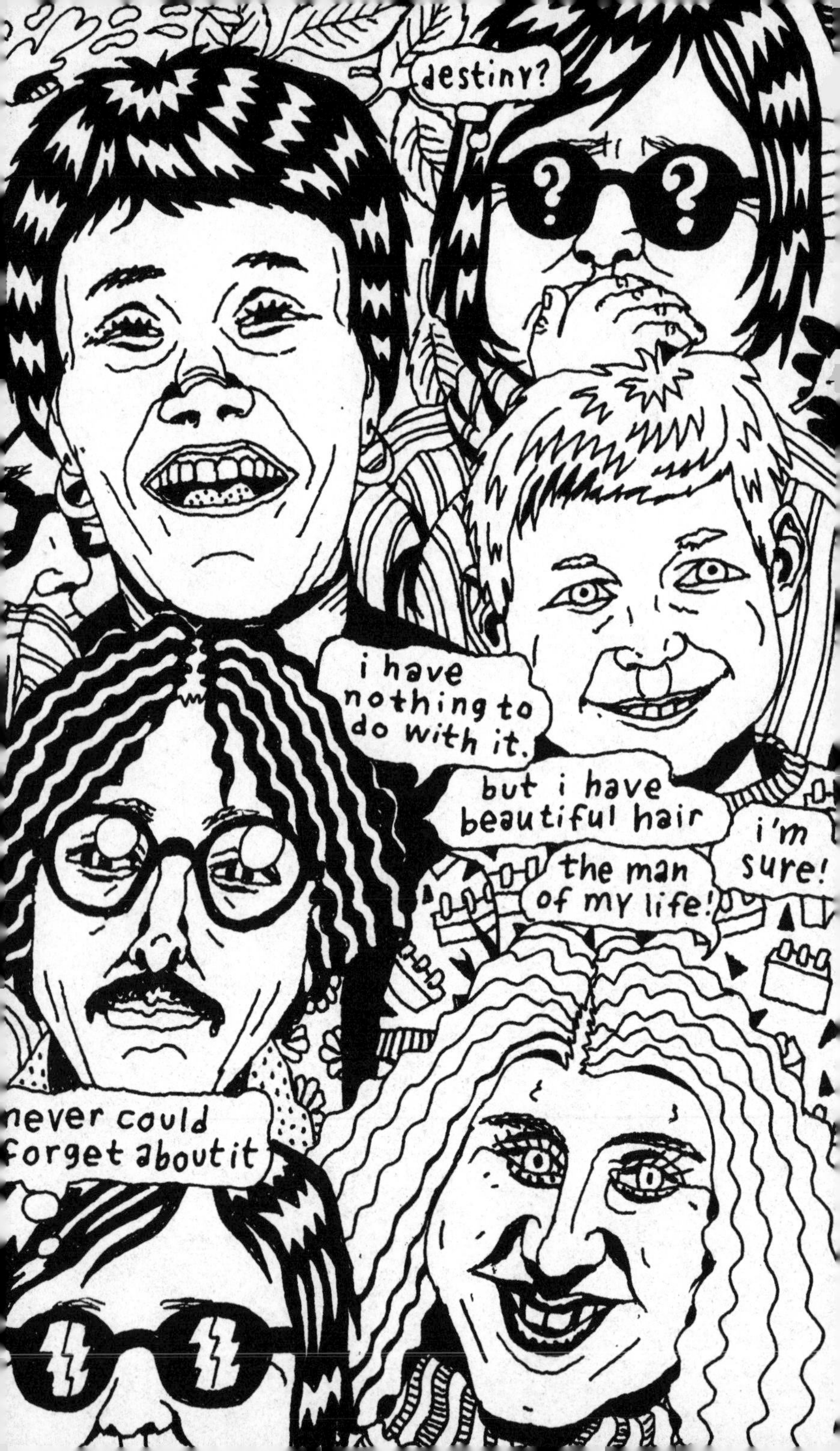
destiny?
i have nothing to do with it.
but i have beautiful hair
the man of my life!
i'm sure!
never could forget aboutit

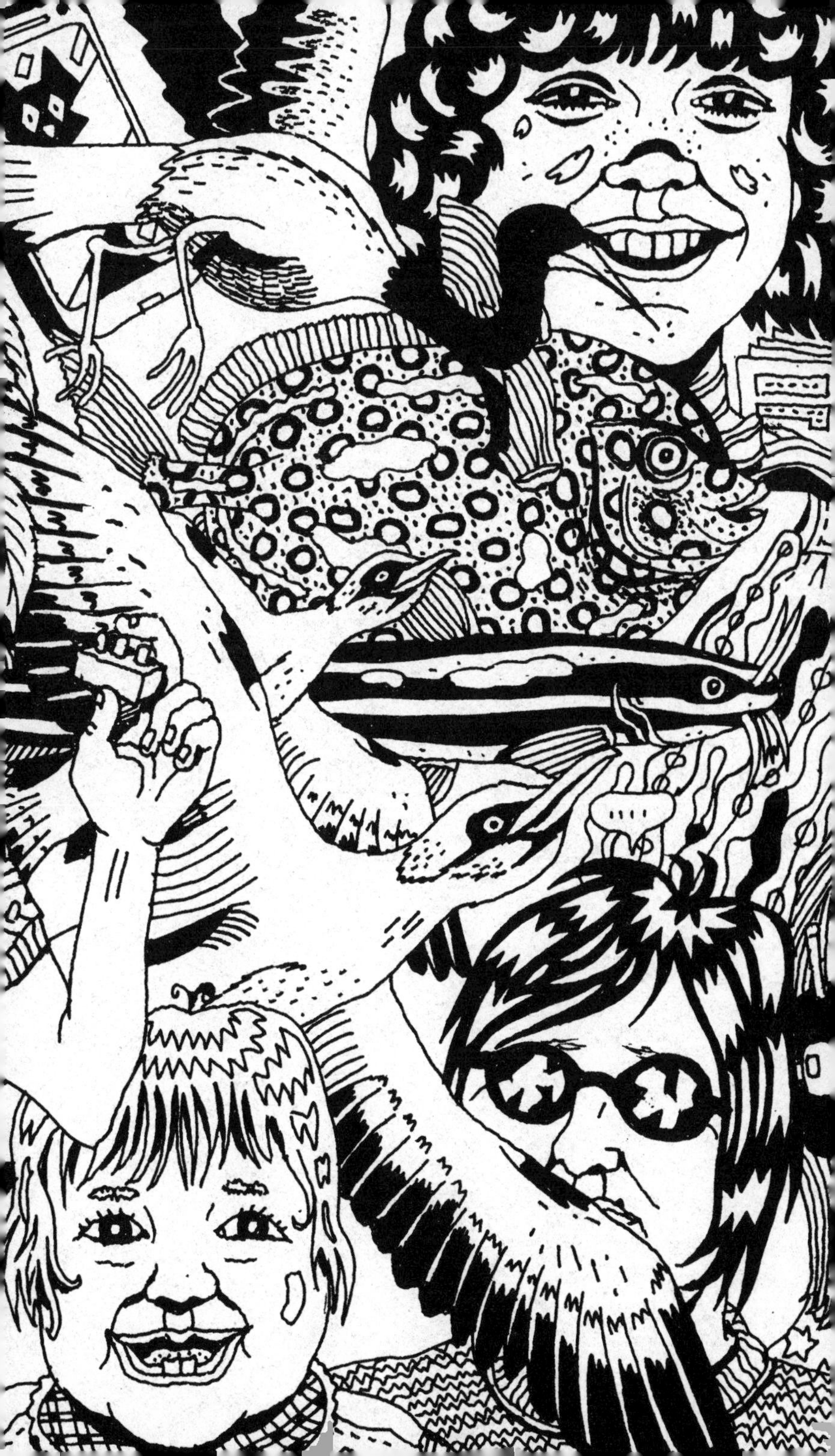

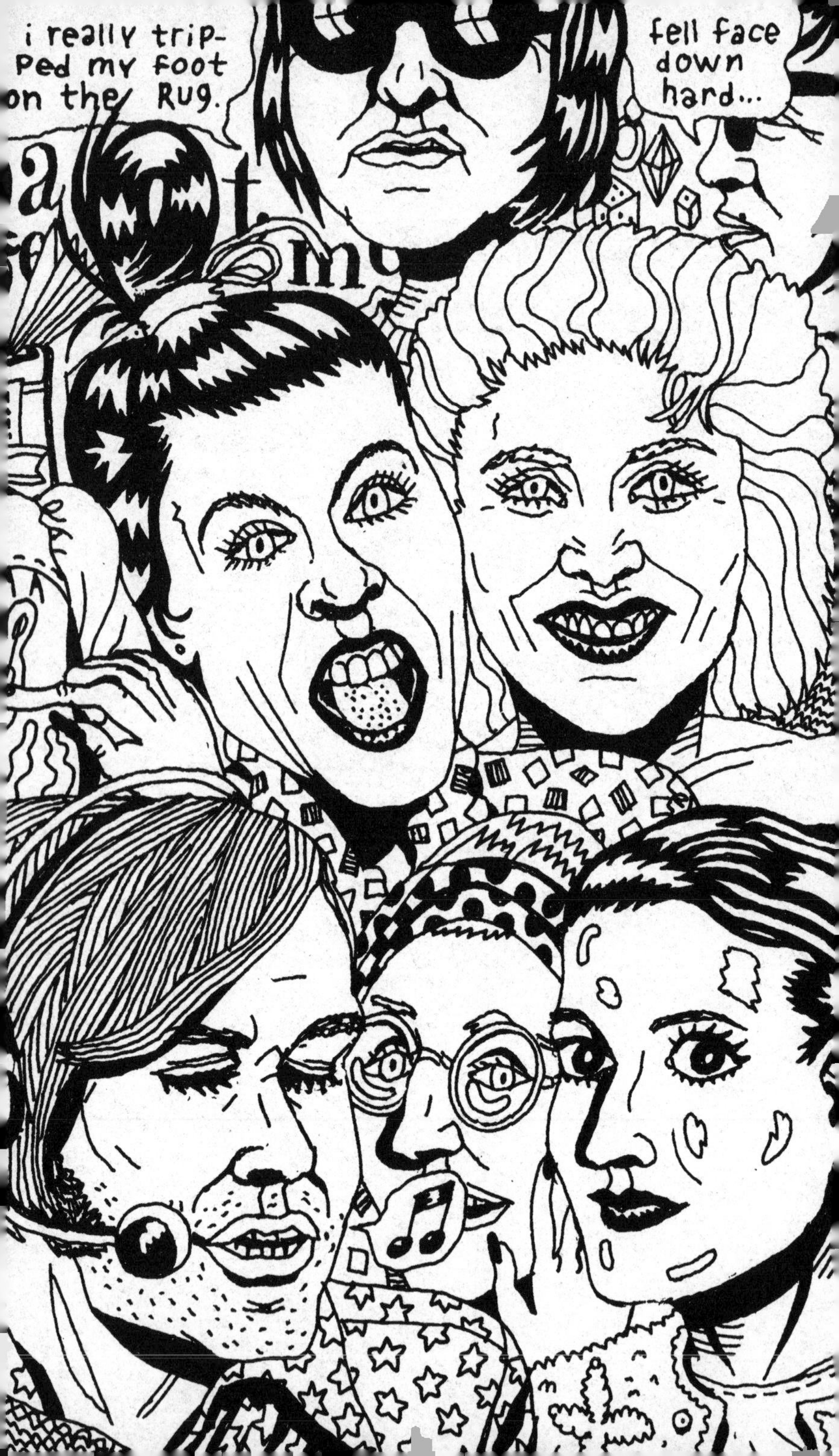
i really tripped my foot on the Rug.
fell face down hard...

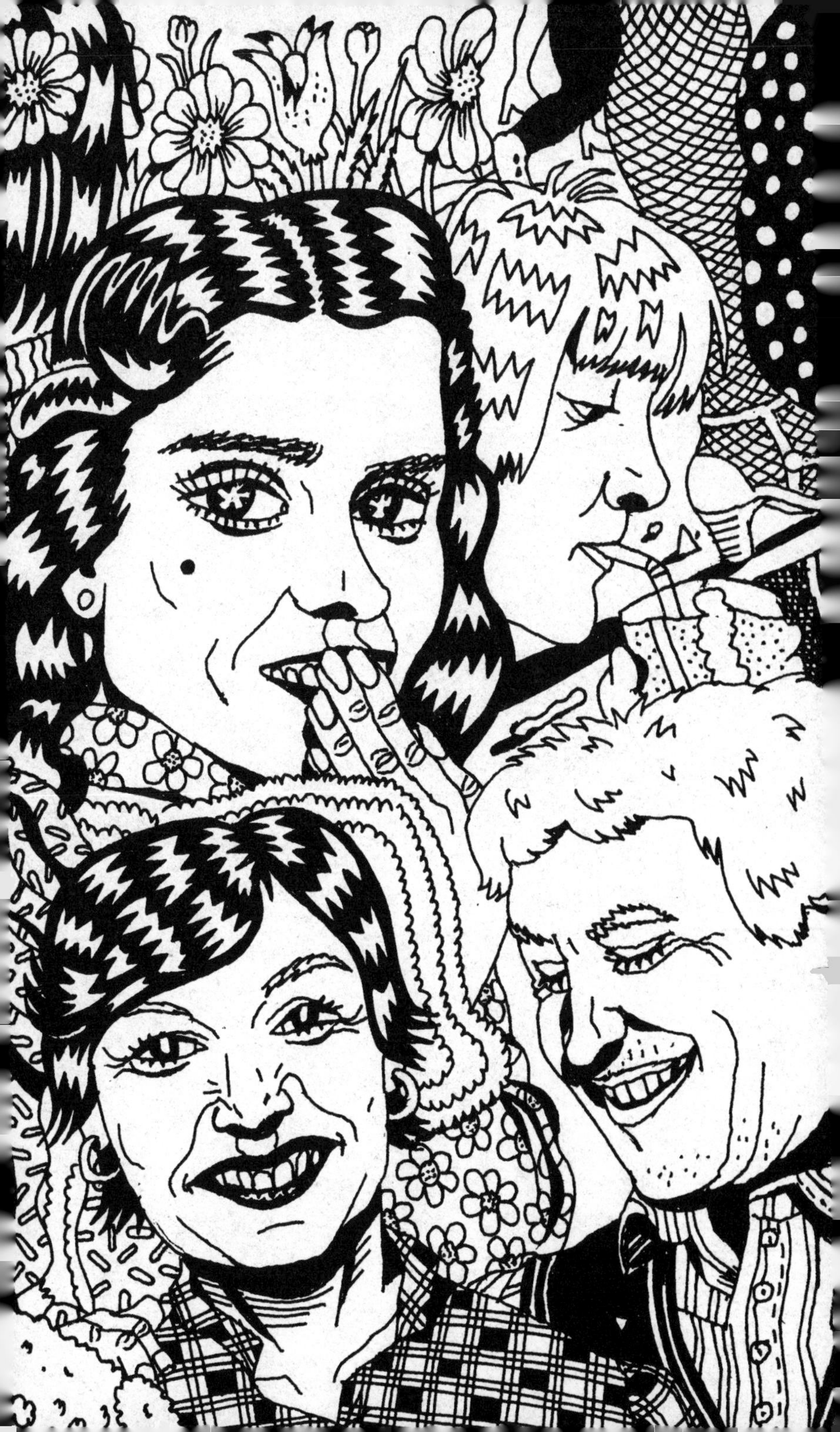

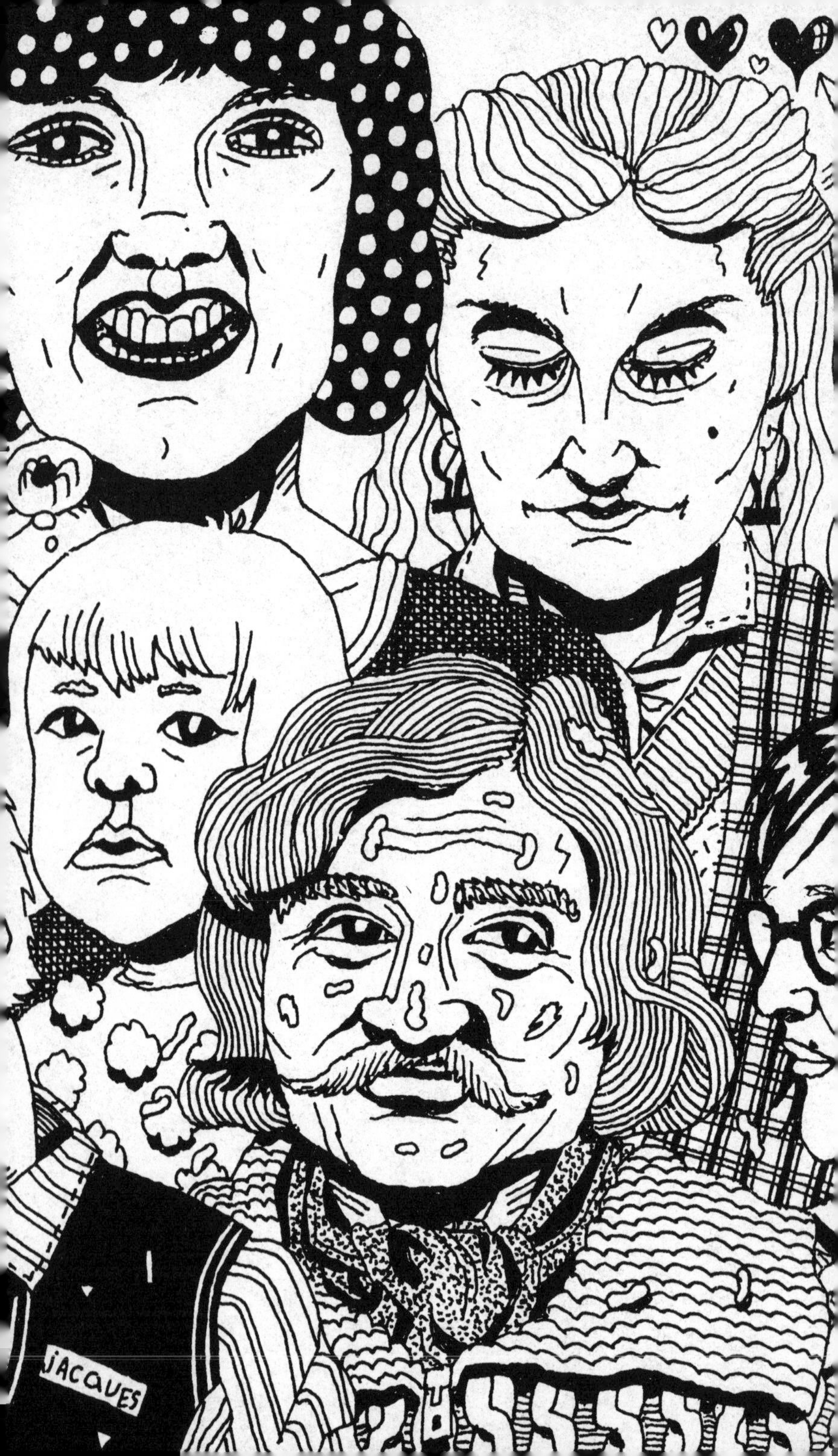
JACQUES

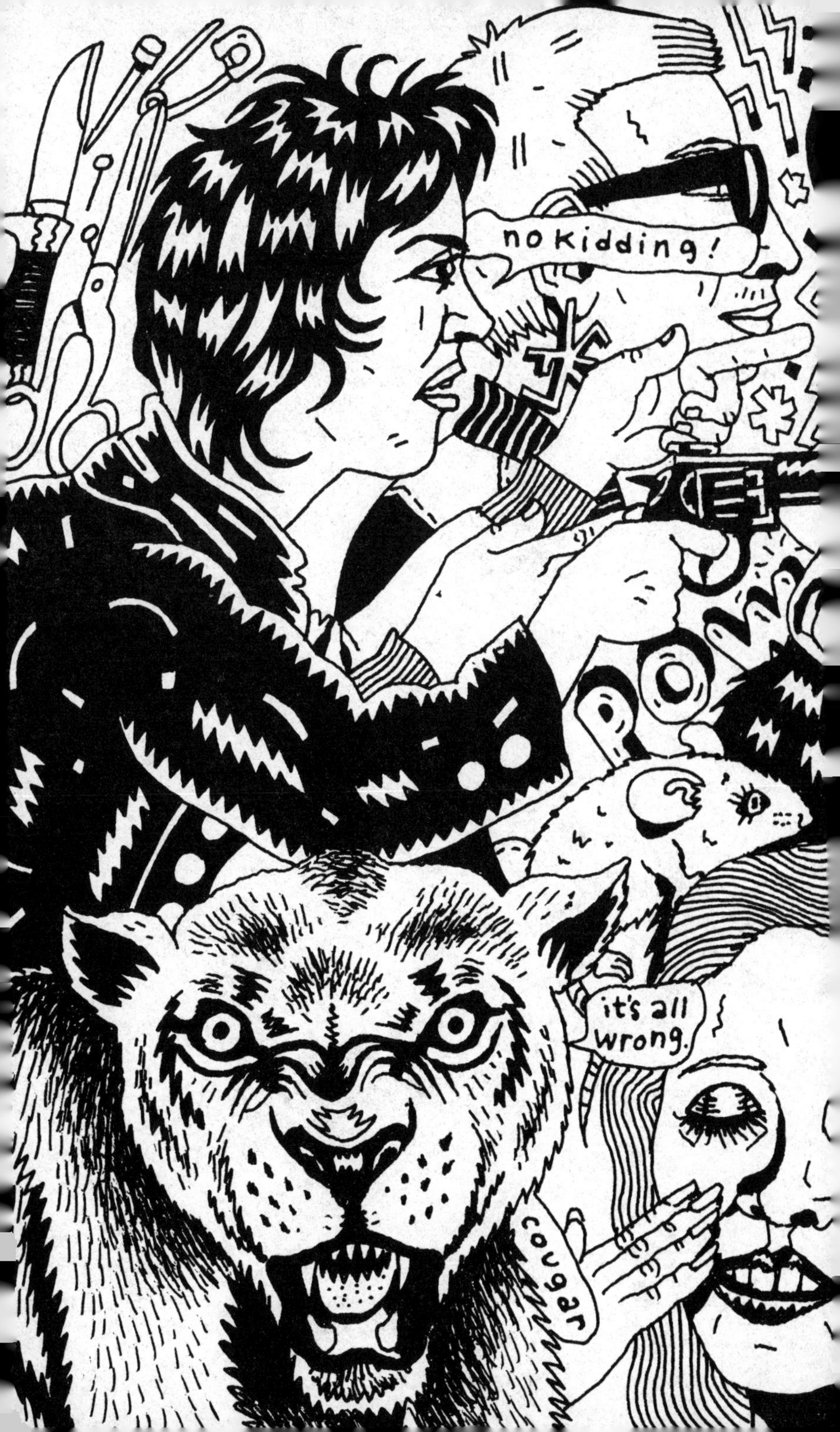
no kidding!
it's all wrong.
cougar

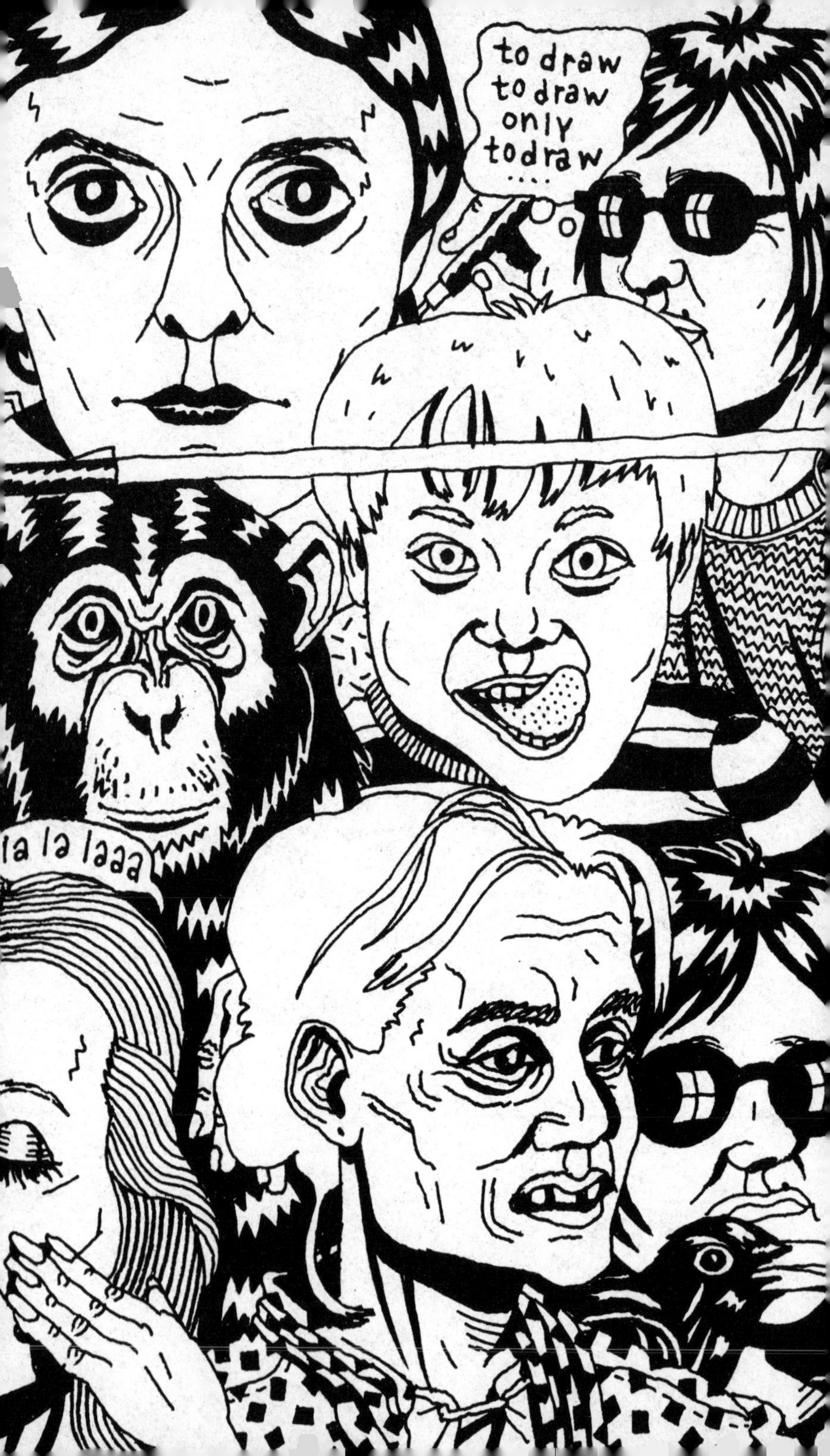
to draw
to draw
only
todraw
....
la la laaa

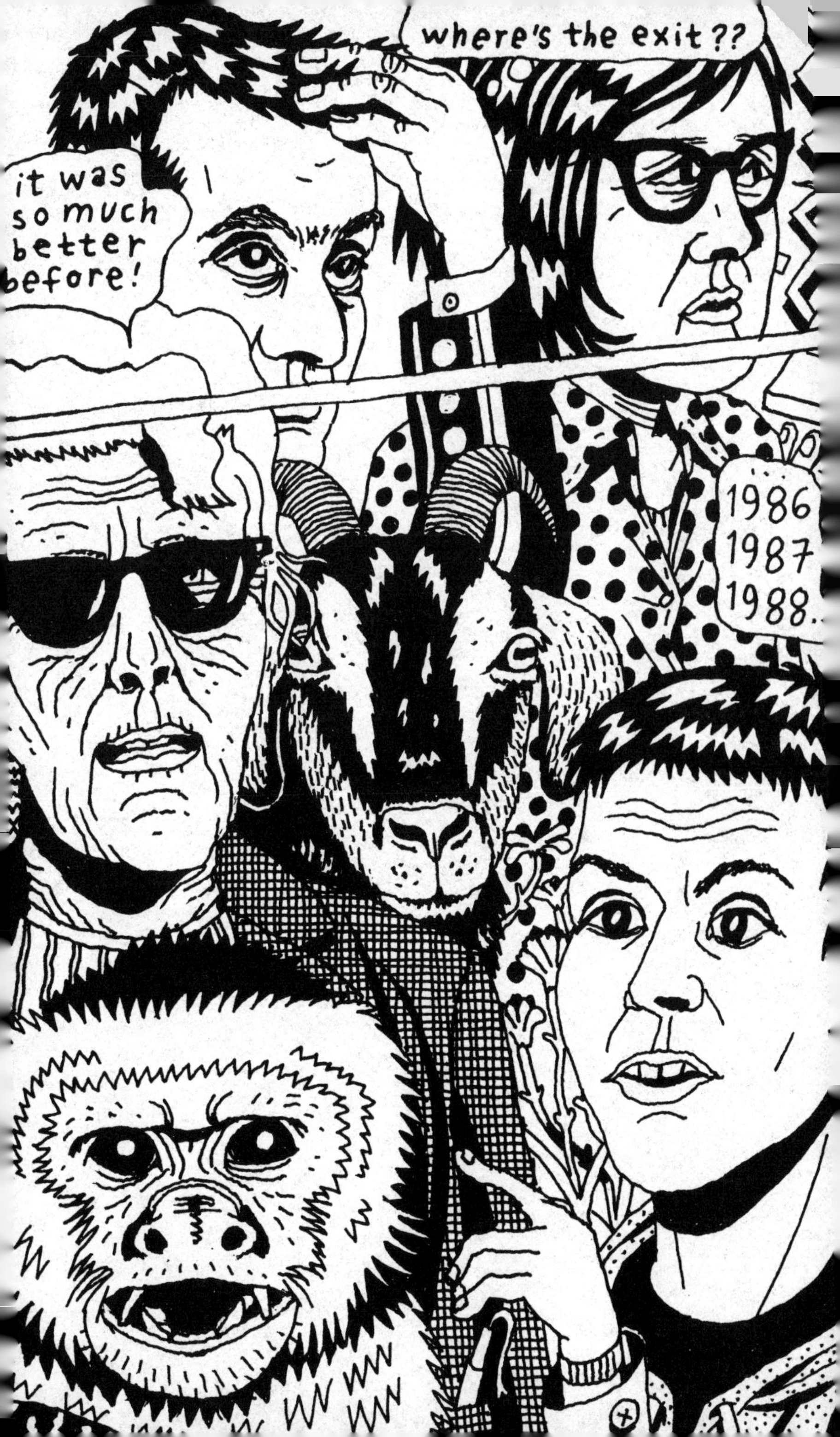
where's the exit??
it was so much better before!
1986 1987 1988...

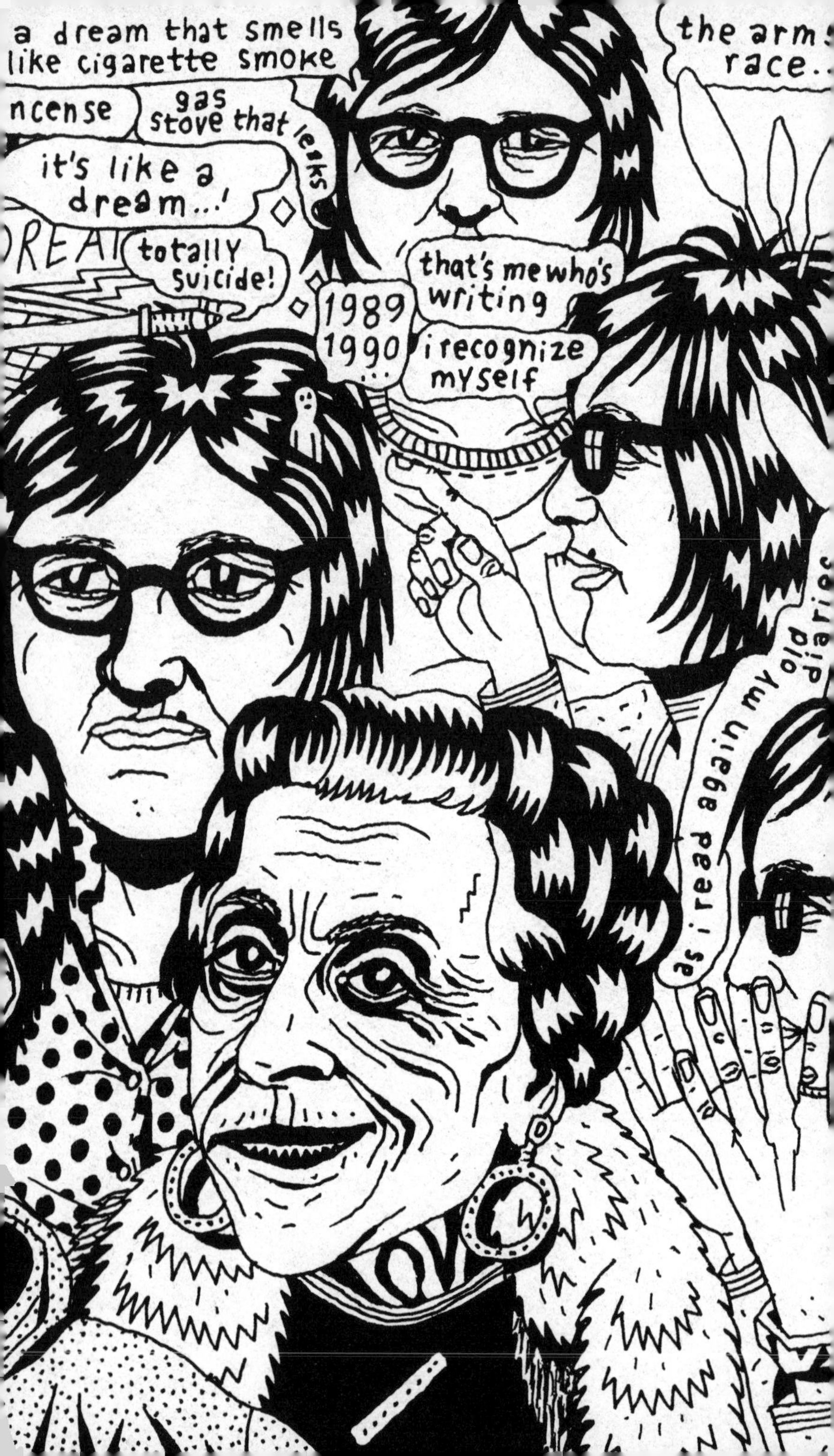
a dream that smells like cigarette smoke
the arms race...
ncense
gas stove that leaks
it's like a dream...!
REA
totally suicide!
that's me who's writing
1989 1990 ...
i recognize myself
as i read again my old diaries

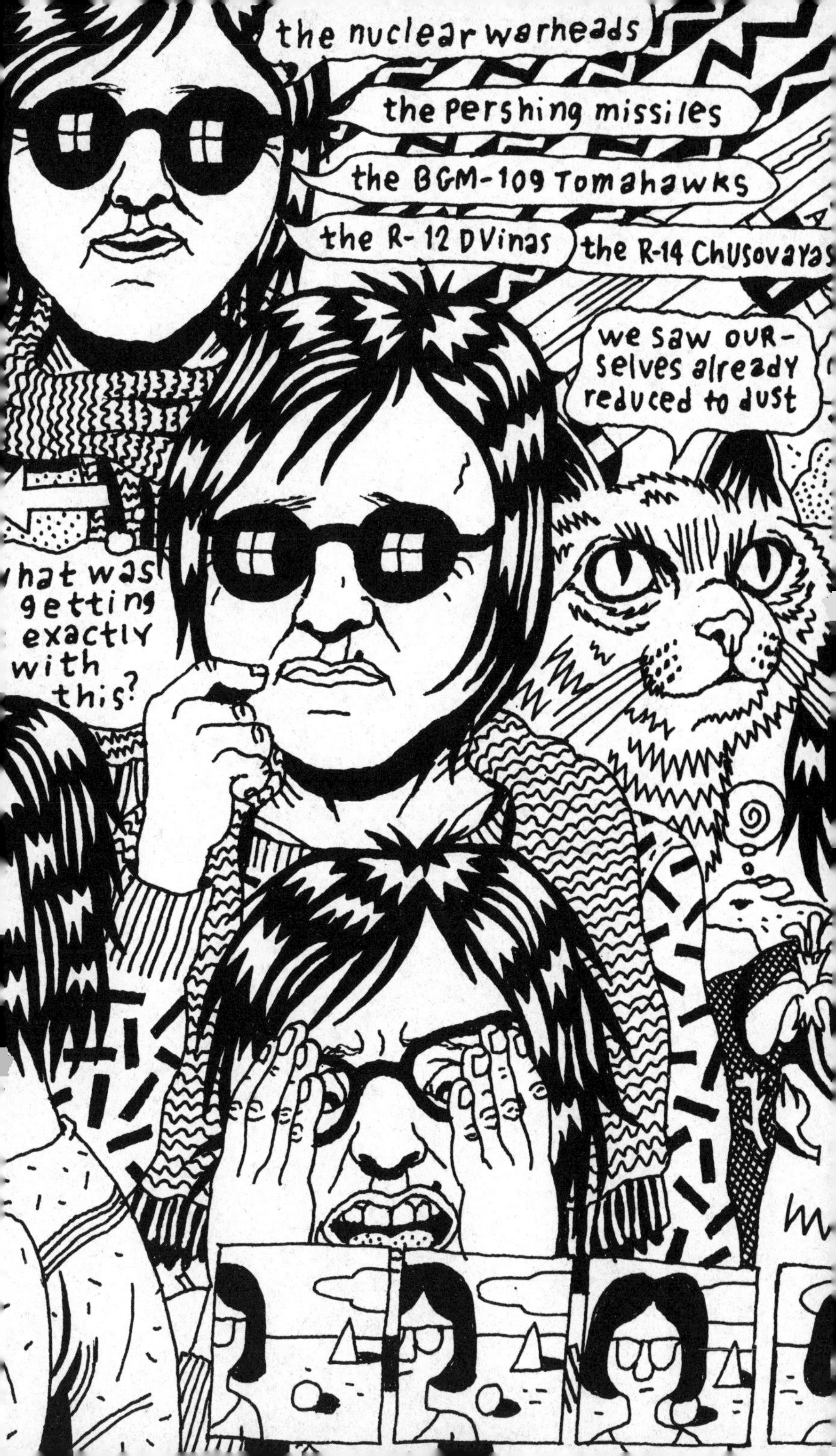
the nuclear warheads
the Pershing missiles
the BGM-109 Tomahawks
the R-12 Dvinas
the R-14 Chusovayas
we saw our-selves already reduced to dust
hat was getting exactly with this?

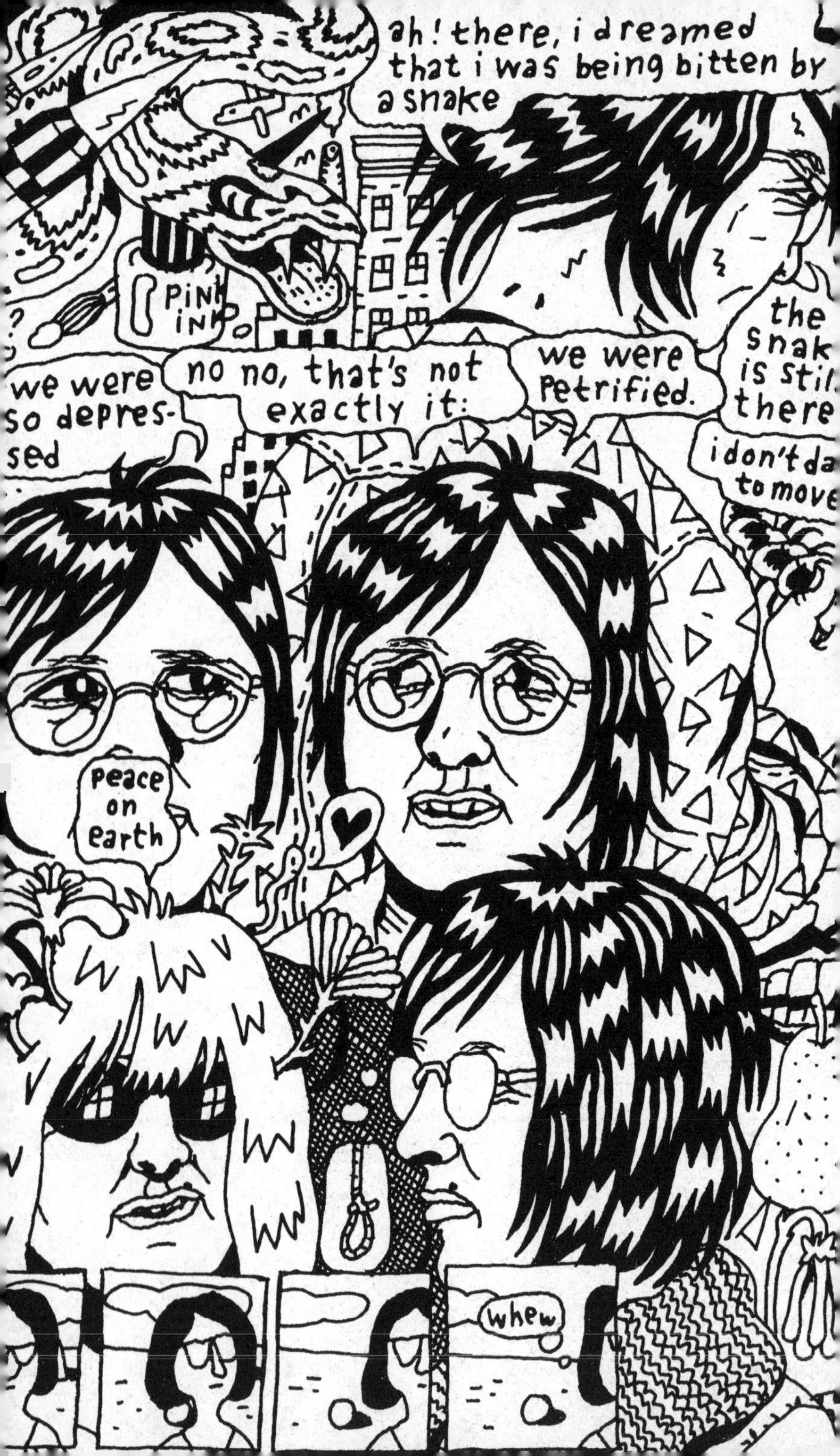
ah! there, i dreamed that i was being bitten by a snake
PINK INK
we were so depres-sed
no no, that's not exactly it:
we were petrified.
peace on earth
whew

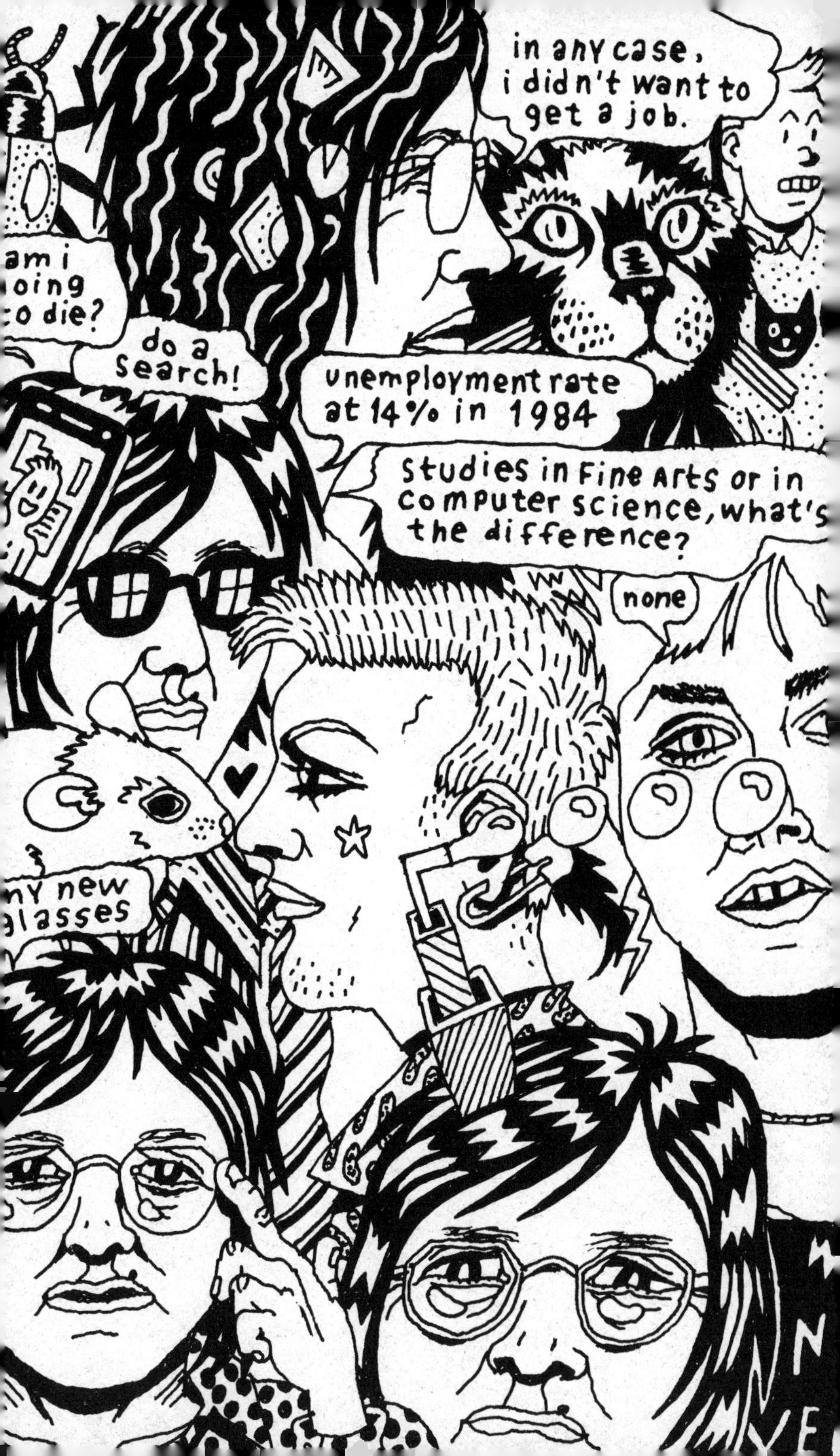
in any case, i didn't want to get a job.
am i oing o die?
do a search!
unemployment rate at 14% in 1984
Studies in Fine Arts or in computer science, what's the difference?
none
ny new lasses

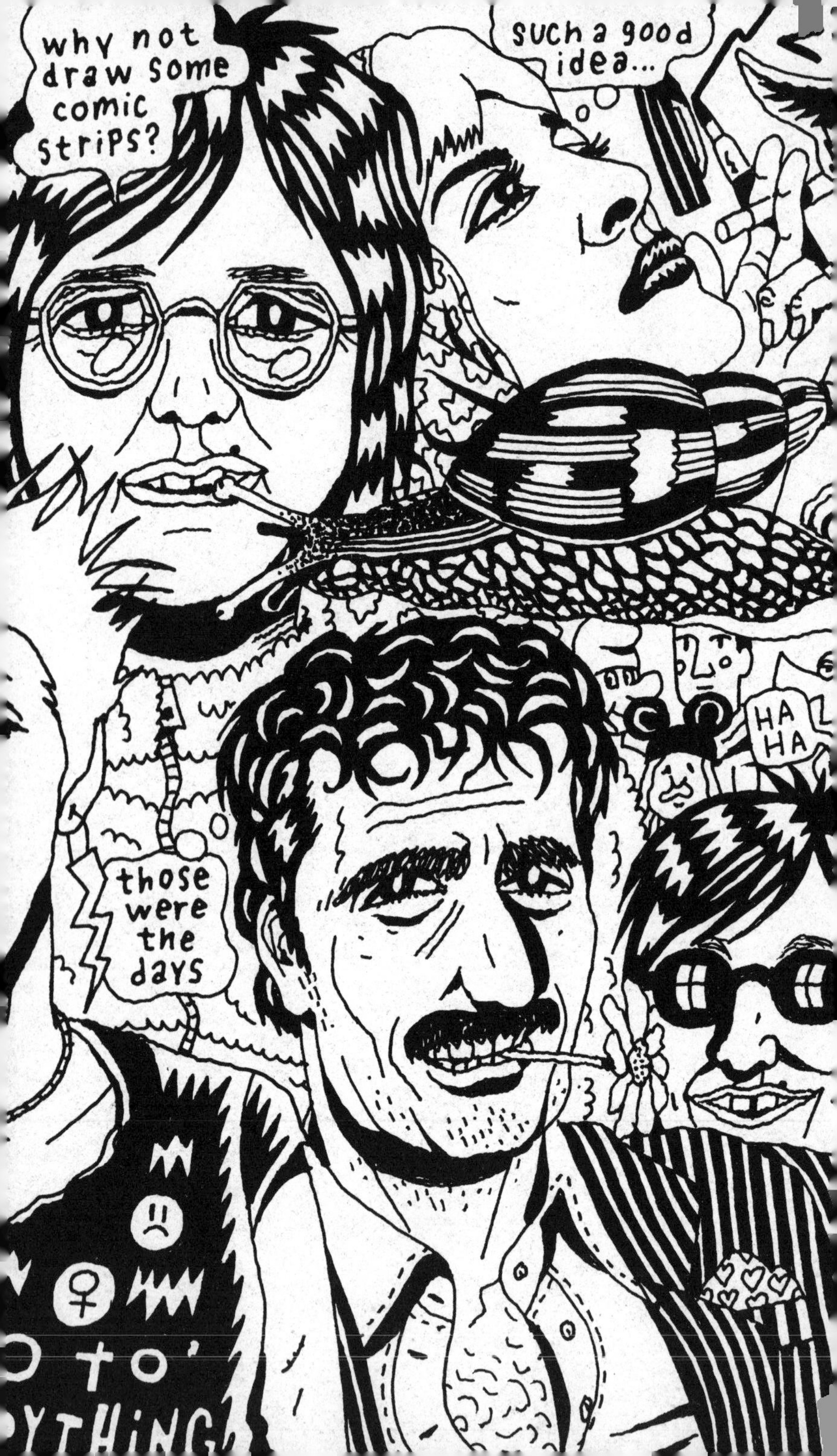
why not draw some comic strips?
such a good idea...
HA HA HA
those were the days

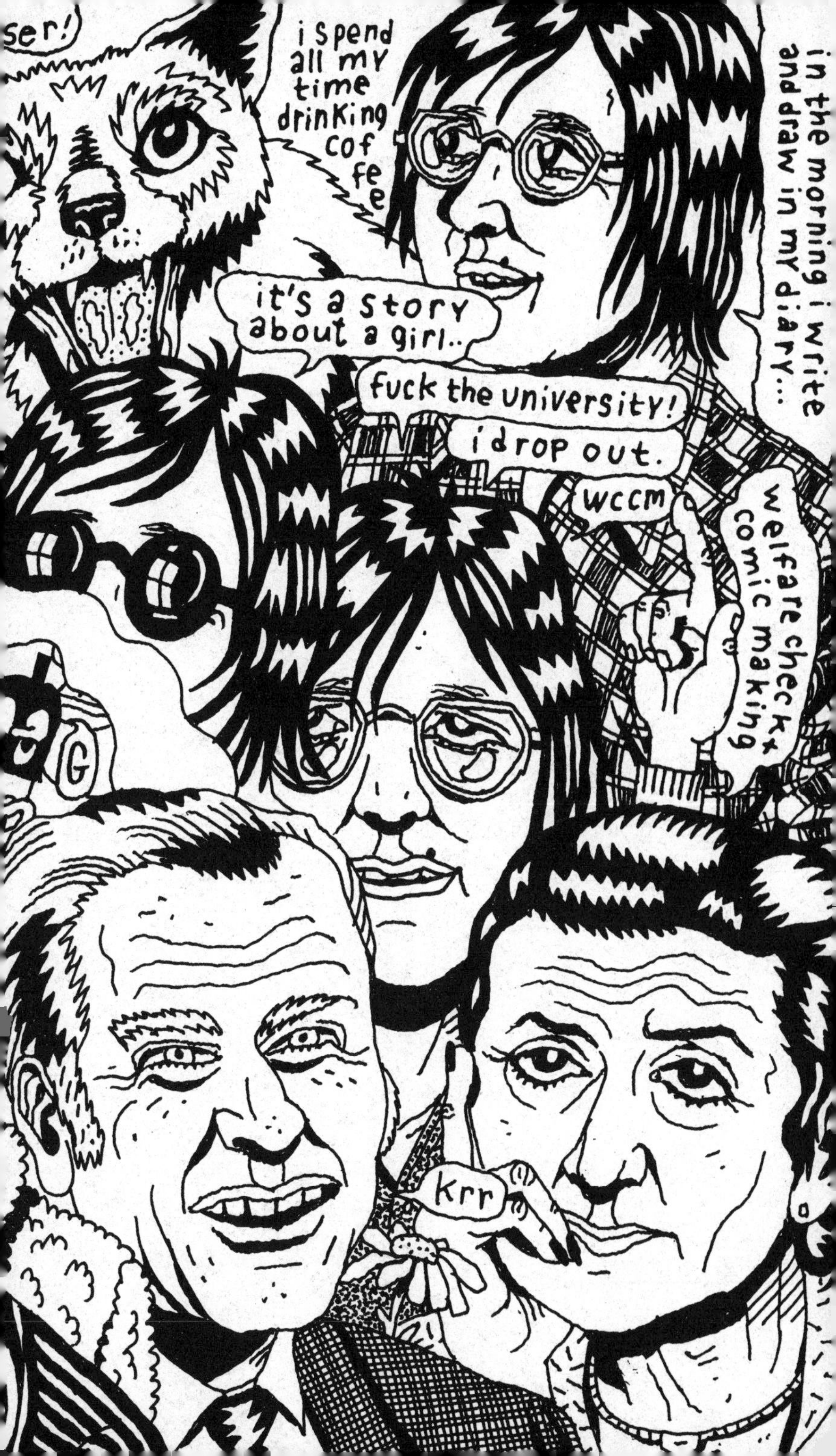
ser!)
i spend all my time drinking cof fe e
in the morning i write and draw in my diary...
it's a story about a girl..
fuck the university!
i drop out.
wccm
welfare check + comic making
G
krr

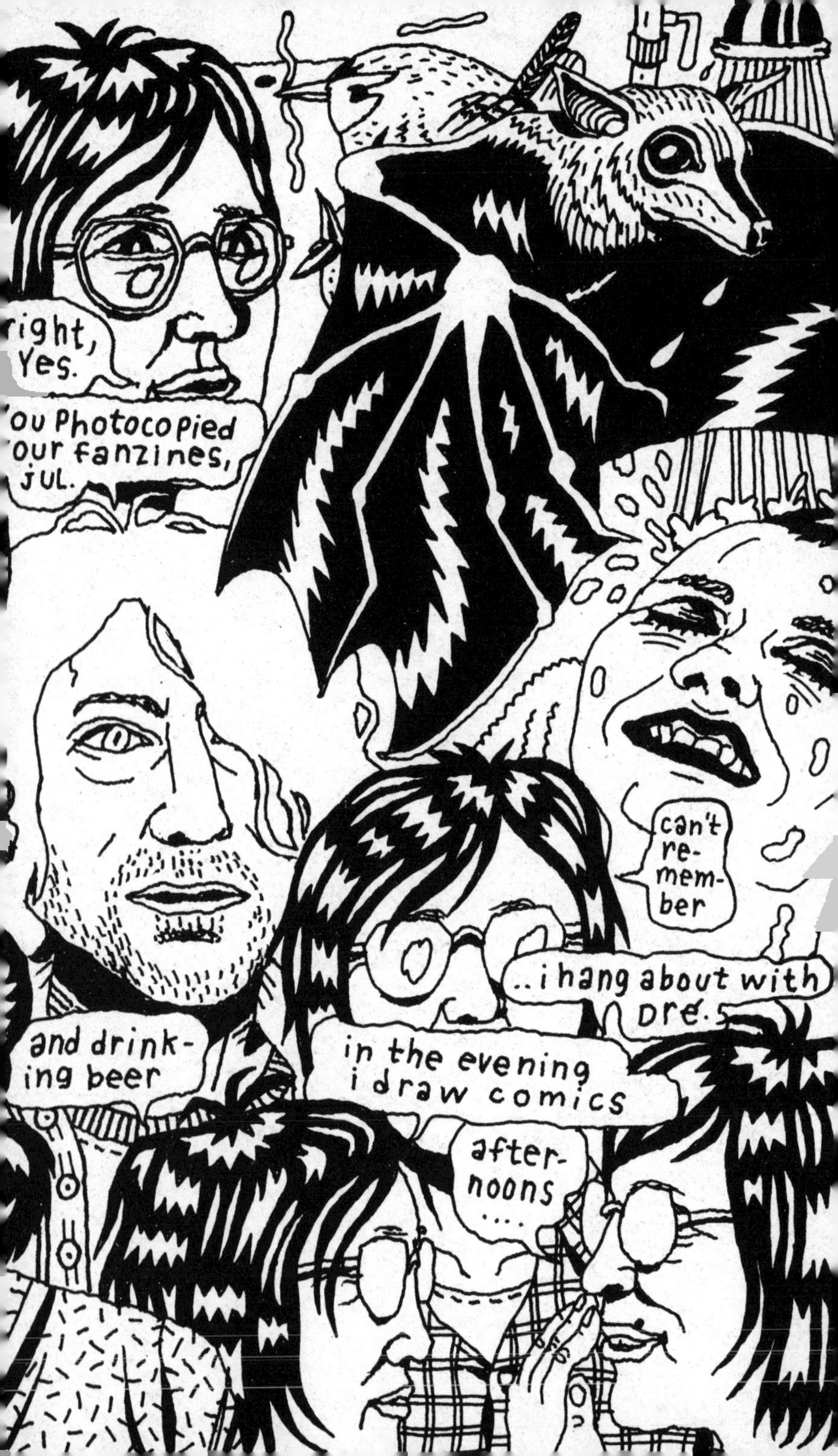
right, yes.
ou photocopied our fanzines, jul.
can't re-mem-ber
...i hang about with pré.
and drink-ing beer
in the evening i draw comics
after-noons ....

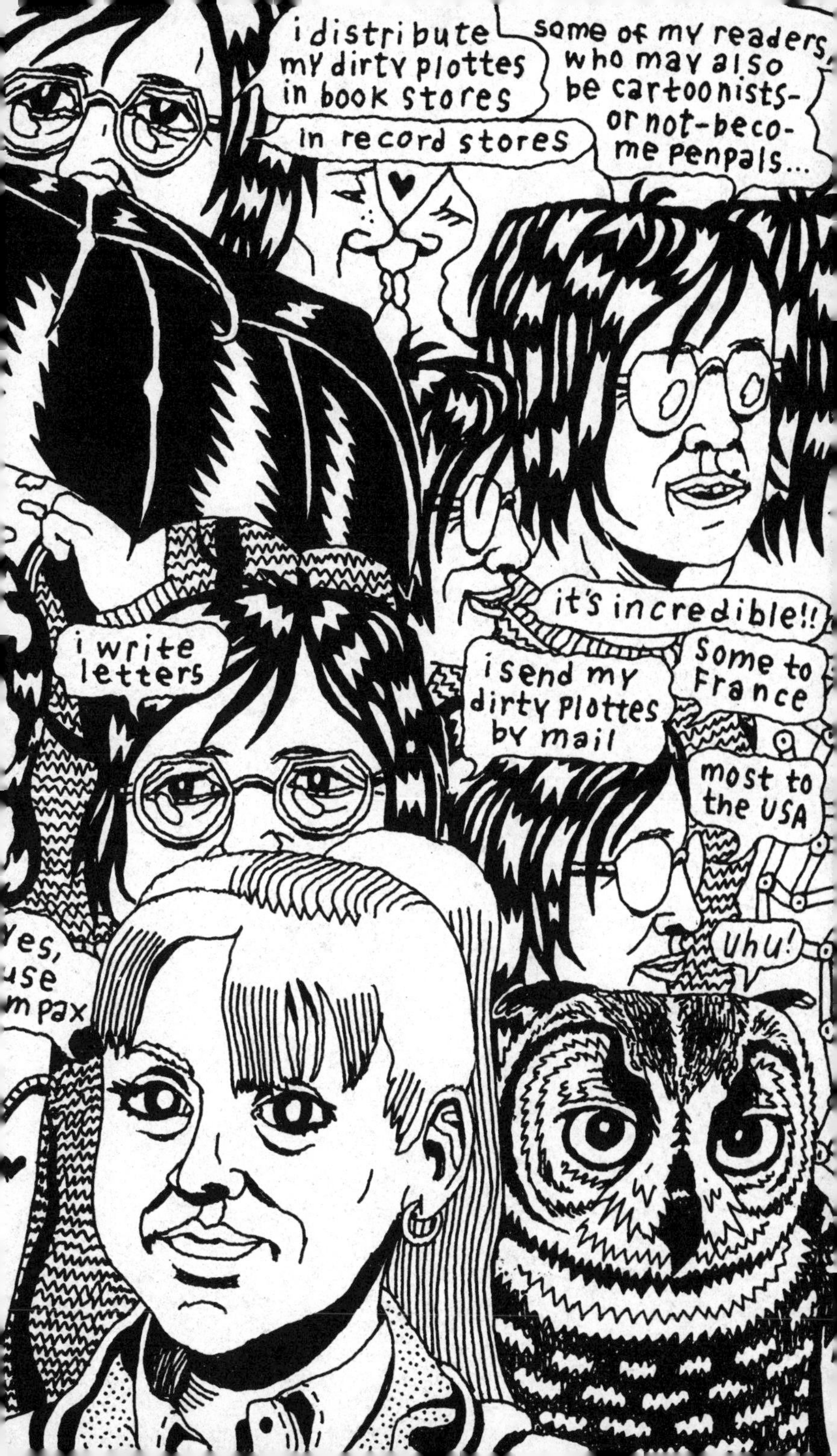
i distribute my dirty plottes in book stores
in record stores
some of my readers, who may also be cartoonists- or not-become penpals...
it's incredible!!
i write letters
i send my dirty plottes by mail
Some to France
most to the USA
uhu!
yes,
use
mpax

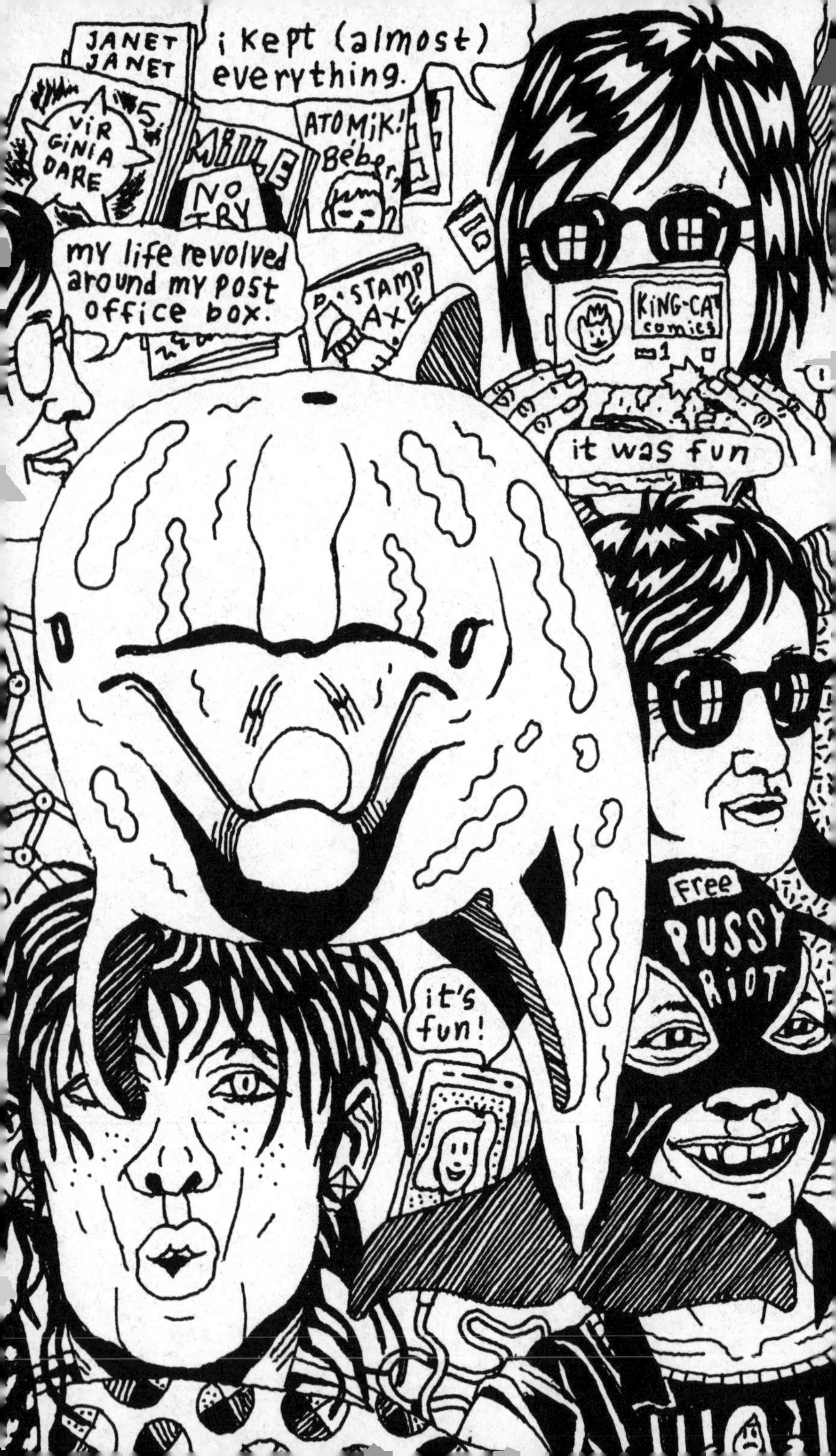
JANET JANET
i kept (almost) everything.
VIRGINIA DARE
ATOMIK! Bébert
NO TRY
my life revolved around my post office box.
STAMP AXE
KING-CAT comics
it was fun
Free PUSSY RIOT
it's fun!

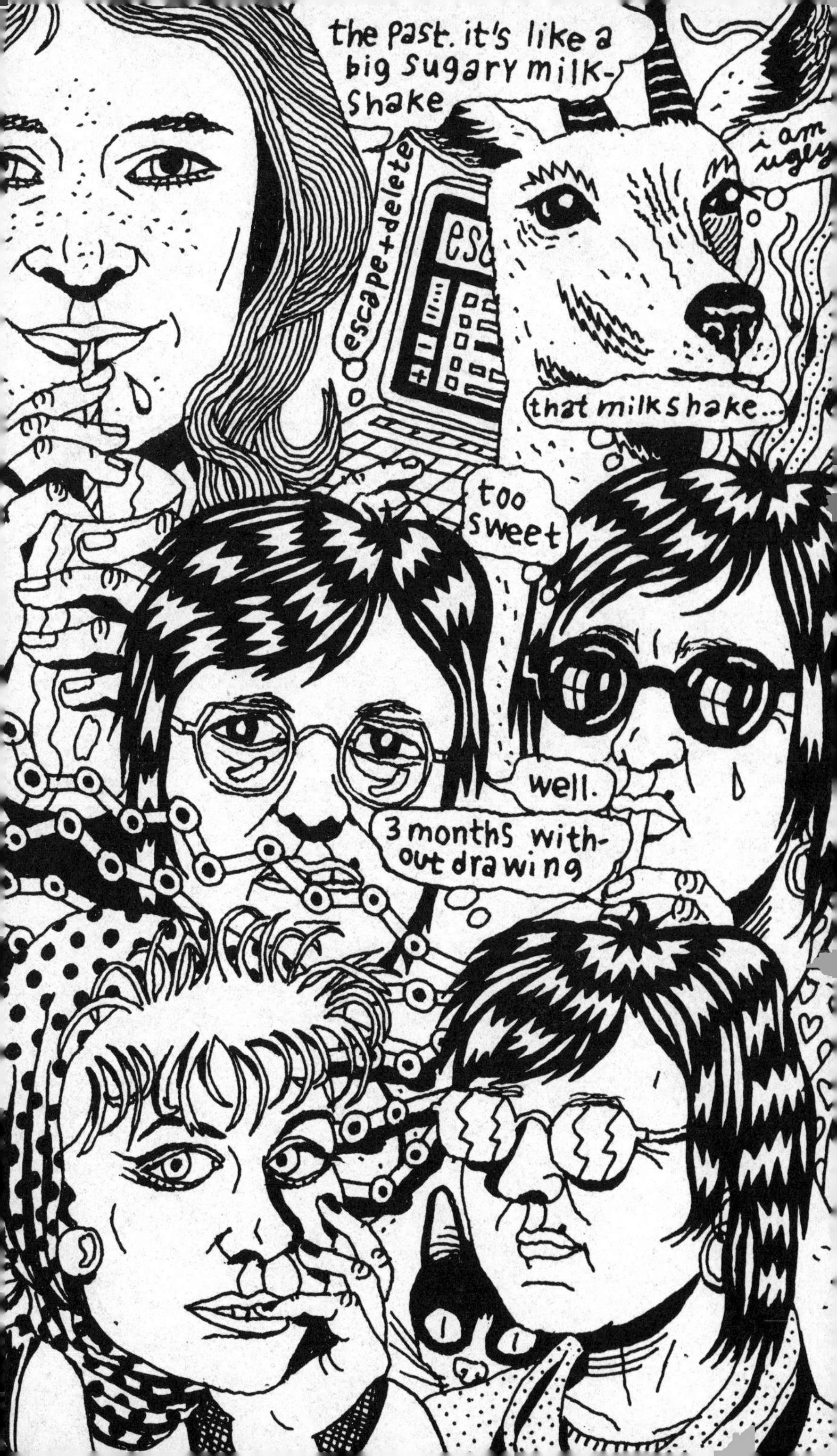
the past. it's like a big sugary milk-shake
escape+delete
i am ugly
that milkshake...
too sweet
well.
3 months with-out drawing

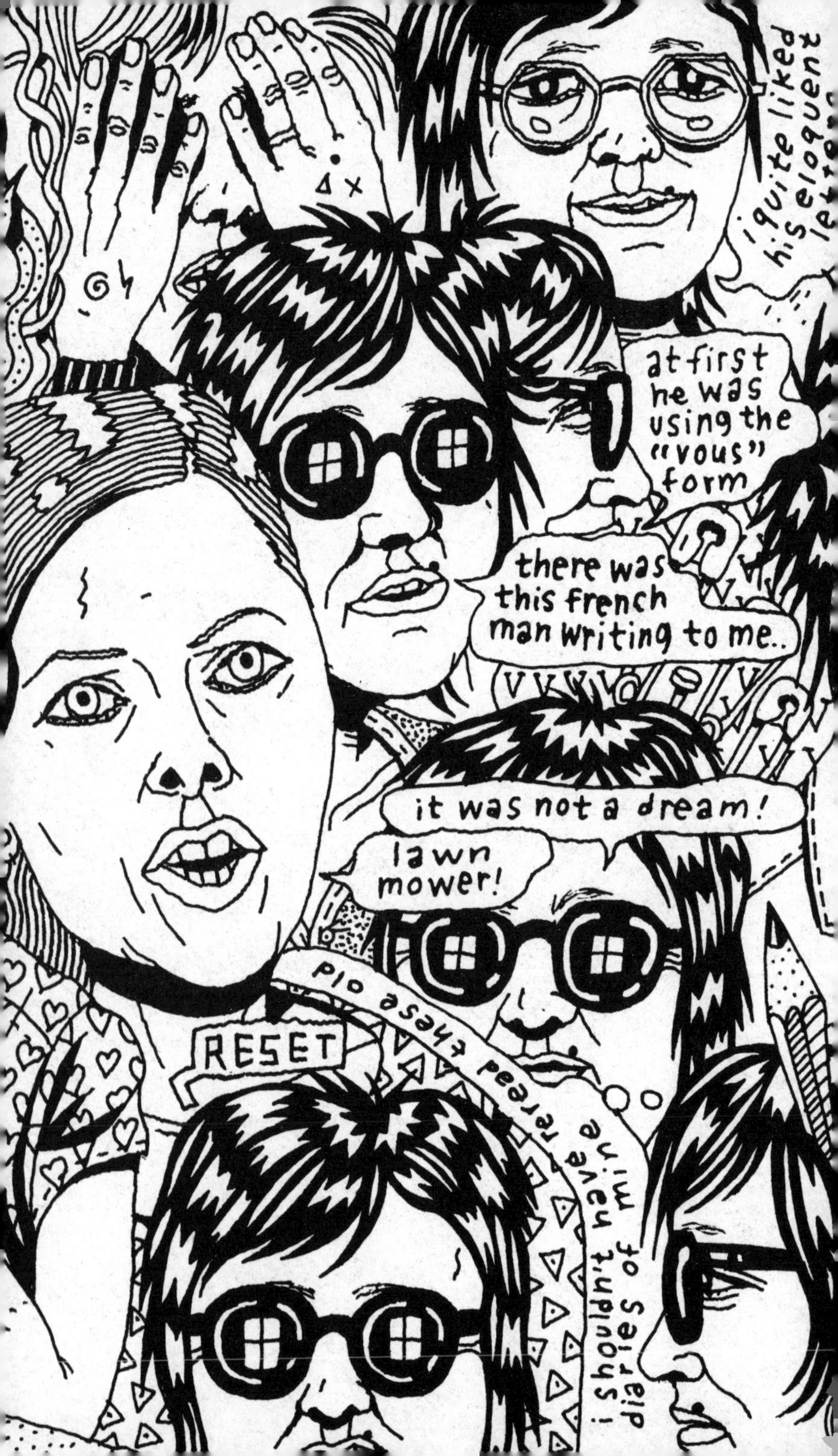
there was this french man writing to me..
at first he was using the "vous" form
i quite liked his eloquent
it was not a dream!
lawn mower!
RESET
i shouldn't have reread these old diaries of mine

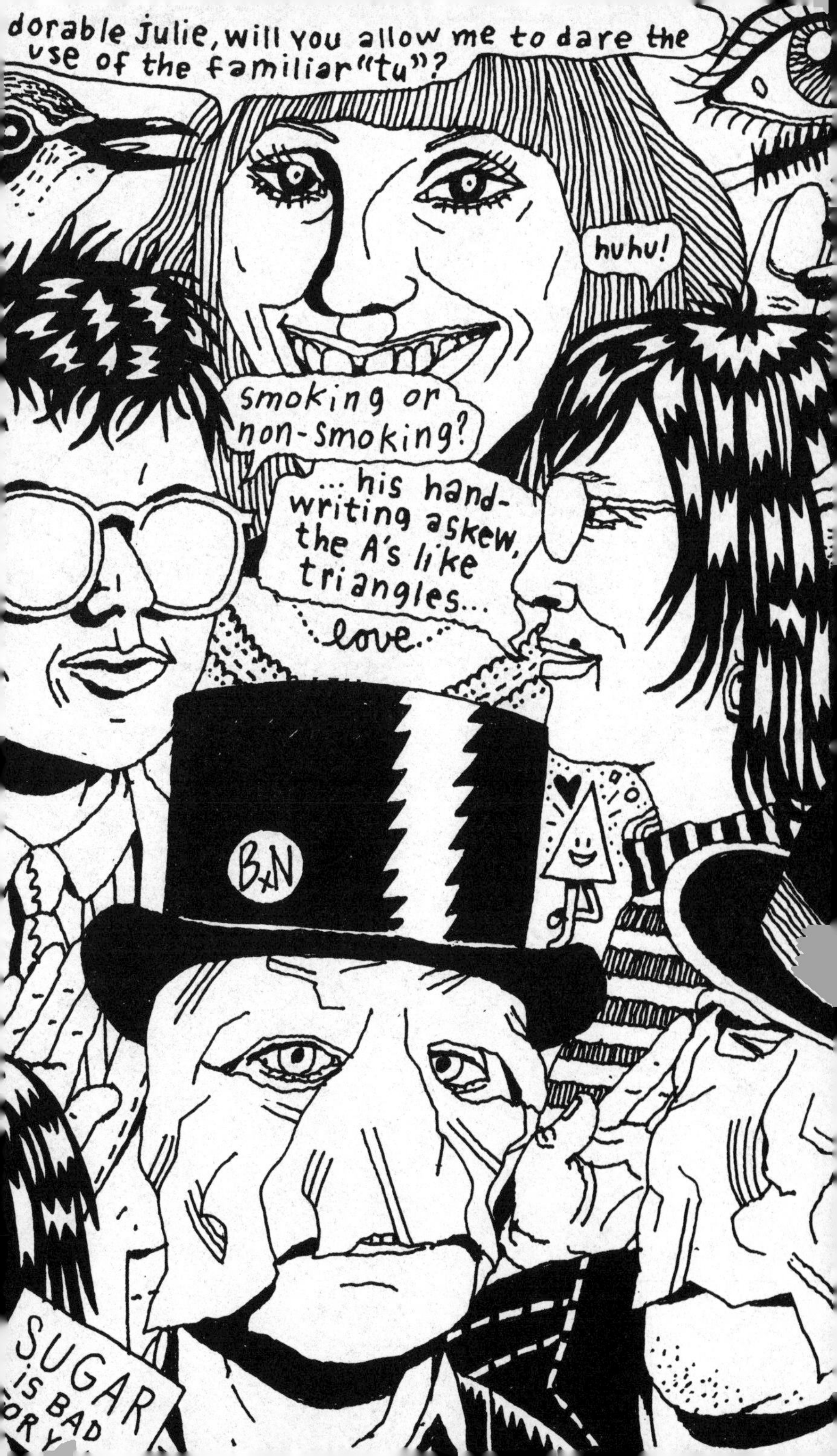
dorable Julie, will you allow me to dare the use of the familiar "tu"?
huhu!
smoking or non-smoking?
...his hand-writing askew, the A's like triangles...
love
B+N
SUGAR IS BAD
ORY

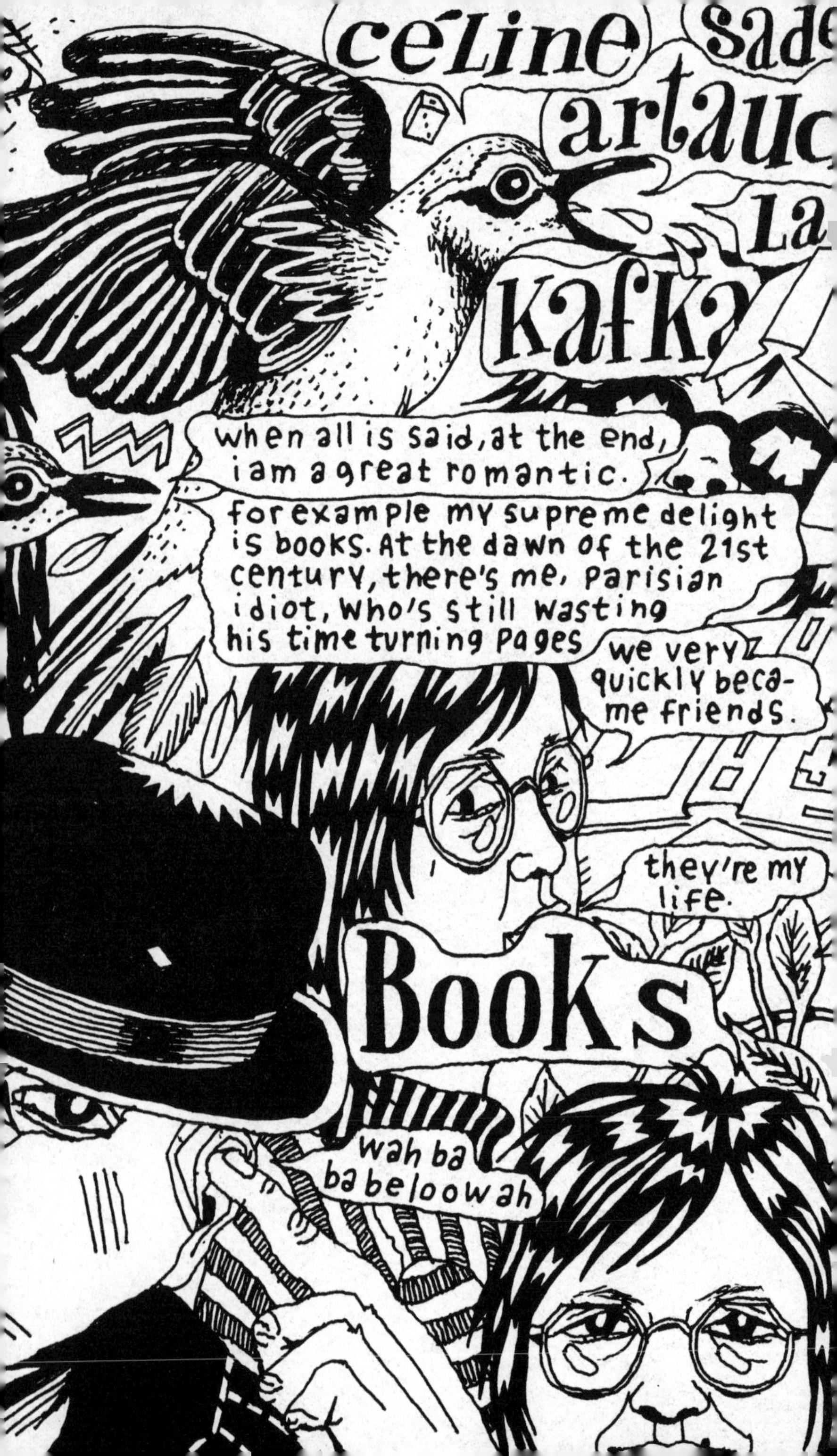
céline
sade
artaud
La
kafka
when all is said, at the end, i am a great romantic.
for example my supreme delight is books. At the dawn of the 21st century, there's me, parisian idiot, who's still wasting his time turning pages
we very quickly became friends.
they're my life.
Books
wah ba ba beloowah

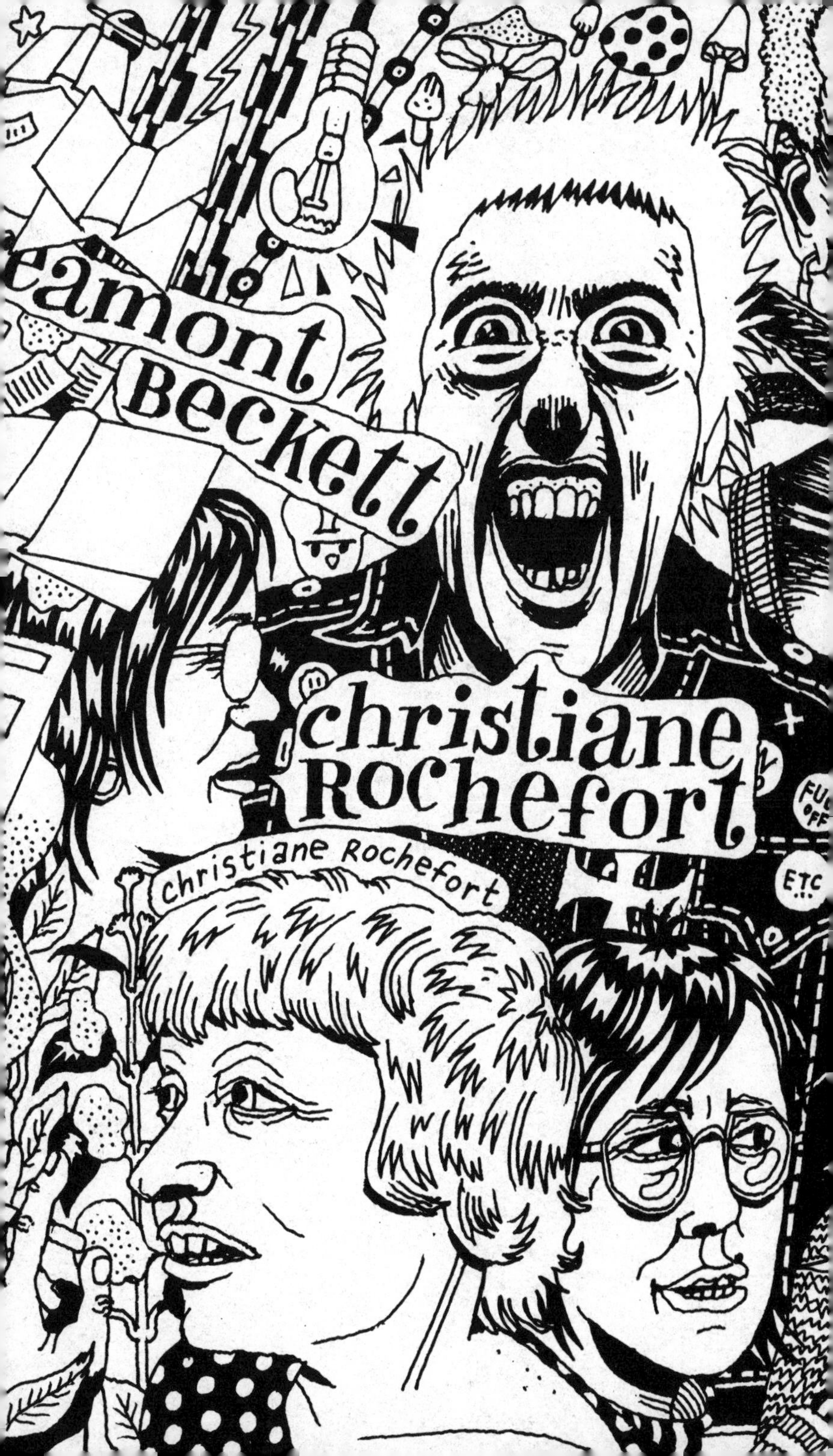

eamont
Beckett
christiane
Rochefort
christiane Rochefort
ETC

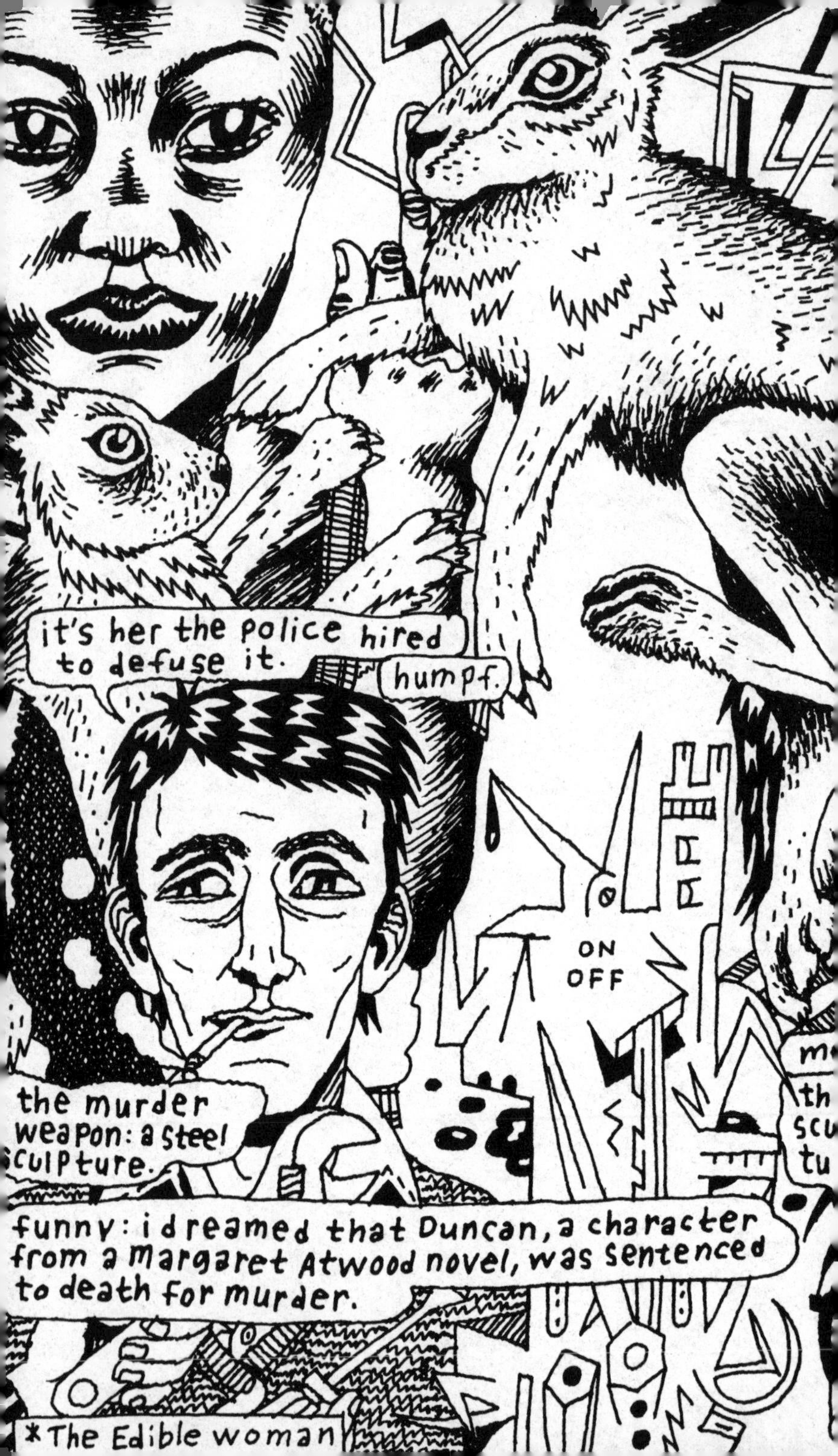
it's her the police hired to defuse it.
humpf.
ON
OFF
the murder weapon: a steel sculpture.
funny: i dreamed that Duncan, a character from a Margaret Atwood novel, was sentenced to death for murder.
*The Edible woman

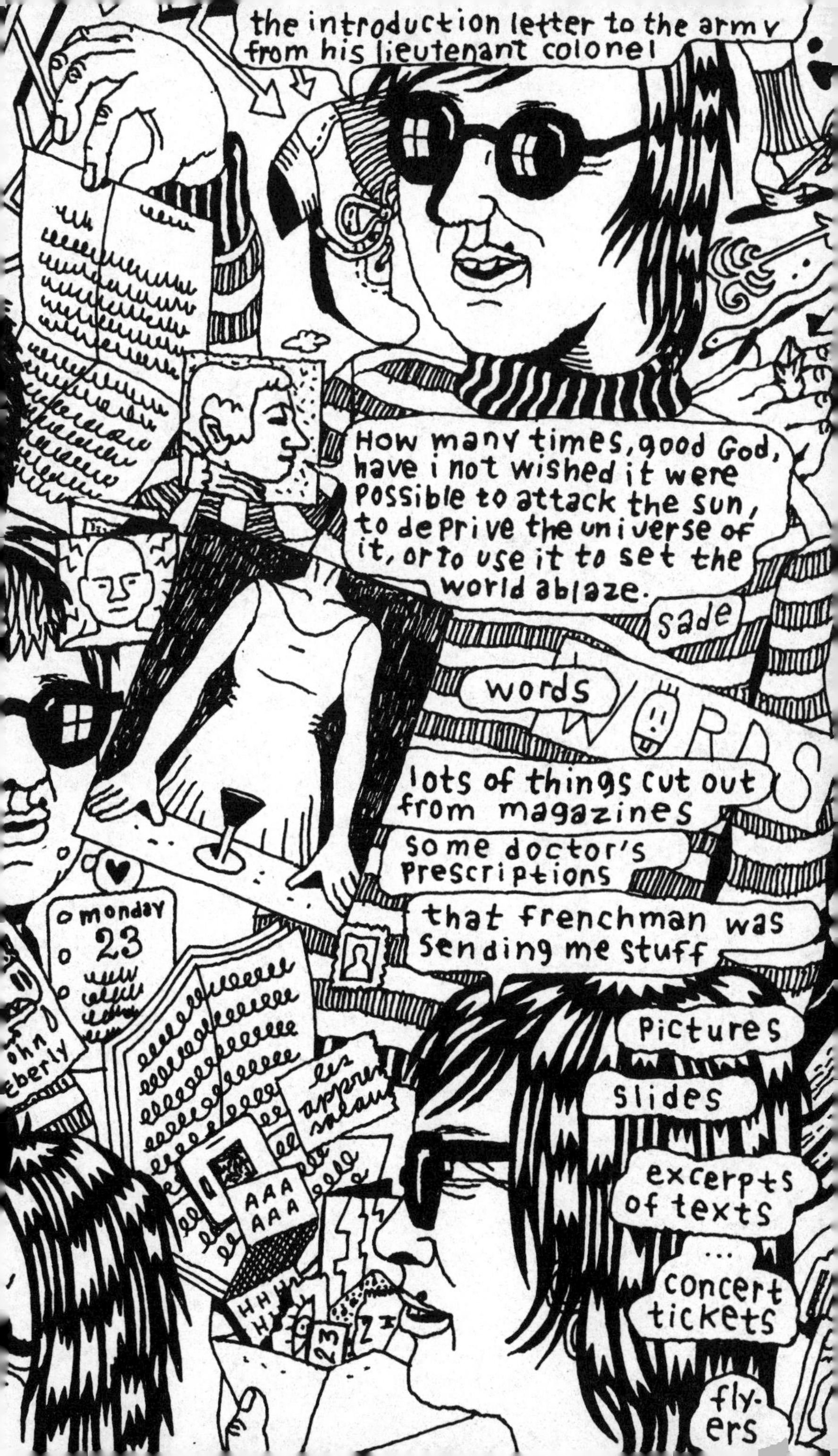
the introduction letter to the army from his lieutenant colonel
How many times, good God, have i not wished it were possible to attack the sun, to deprive the universe of it, or to use it to set the world ablaze.
sade
words
lots of things cut out from magazines
some doctor's prescriptions
that frenchman was sending me stuff
monday 23
pictures
slides
excerpts of texts
...
concert tickets
fly-ers

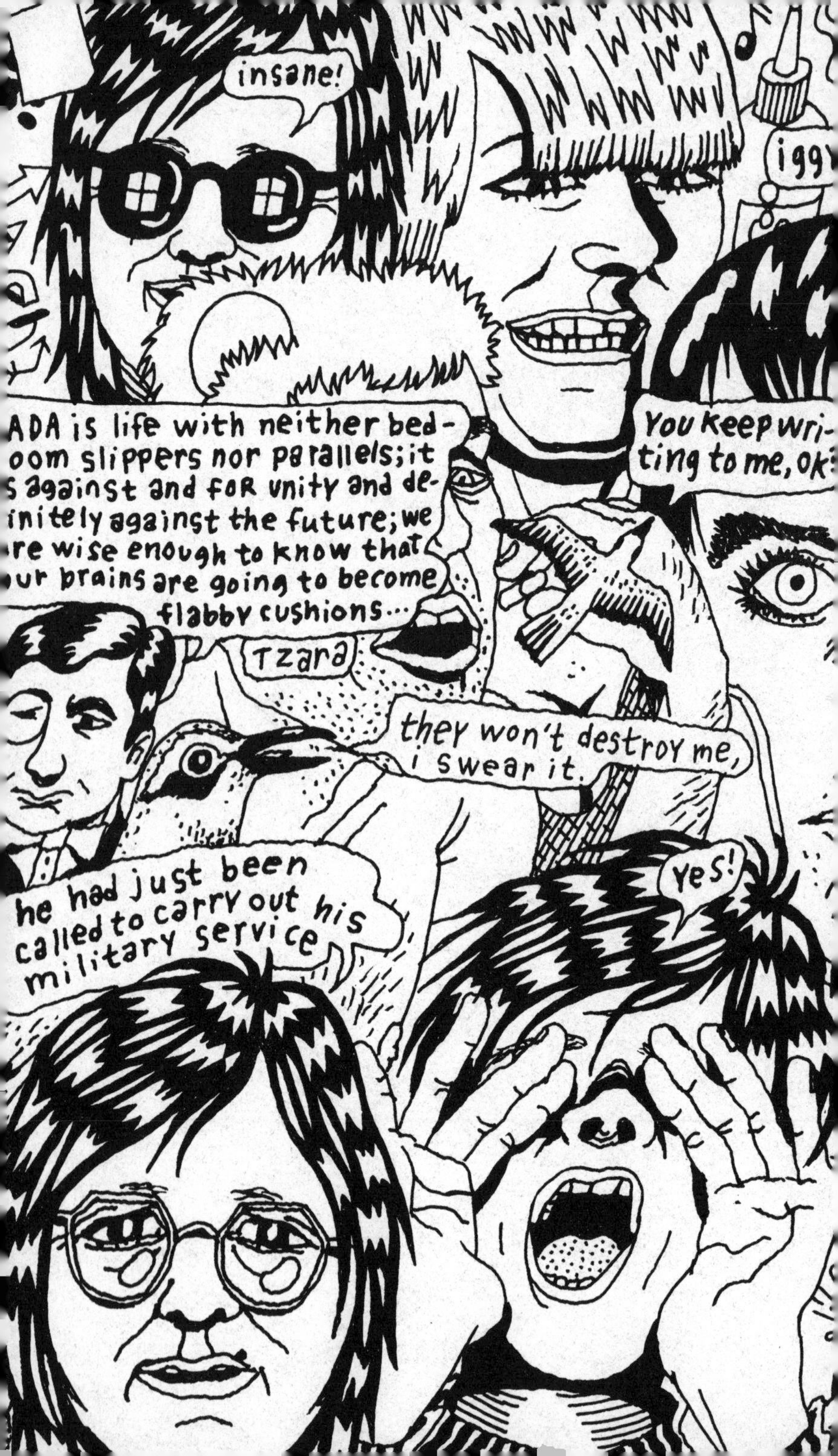
insane!
iggy
ADA is life with neither bed-
oom slippers nor parallels; it
s against and FOR unity and de-
initely against the future; we
re wise enough to know that
ur brains are going to become
flabby cushions...
TZARA
You keep wri-
ting to me, ok
they won't destroy me,
i swear it.
he had just been
called to carry out his
military service
YES!

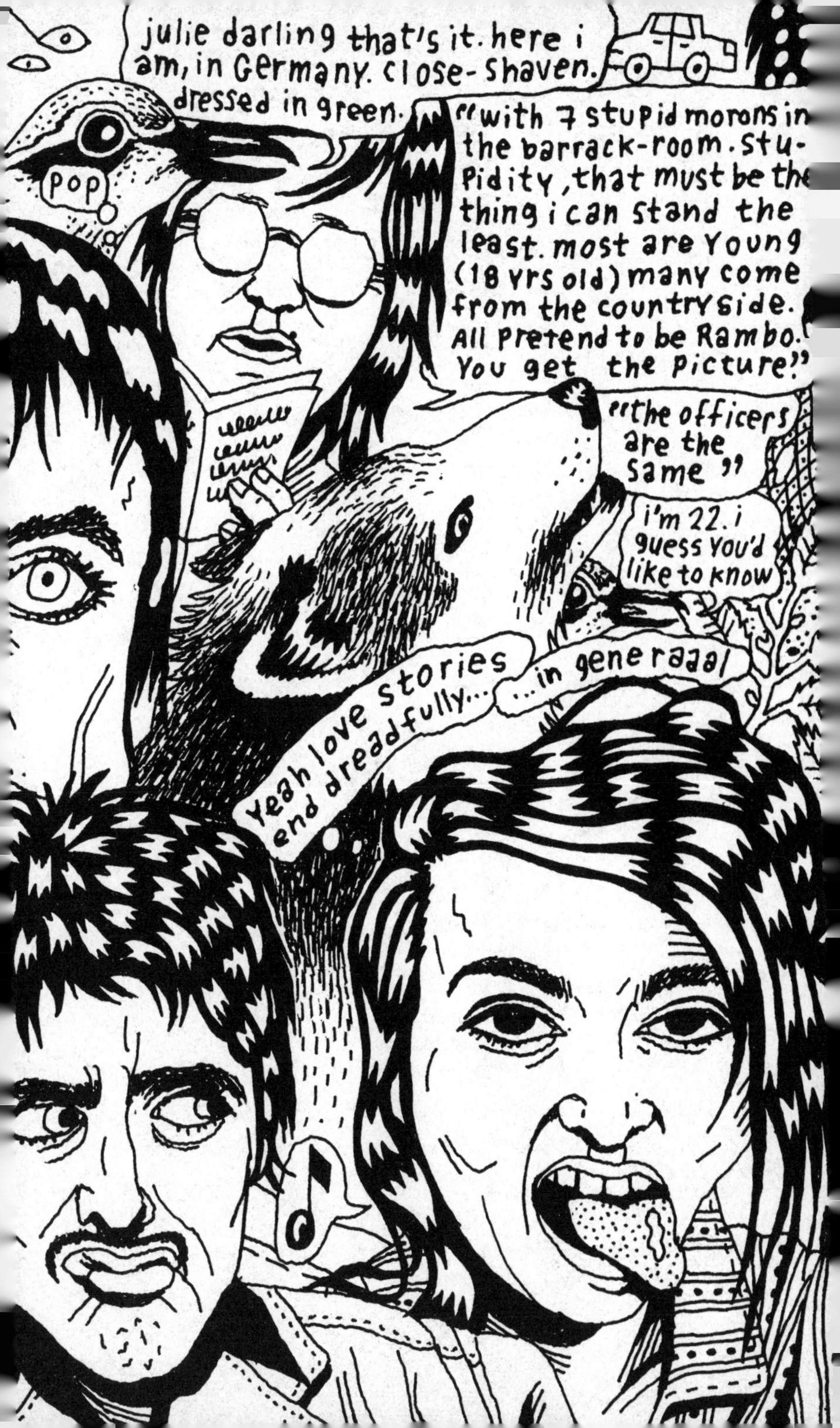
julie darling that's it. here i am, in Germany. close-shaven. dressed in green.
"with 7 stupid morons in the barrack-room. stupidity, that must be the thing i can stand the least. most are young (18 yrs old) many come from the countryside. All pretend to be Rambo. You get the picture"
pop
"the officers are the same"
i'm 22. i guess you'd like to know
yeah love stories end dreadfully...
...in generaaal

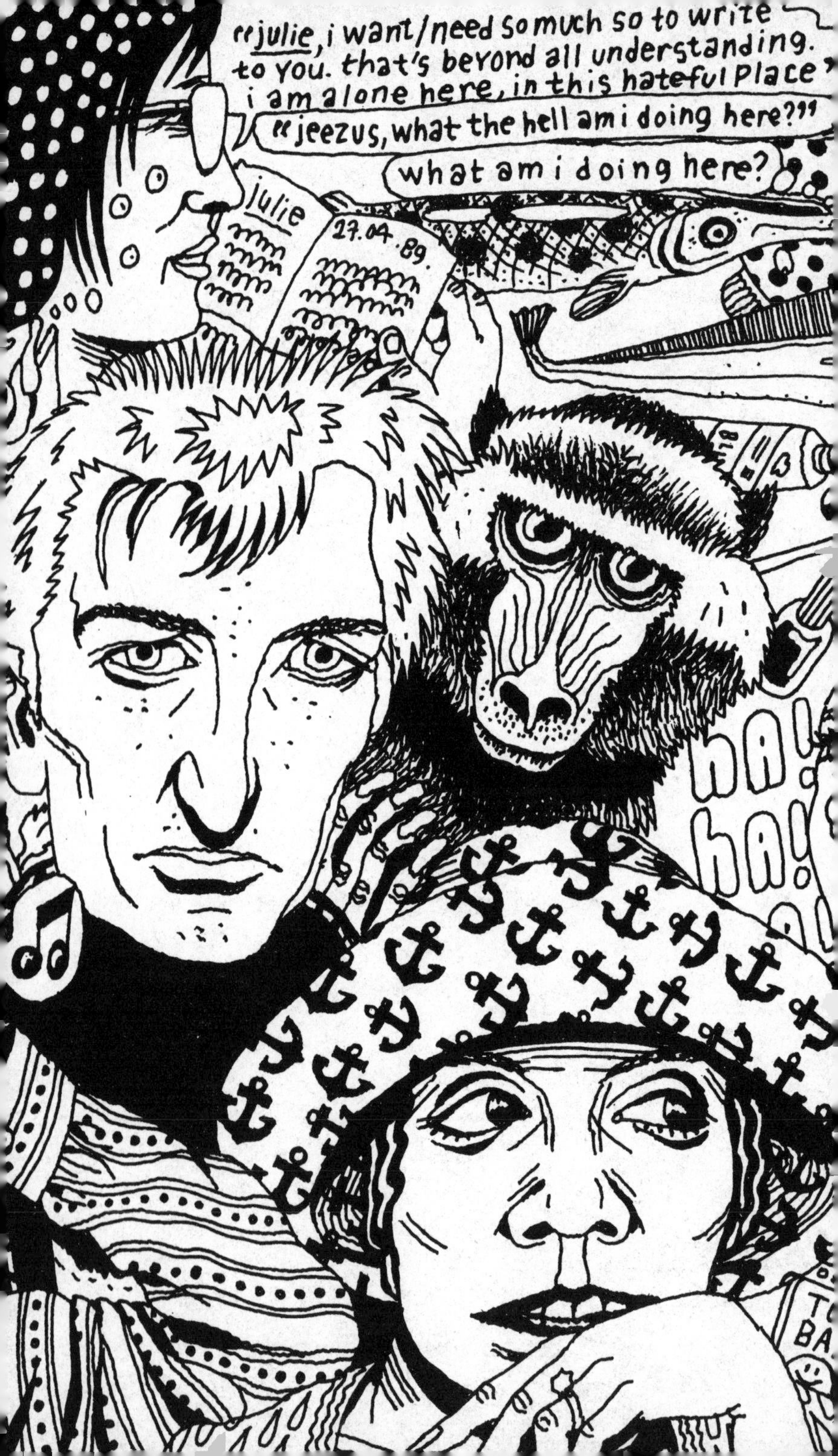
"julie, i want/need so much so to write to you. that's beyond all understanding. i am alone here, in this hateful place"
"jeezus, what the hell am i doing here?"
what am i doing here?
julie
27.04.89
ha! ha!

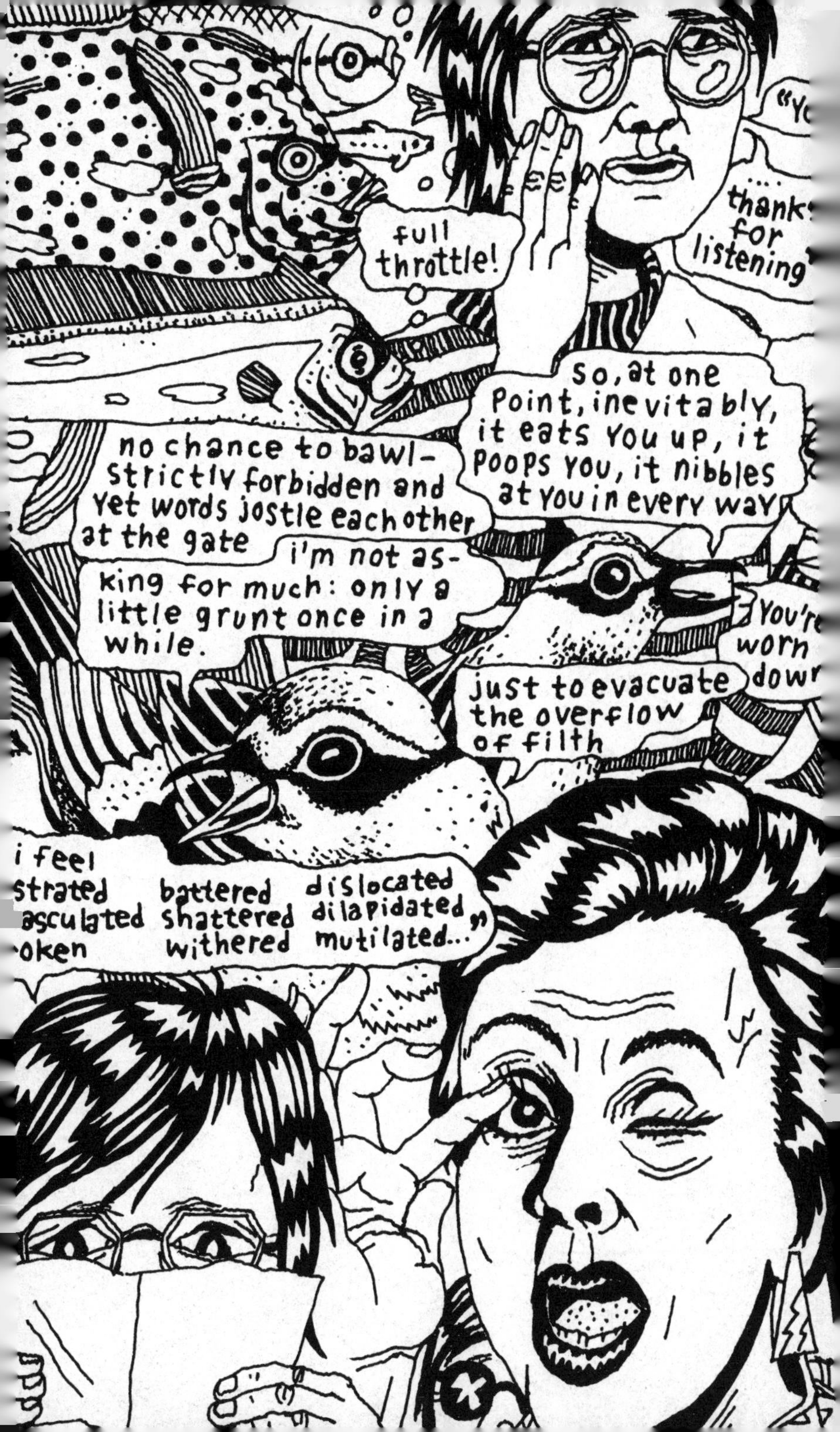
full throttle!
... thanks for listening"
"Yo
So, at one point, inevitably, it eats you up, it poops you, it nibbles at you in every way
no chance to bawl-strictly forbidden and yet words jostle each other at the gate
i'm not asking for much: only a little grunt once in a while.
just to evacuate the overflow of filth
You're worn down
i feel
strated asculated oken
battered shattered withered
dislocated dilapidated mutilated..."

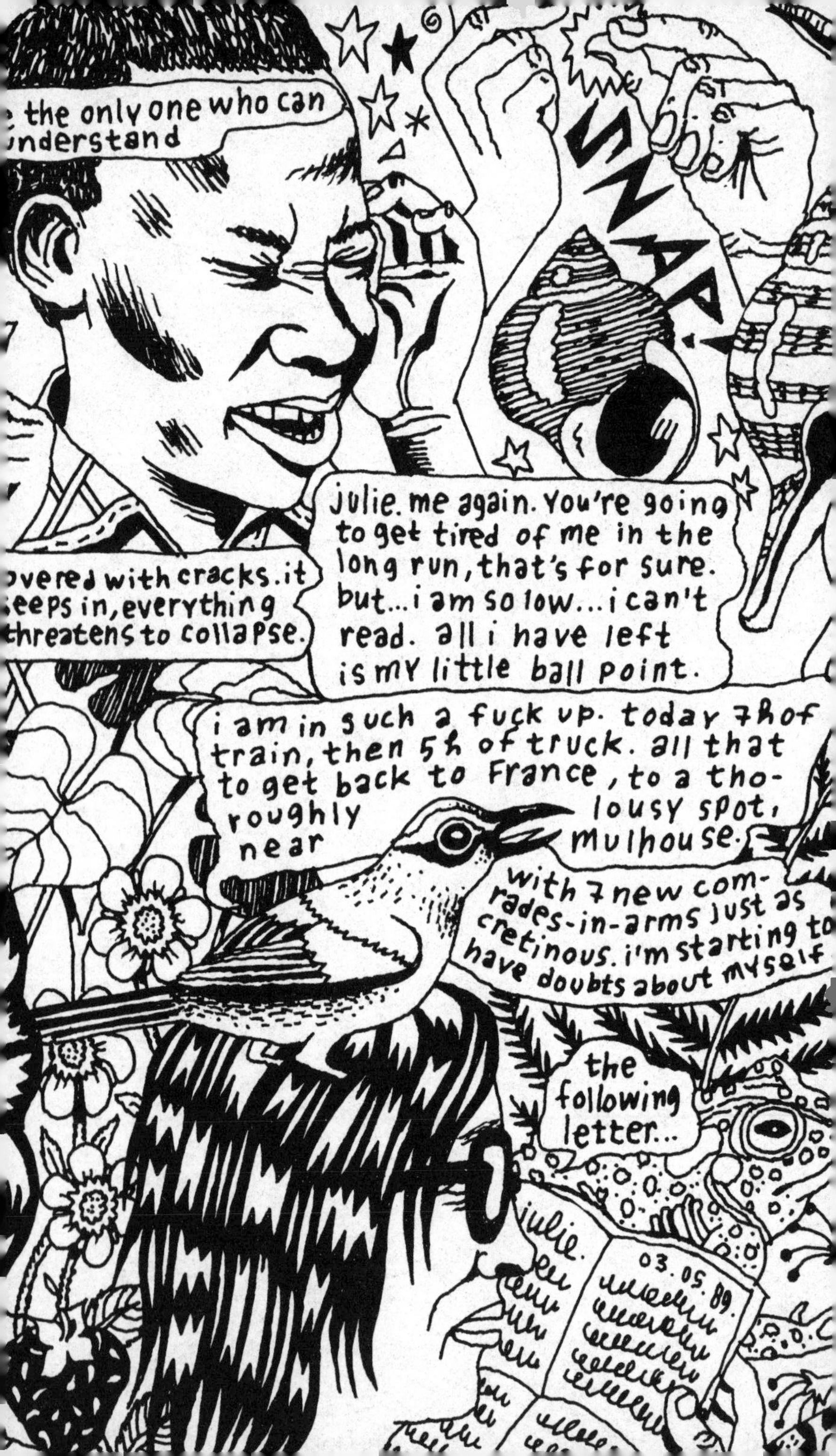
the only one who can understand
overed with cracks. it seeps in, everything threatens to collapse.
SNAP
julie. me again. you're going to get tired of me in the long run, that's for sure. but... i am so low... i can't read. all i have left is my little ball point.
i am in such a fuck up. today 7h of train, then 5h of truck. all that to get back to France, to a thoroughly lousy spot, near mulhouse.
with 7 new comrades-in-arms just as cretinous. i'm starting to have doubts about myself
the following letter...
julie.
03.05.89.

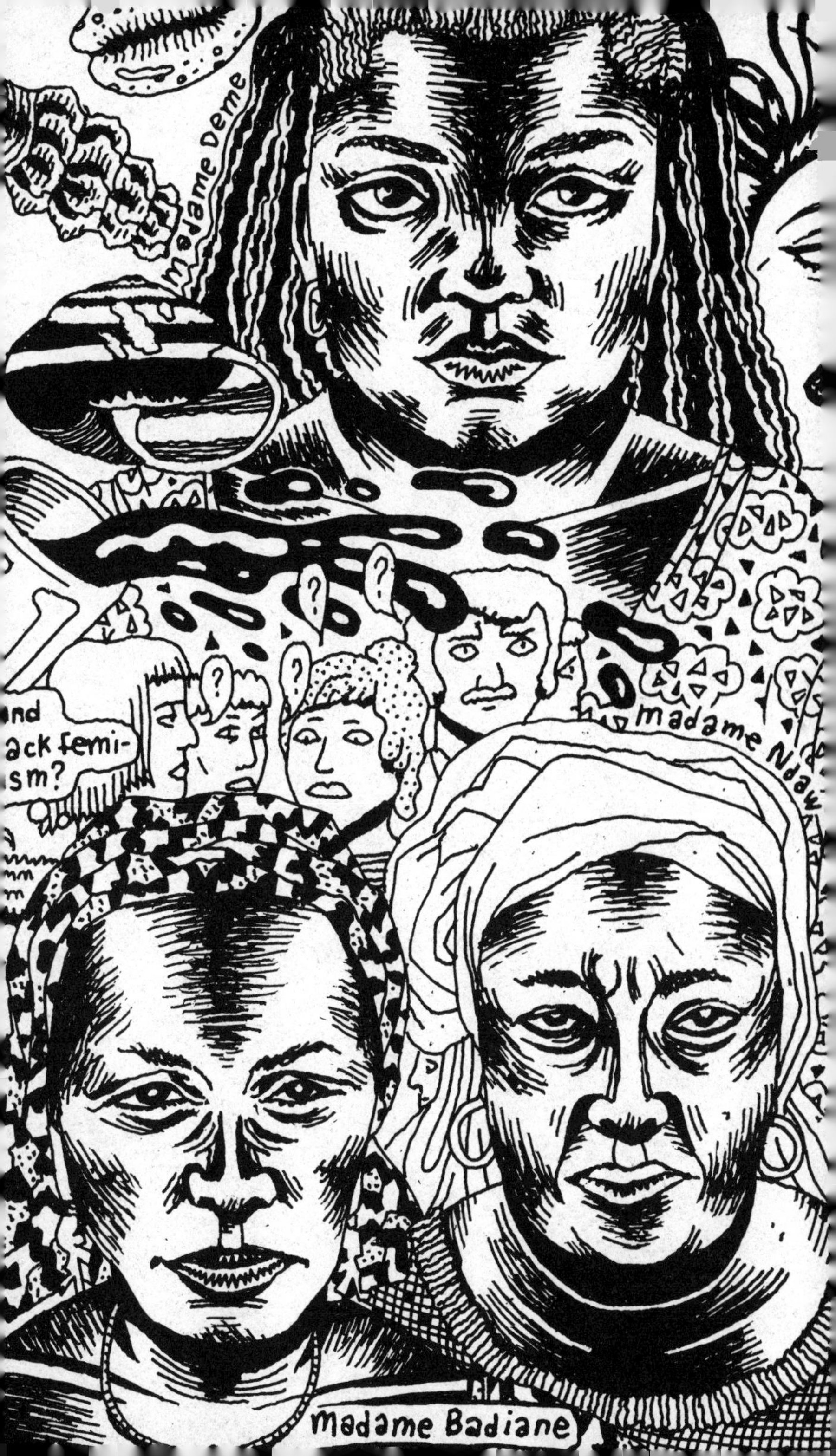

Madame Deme
?
?
?
?
nd
ack femi-
sm?
madame Ndaw
Madame Badiane

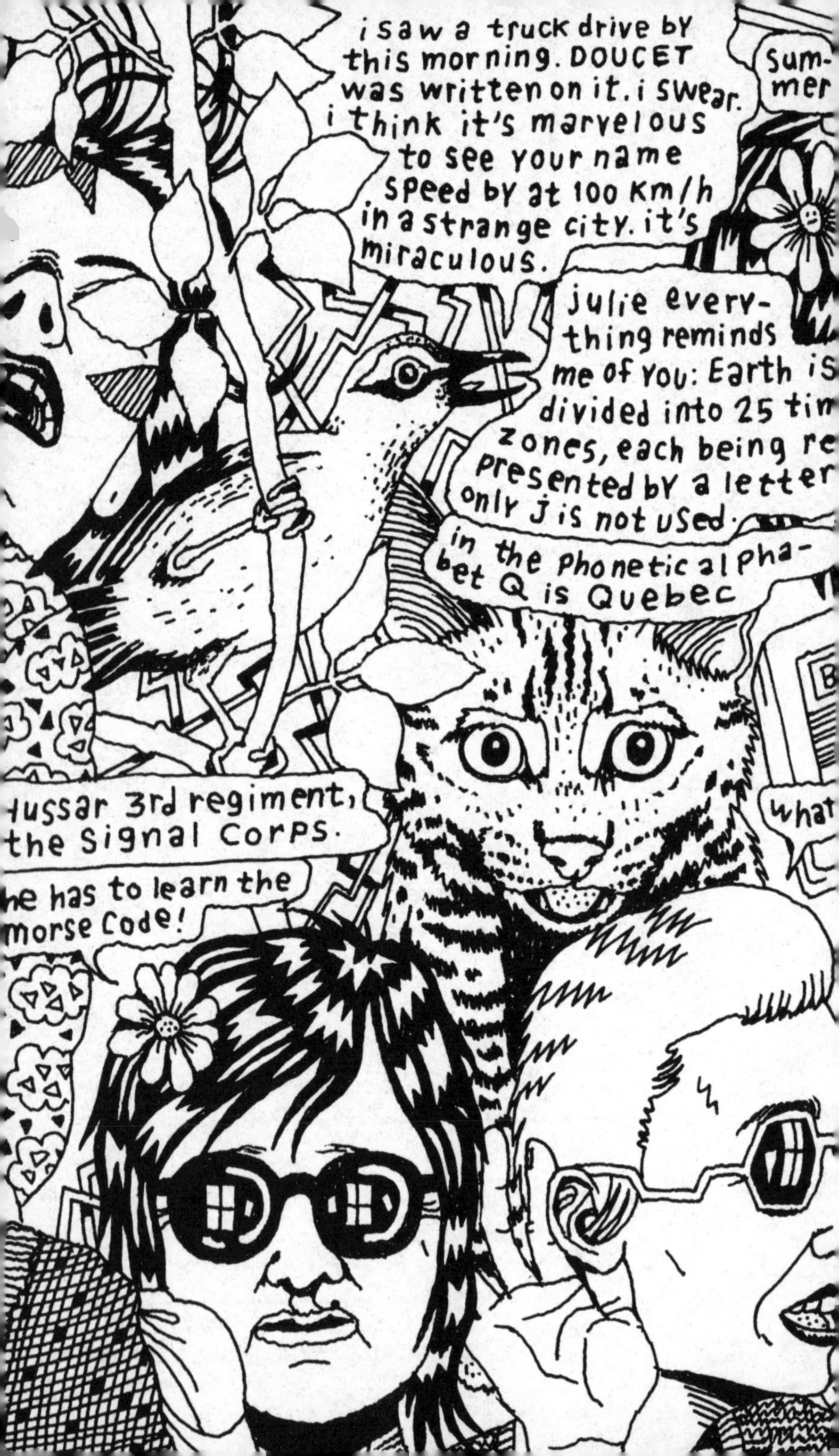

i saw a truck drive by this morning. DOUCET was written on it. i swear. i think it's marvelous to see your name speed by at 100 km/h in a strange city. it's miraculous.
Sum-mer
julie every-thing reminds me of you: Earth is divided into 25 tim zones, each being re presented by a letter only J is not used.
in the phonetic alpha-bet Q is Quebec
Hussar 3rd regiment, the Signal Corps.
what
he has to learn the morse code!

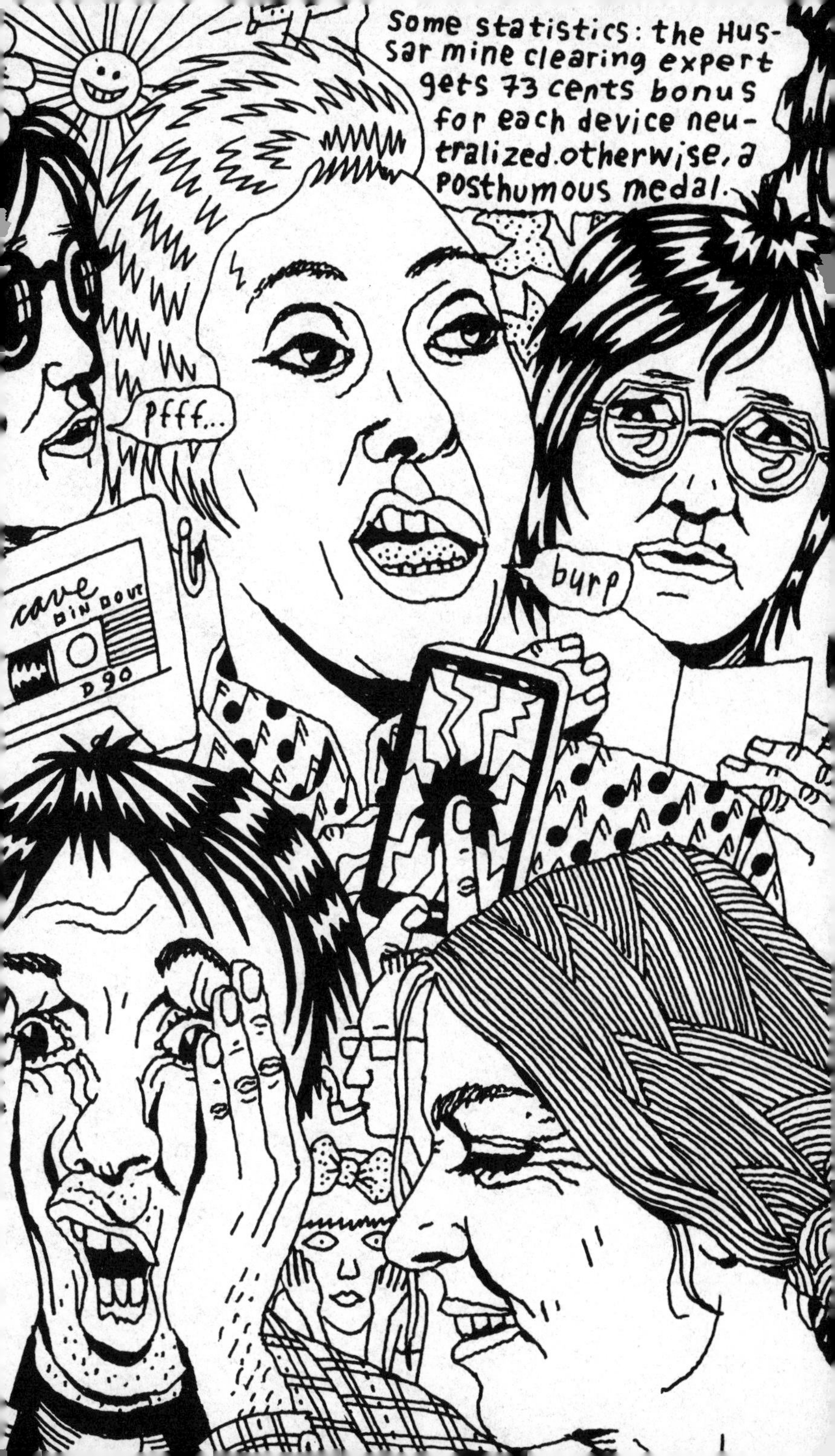
Some statistics: the Hussar mine clearing expert gets 73 cents bonus for each device neutralized. otherwise, a posthumous medal.
pfff...
burp
cave
IN DOUT
D90

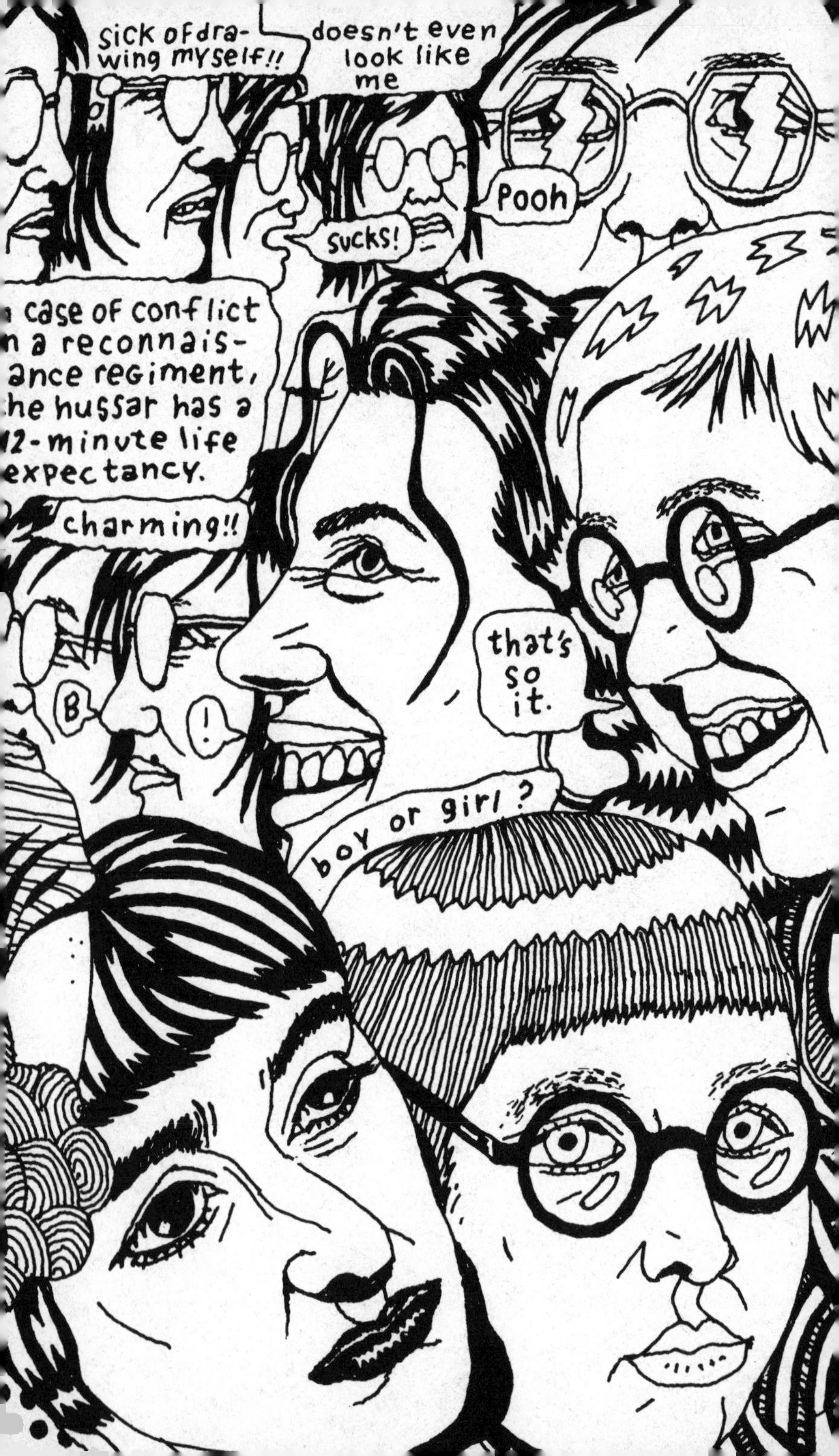
sick of drawing myself!!
doesn't even look like me
Pooh
sucks!
case of conflict
n a reconnais-
ance regiment,
he hussar has a
2-minute life
expectancy.
charming!!
that's so it.
B
!
boy or girl?

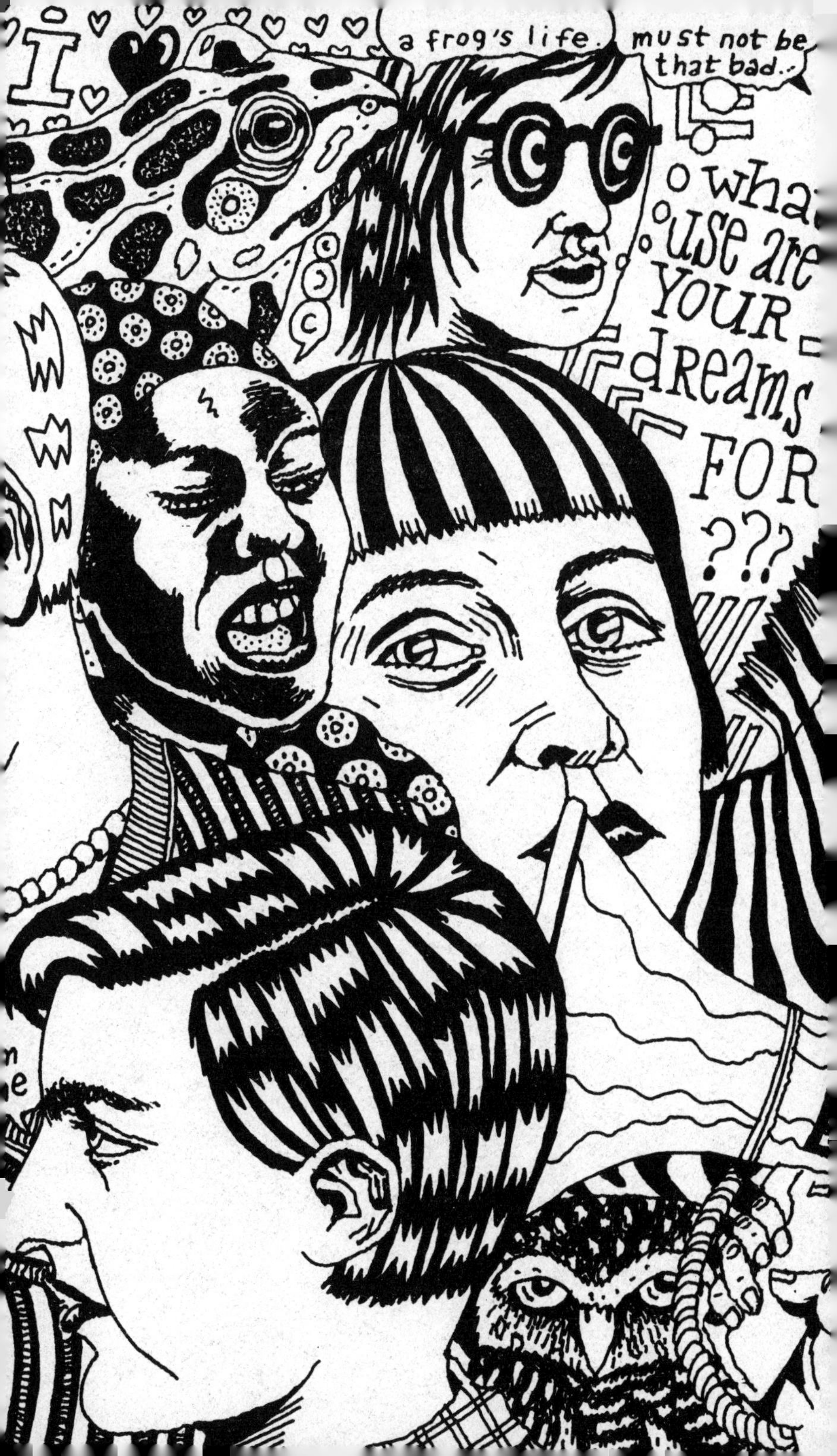
I
a frog's life.
must not be that bad..
what use are YOUR dreams FOR ???

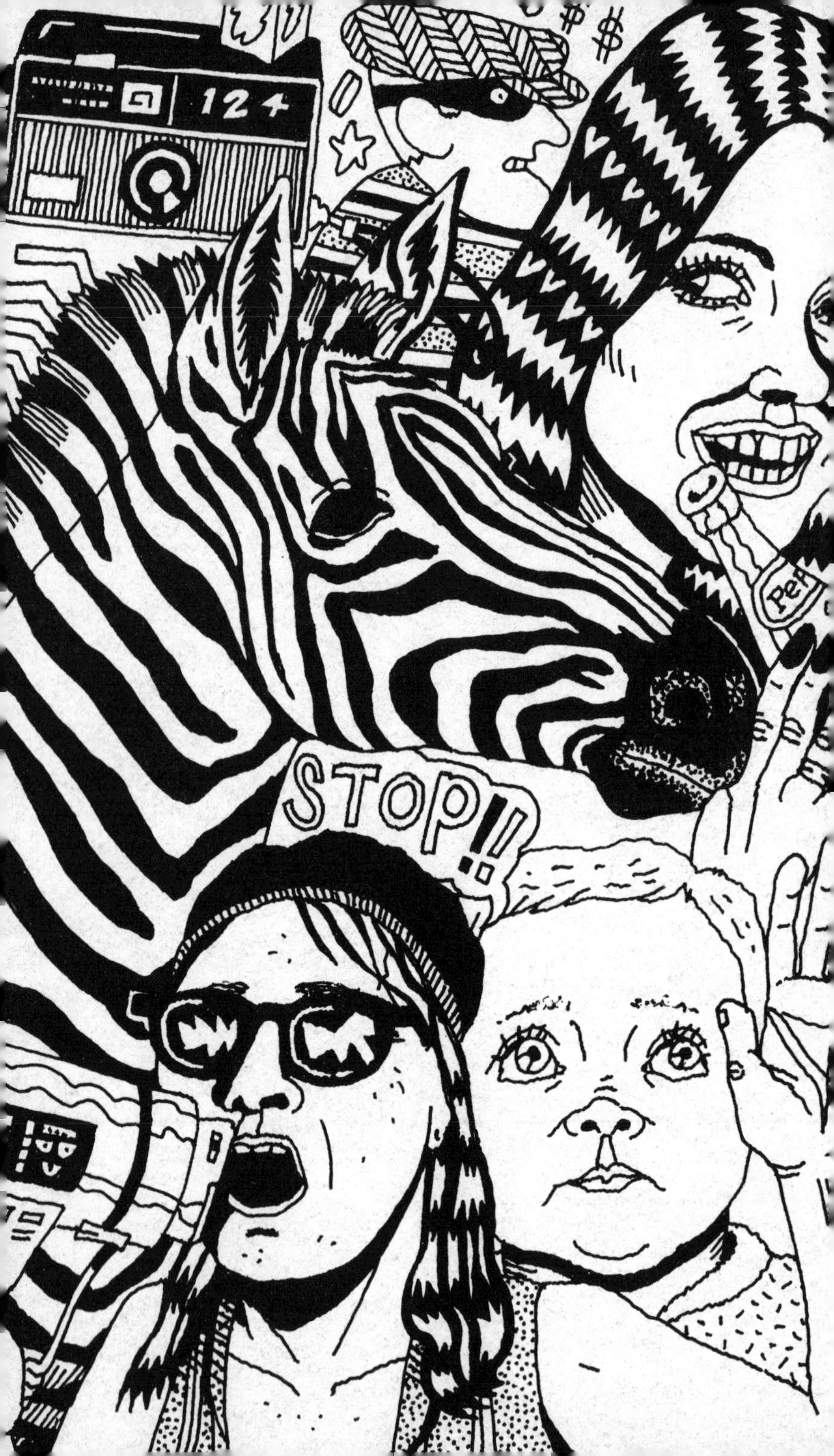
124
STOP!!

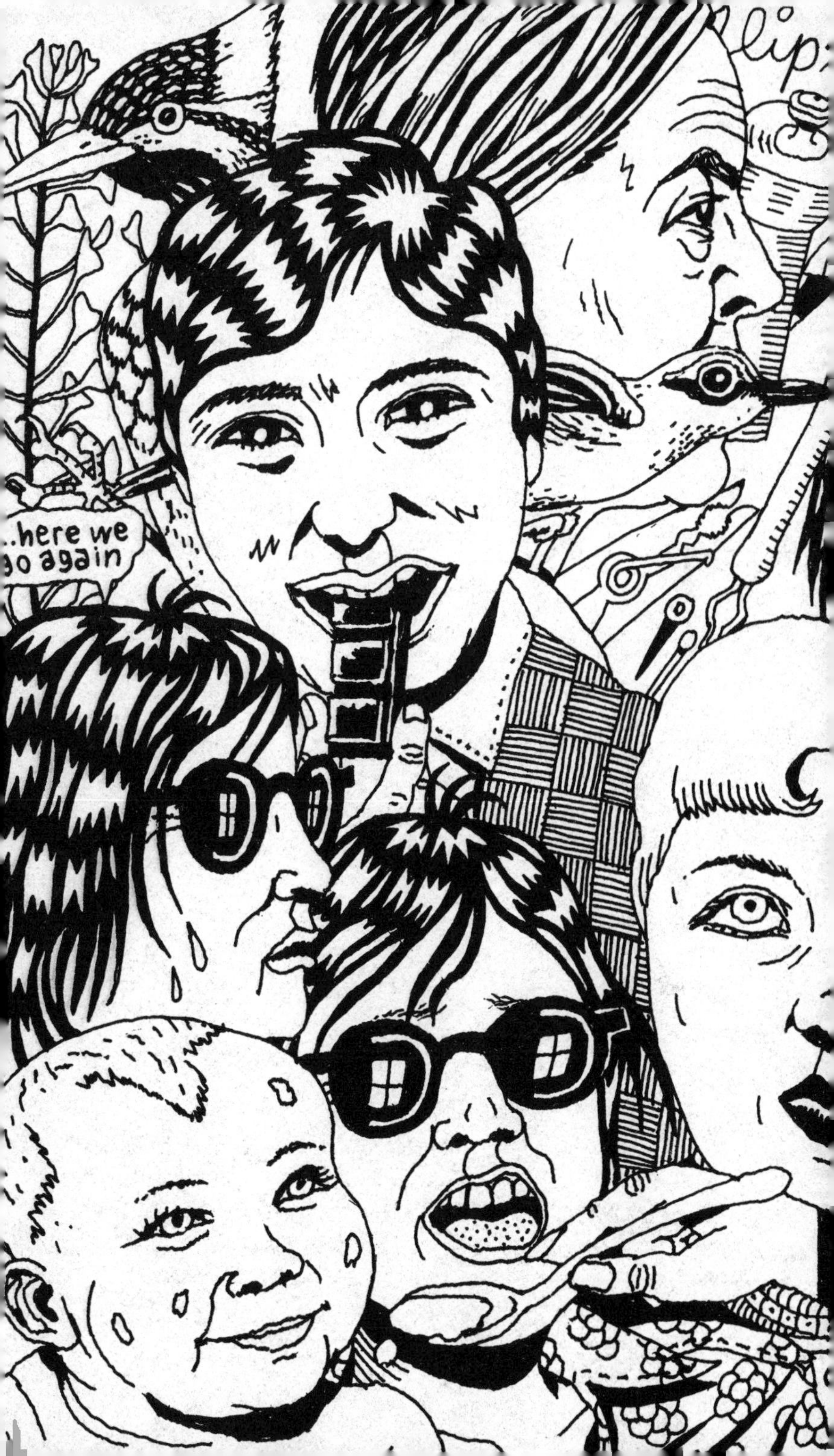
..here we go again

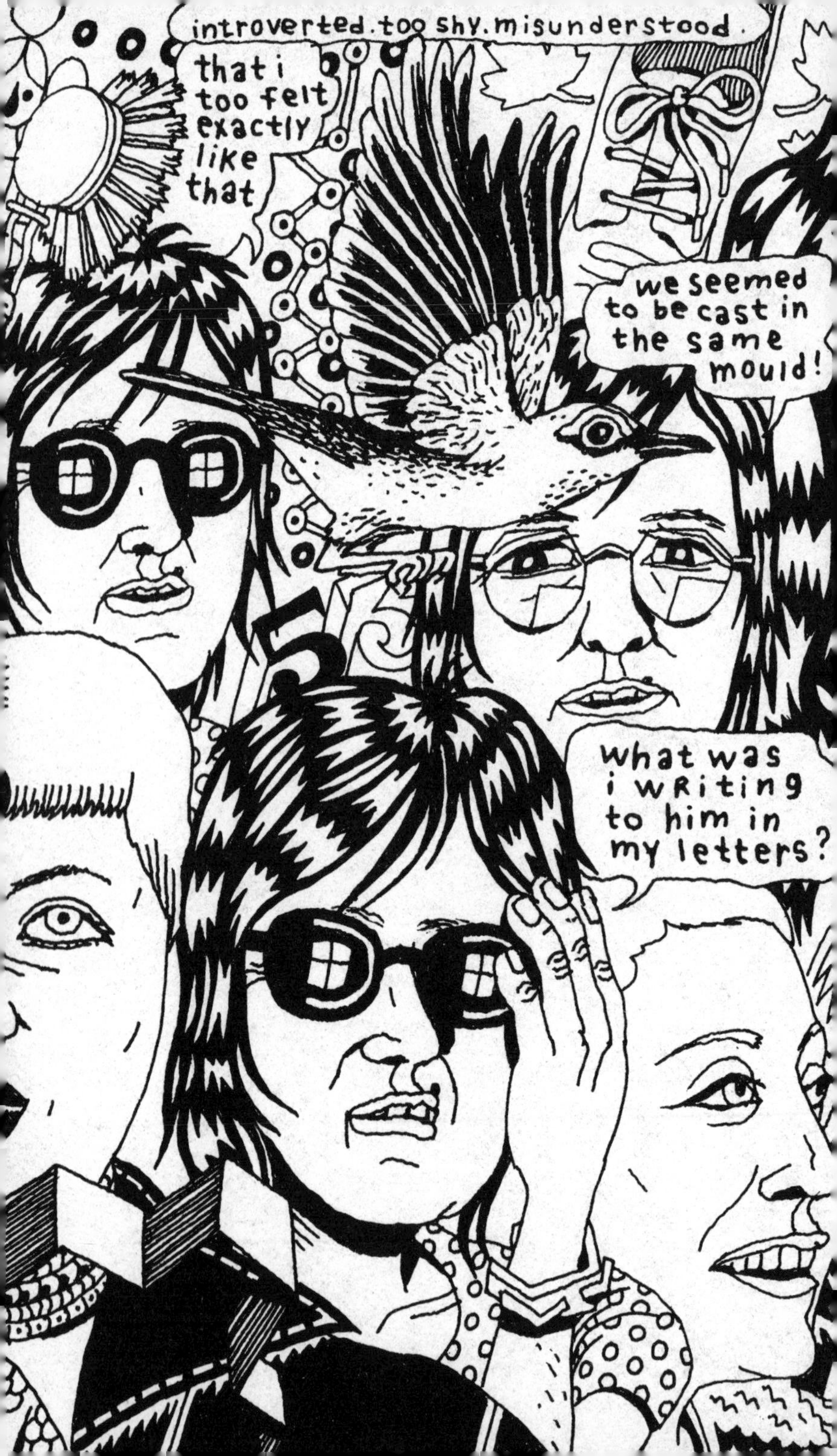
introverted. too shy. misunderstood.
that i too felt exactly like that
we seemed to be cast in the same mould!
what was i writing to him in my letters?

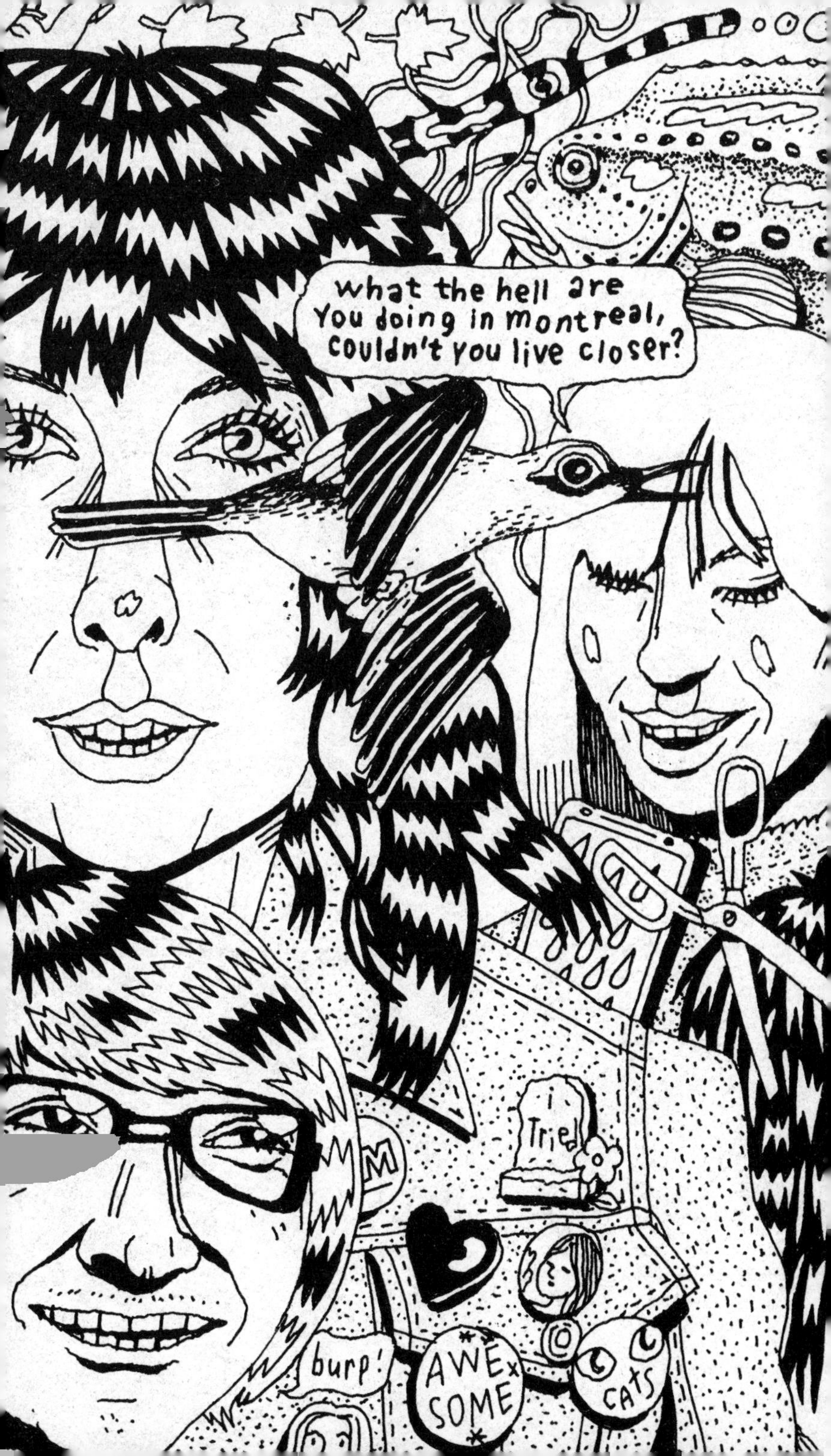
what the hell are you doing in montreal, couldn't you live closer?
I Tried
burp!
AWESOME
CATS

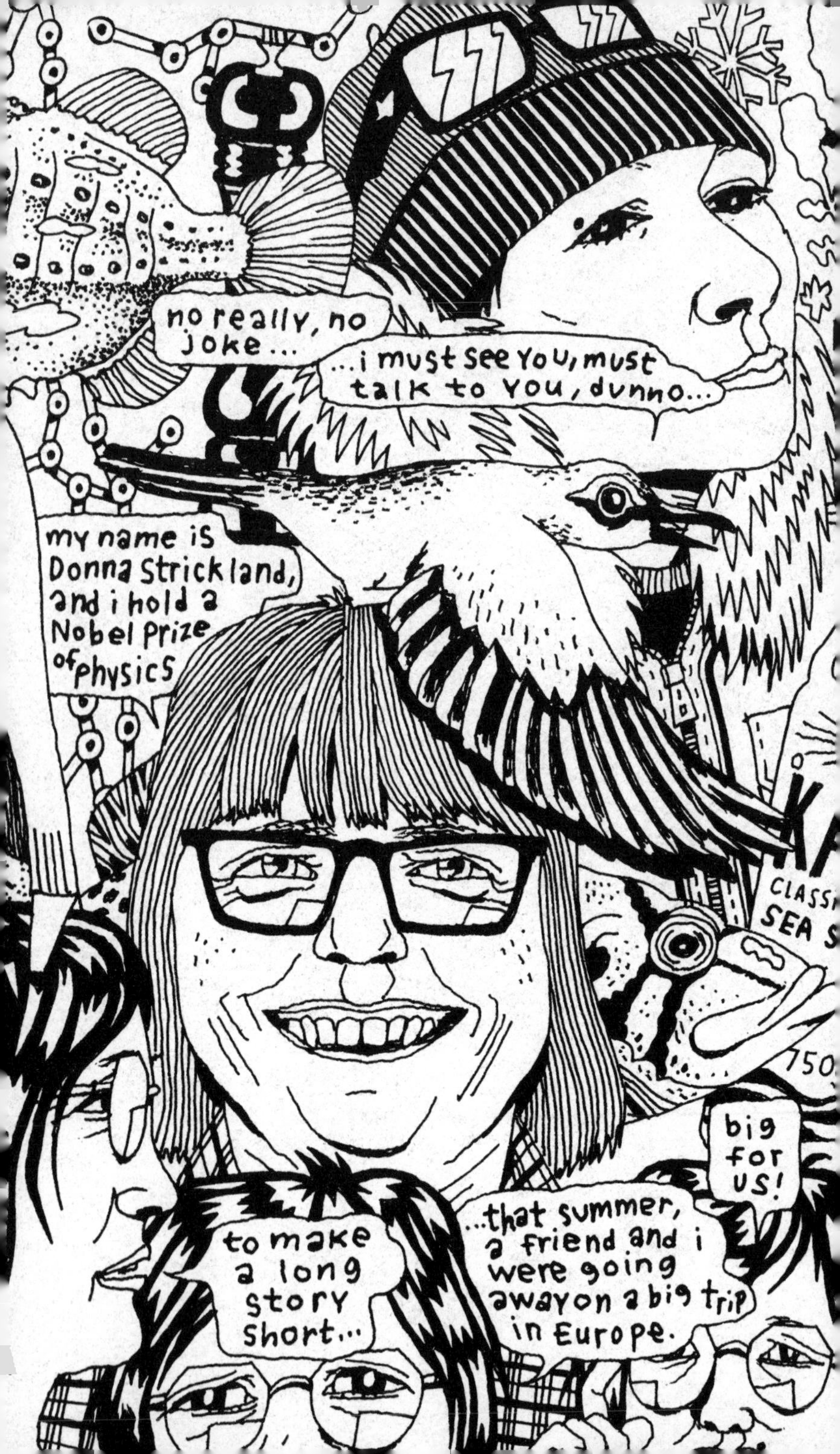
no really, no joke...
...i must see you, must talk to you, dunno...
my name is Donna Strickland, and i hold a Nobel Prize of physics
to make a long story short...
...that summer, a friend and i were going away on a big trip in Europe.
big for us!

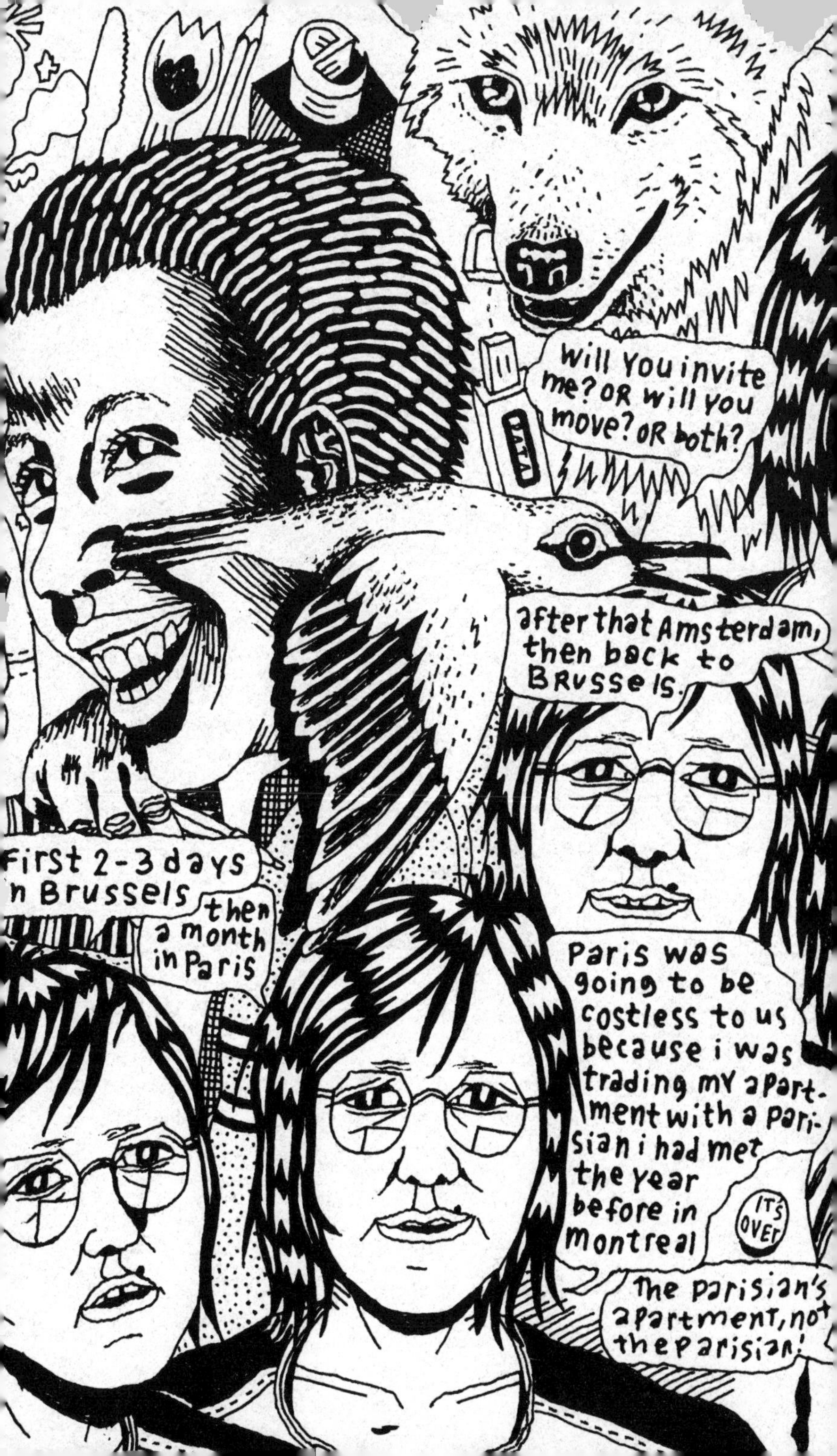
will you invite me? OR will you move? OR both?
after that Amsterdam, then back to Brussels.
first 2-3 days in Brussels
then a month in Paris
Paris was going to be costless to us because i was trading my apartment with a parisian i had met the year before in montreal
IT'S OVER
The parisian's apartment, not the parisian!

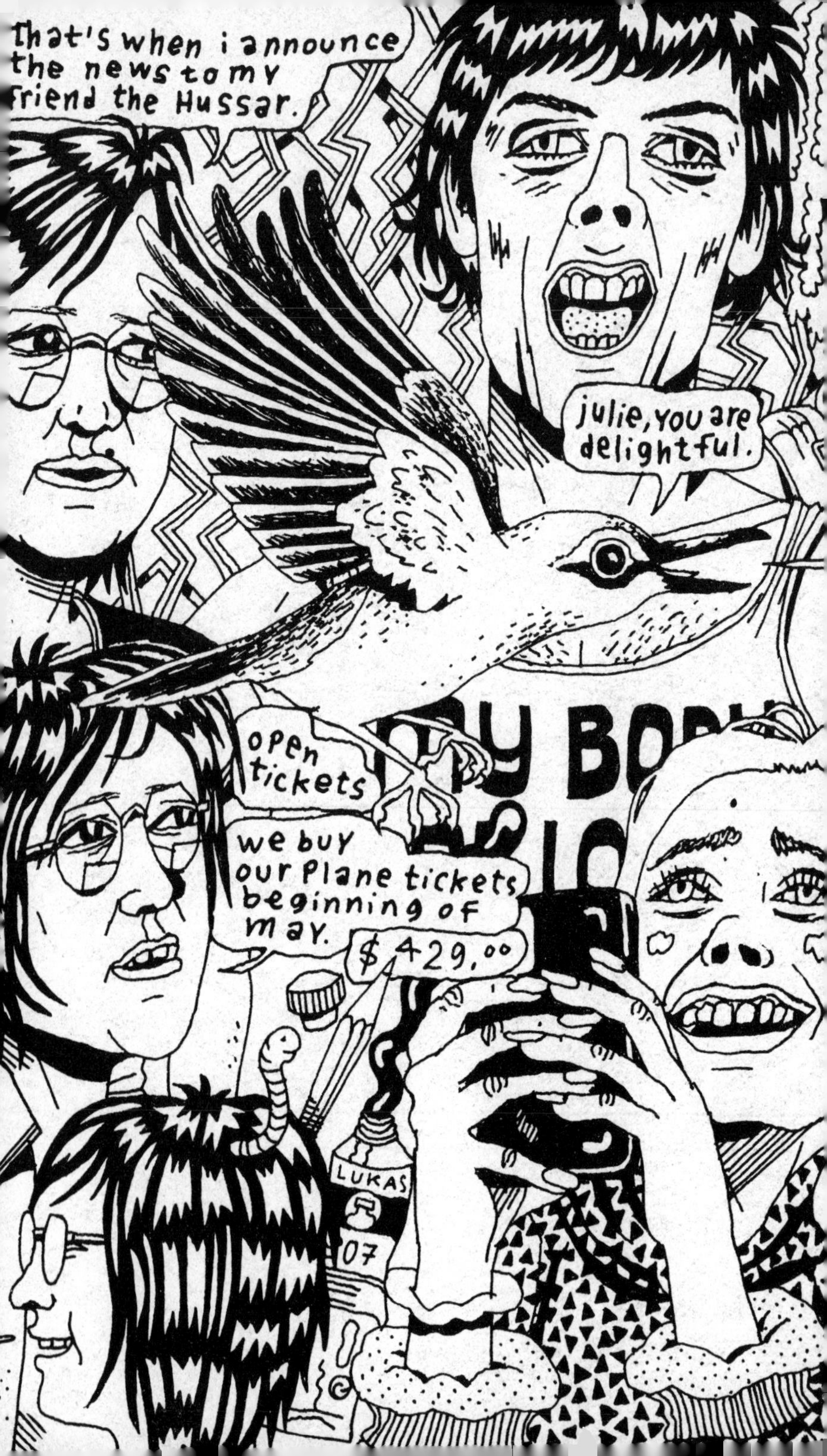
That's when i announce the news to my friend the Hussar.
julie, you are delightful.
open tickets
we buy our plane tickets beginning of may.
$429,00
LUKAS
07

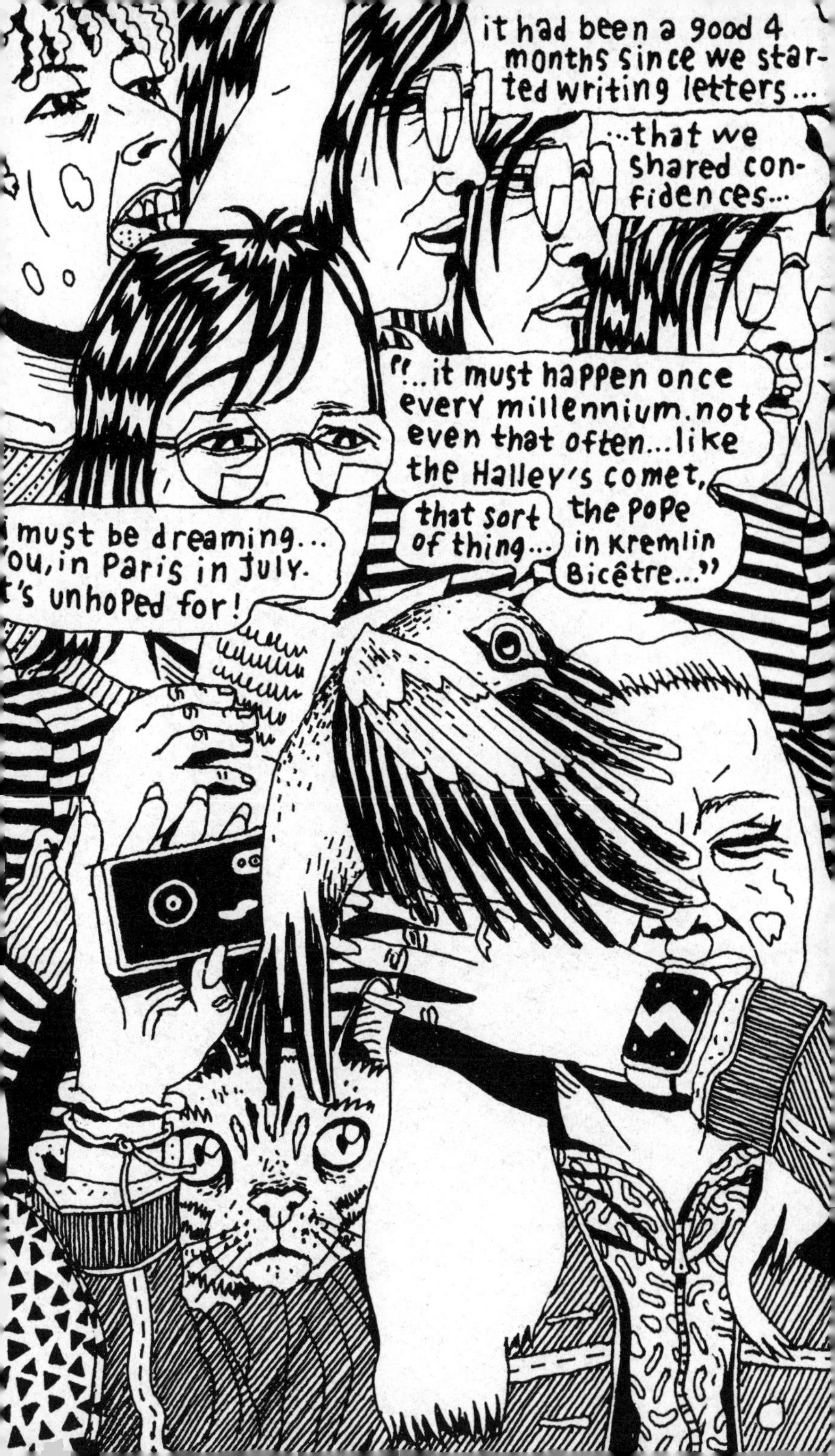
it had been a good 4 months since we started writing letters...
...that we shared confidences...
"...it must happen once every millennium. not even that often... like the Halley's comet,
that sort of thing...
the pope in Kremlin Bicêtre..."
must be dreaming... ou, in Paris in July. t's unhoped for!

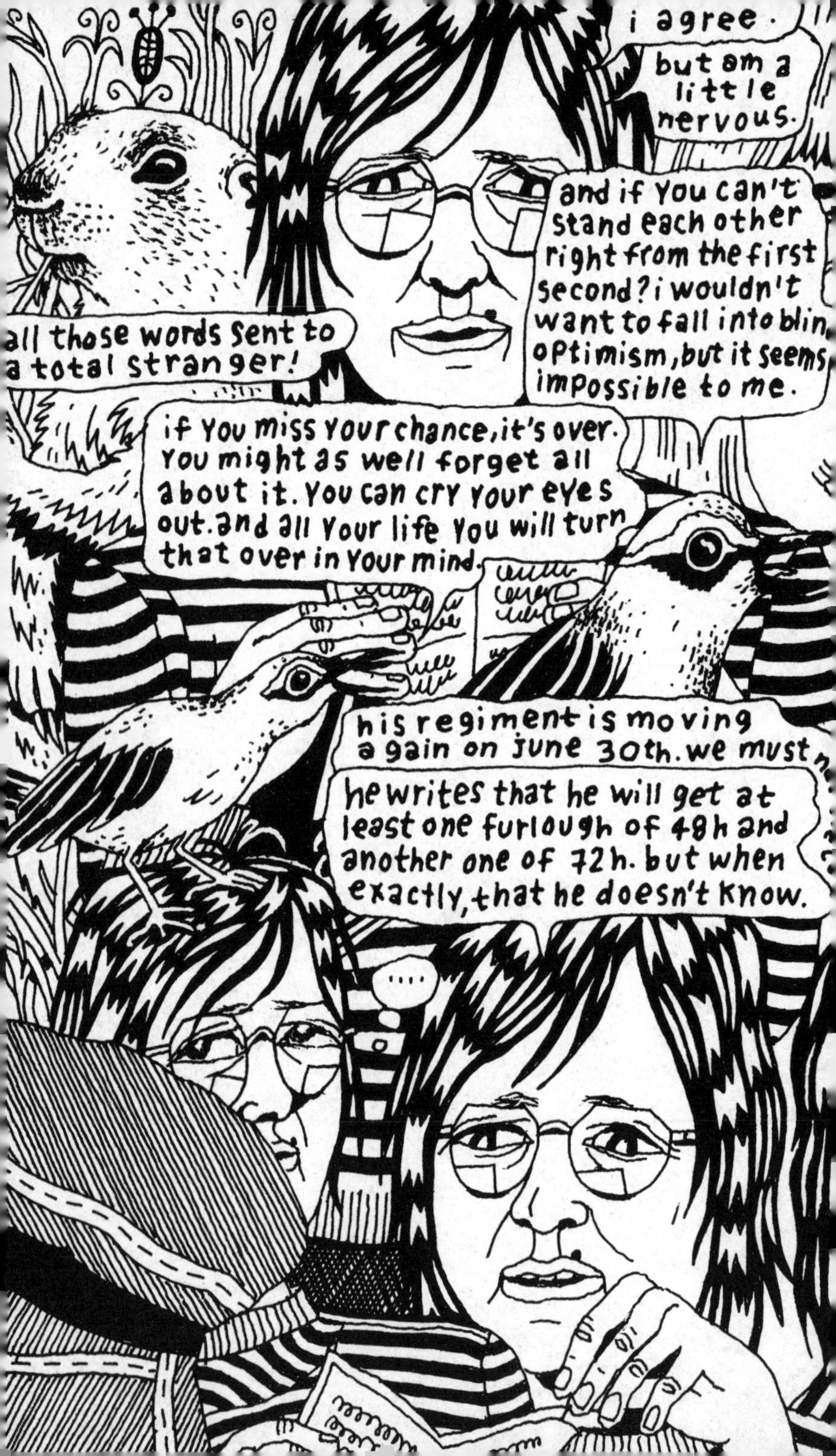
i agree.
but am a little nervous.
and if you can't stand each other right from the first second? i wouldn't want to fall into blin optimism, but it seems impossible to me.
all those words sent to a total stranger!
if you miss your chance, it's over. you might as well forget all about it. you can cry your eyes out. and all your life you will turn that over in your mind.
his regiment is moving again on june 30th. we must
he writes that he will get at least one furlough of 48h and another one of 72h. but when exactly, that he doesn't know.
.....

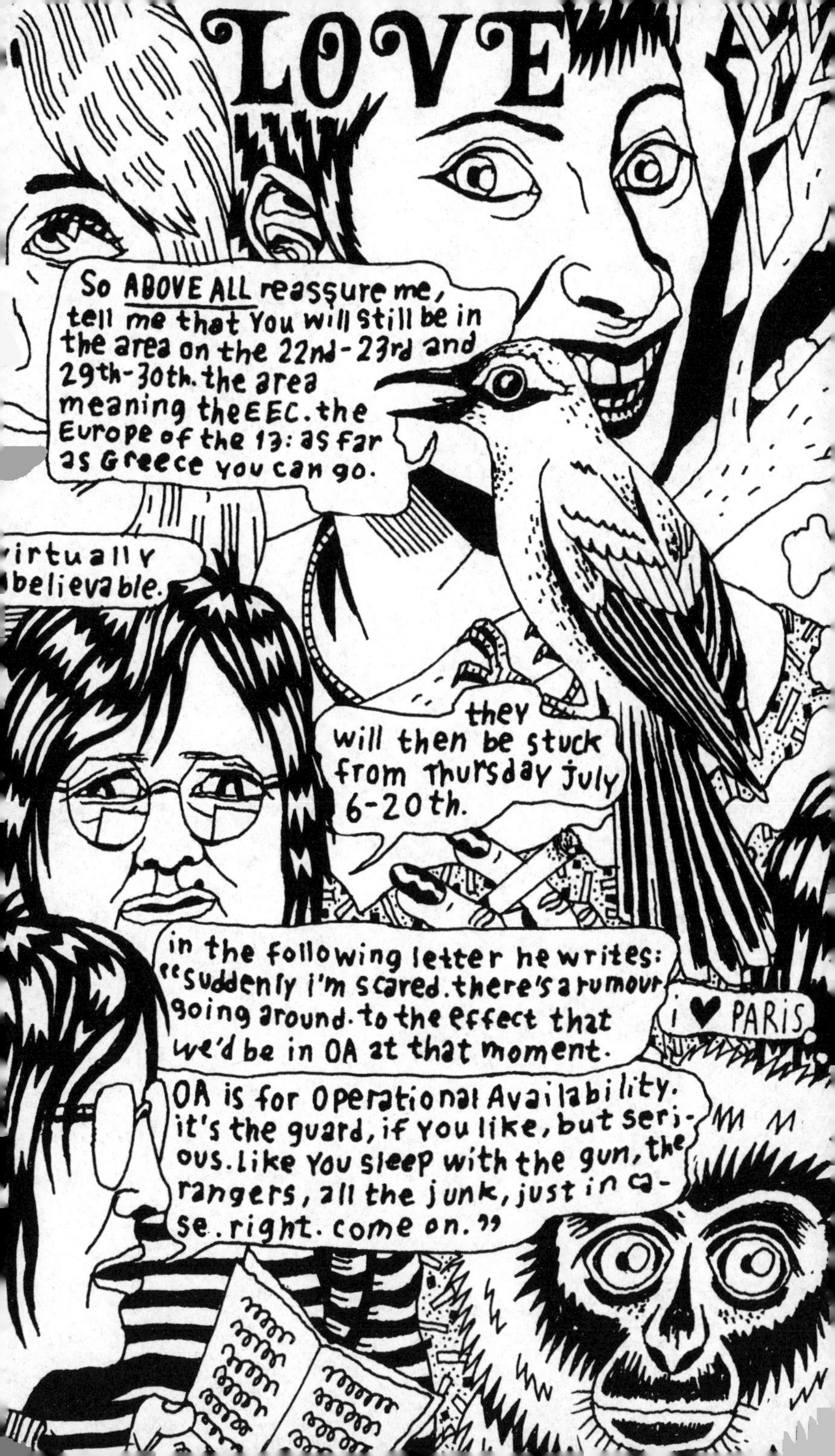
LOVE
So ABOVE ALL reassure me, tell me that you will still be in the area on the 22nd-23rd and 29th-30th. the area meaning the EEC. the Europe of the 13: as far as Greece you can go.
irtually
believable.
they will then be stuck from Thursday July 6-20th.
in the following letter he writes: "suddenly i'm scared. there's a rumour going around. to the effect that we'd be in OA at that moment.
i ♥ PARIS
OA is for Operational Availability. it's the guard, if you like, but serious. like you sleep with the gun, the rangers, all the junk, just in case. right. come on."

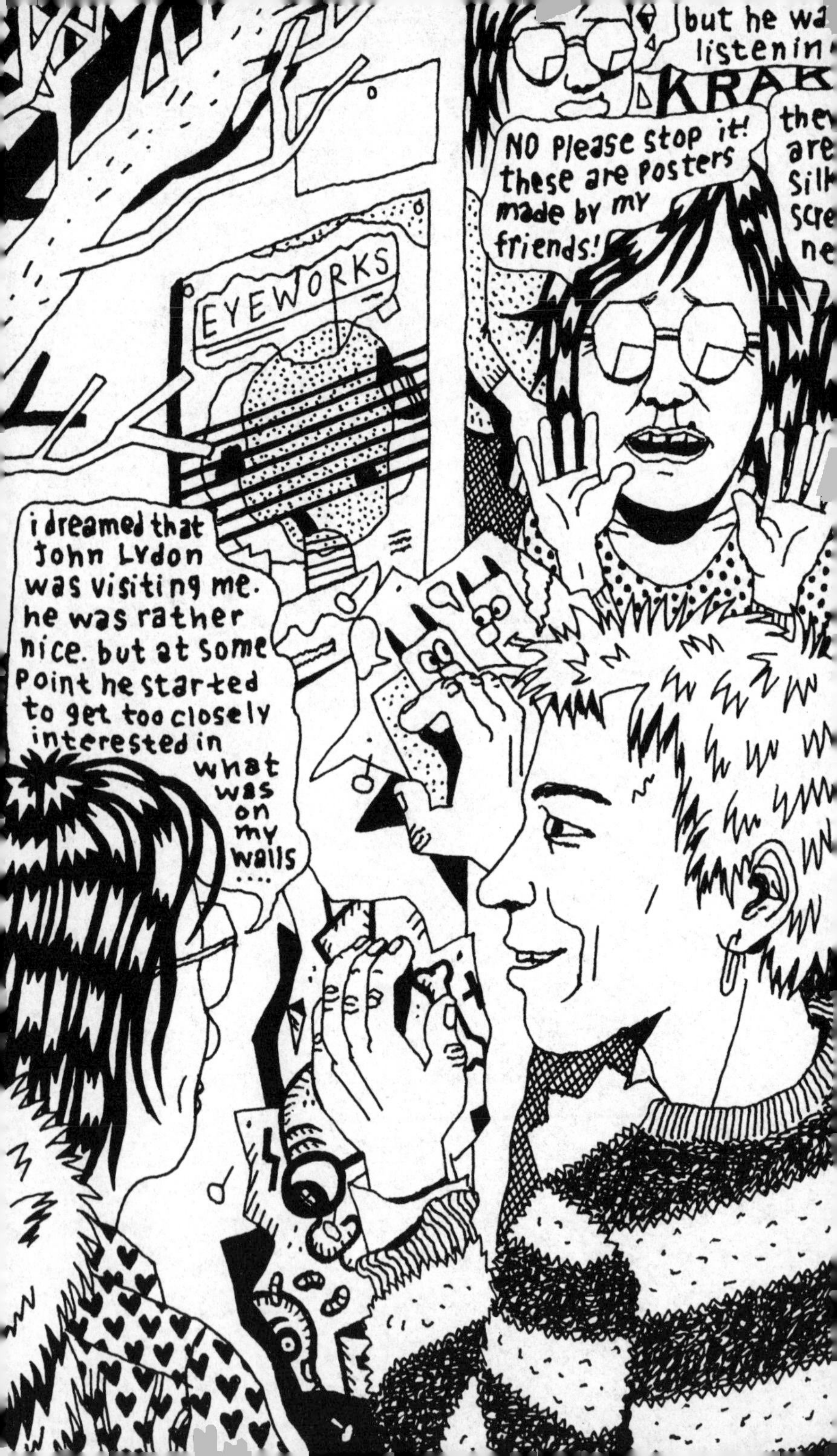
but he wa
listenin
KRAB
NO please stop it! these are posters made by my friends!
they are silk scre ne
EYEWORKS
i dreamed that John Lydon was visiting me. he was rather nice. but at some point he started to get too closely interested in what was on my walls ....

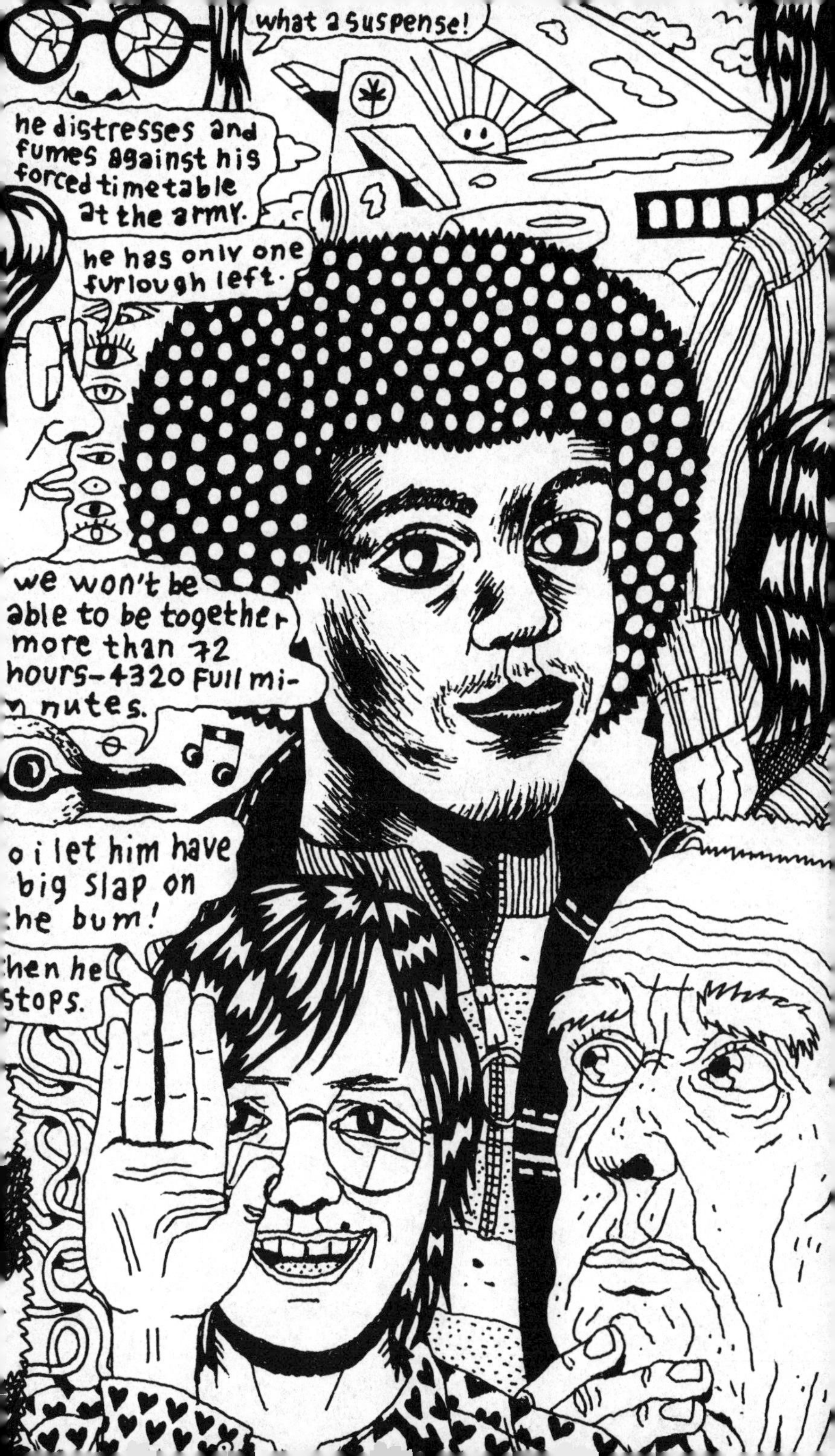
what a suspense!
he distresses and fumes against his forced timetable at the army.
he has only one furlough left.
we won't be able to be together more than 72 hours-4320 full mi-
nutes.
o i let him have big slap on he bum!
hen he stops.

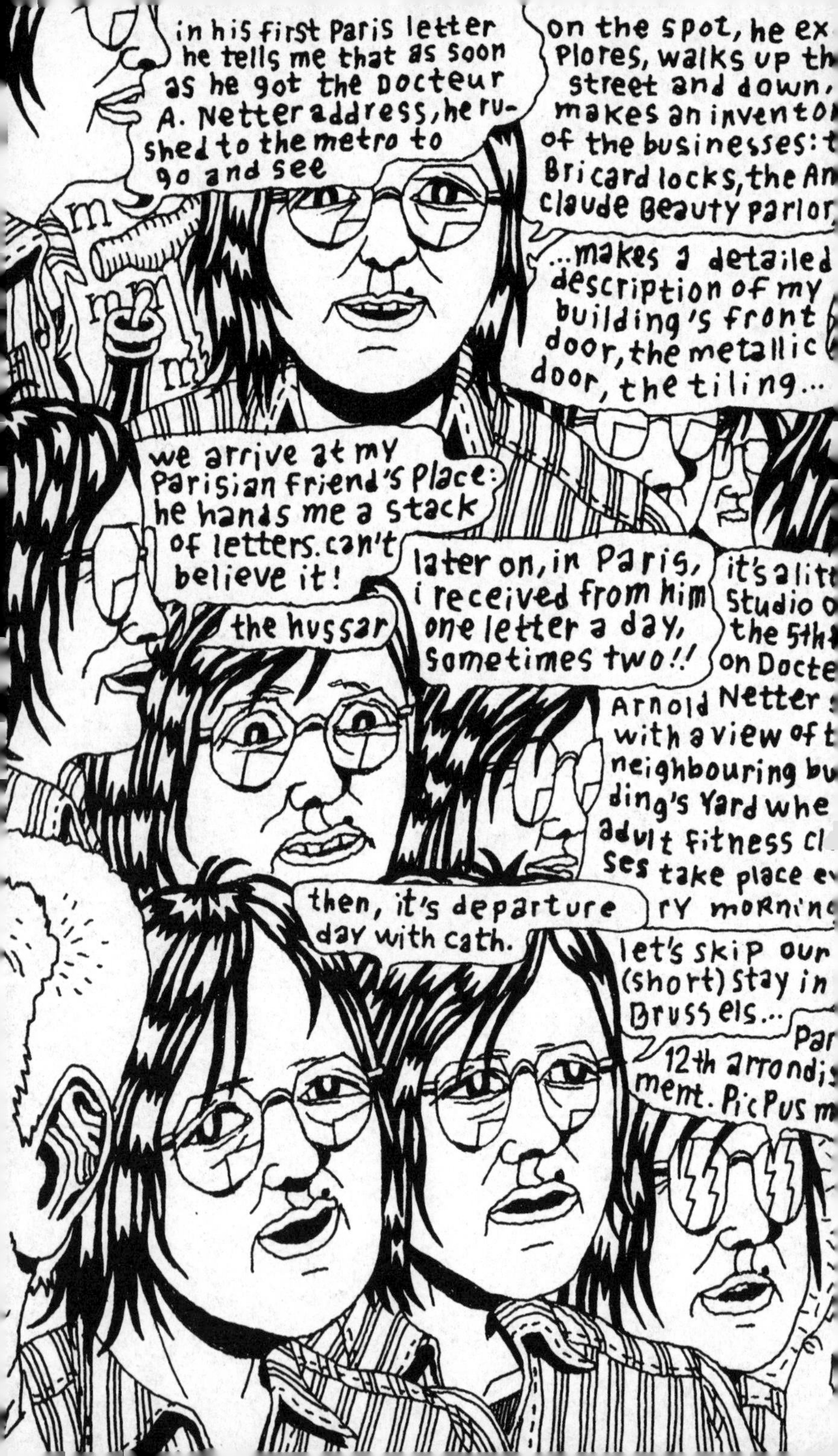
in his first Paris letter he tells me that as soon as he got the Docteur A. Netter address, he rushed to the metro to go and see
on the spot, he ex plores, walks up th street and down, makes an invento of the businesses: t Bricard locks, the An claude Beauty parlor
...makes a detailed description of my building's front door, the metallic door, the tiling...
mm
mm
m
we arrive at my Parisian friend's place: he hands me a stack of letters. can't believe it!
the hussar
later on, in Paris, i received from him one letter a day, sometimes two!!
it's a litt studio o the 5th on Docte Arnold Netter with a view of t neighbouring bu ding's yard whe adult fitness cl ses take place e ry morning
then, it's departure day with cath.
let's skip our (short) stay in Brussels...
Par 12th arrondis ment. Picpus m

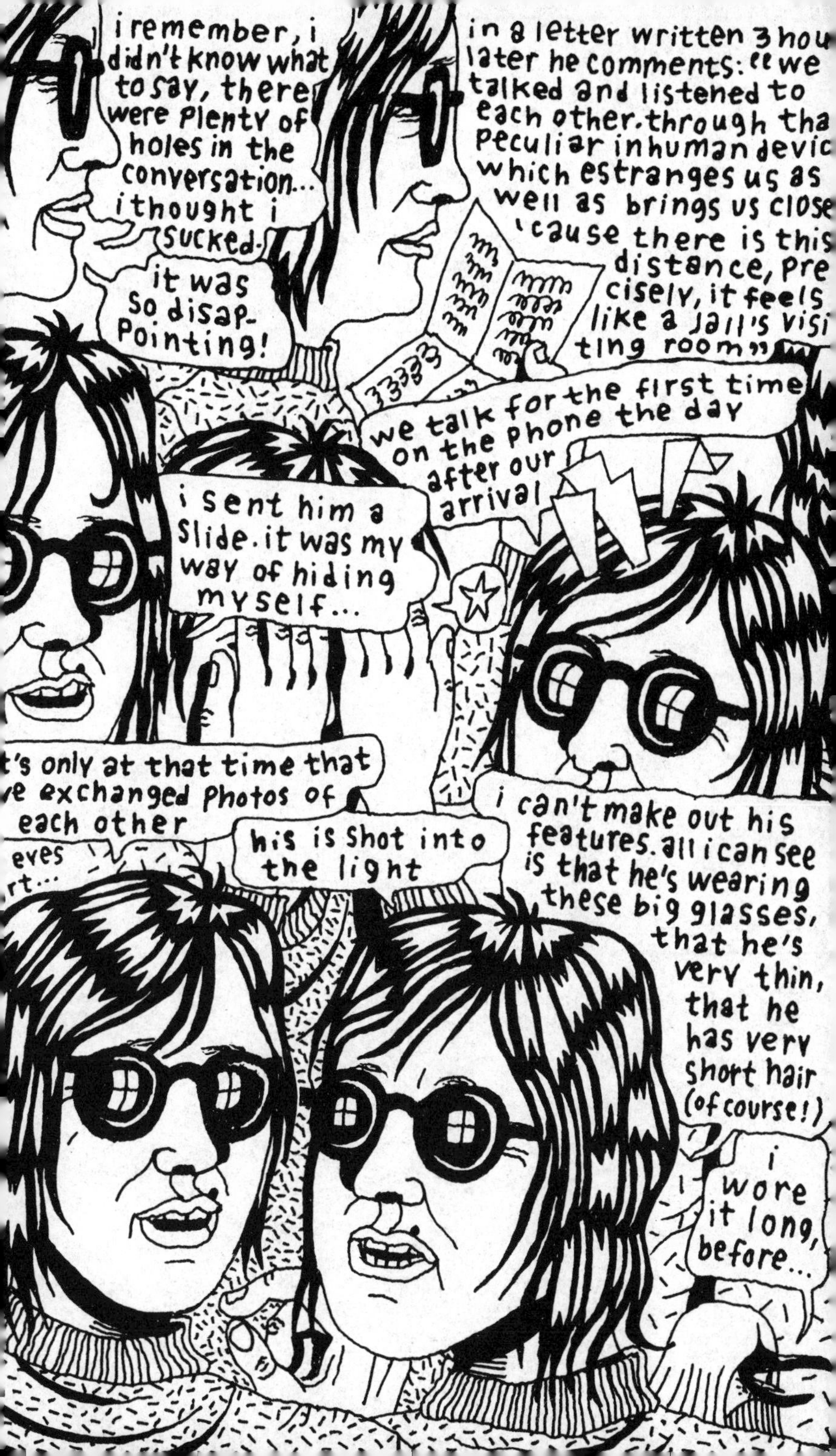
i remember, i didn't know what to say, there were plenty of holes in the conversation... i thought i sucked.
in a letter written 3 hou later he comments: "we talked and listened to each other through tha peculiar inhuman devic which estranges us as well as brings us close 'cause there is this distance, precisely, it feels like a jail's visiting room"
it was so disappointing!
we talk for the first time on the phone the day after our arrival
i sent him a slide. it was my way of hiding myself...
t's only at that time that e exchanged photos of each other
eyes rt...
his is shot into the light
i can't make out his features. all i can see is that he's wearing these big glasses, that he's very thin, that he has very short hair (of course!)
i wore it long, before...

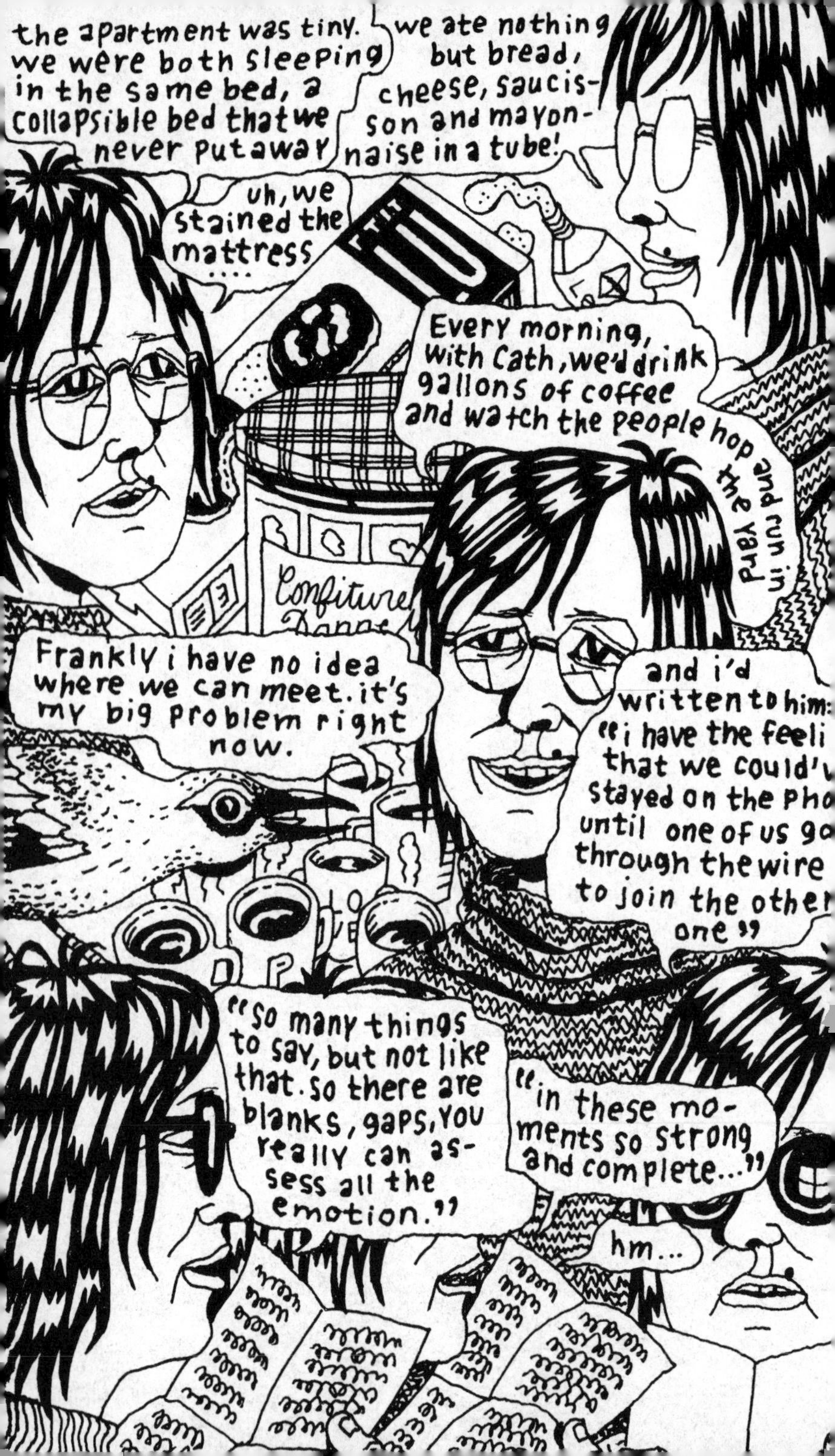
the apartment was tiny. we were both sleeping in the same bed, a collapsible bed that we never put away
we ate nothing but bread, cheese, saucisson and mayonnaise in a tube!
uh, we stained the mattress ....
Every morning, with Cath, we'd drink gallons of coffee and watch the people hop and run in the yard
Confiture
Frankly i have no idea where we can meet. it's my big problem right now.
and i'd written to him: "i have the feeli that we could'v stayed on the pho until one of us go through the wire to join the othe one"
"so many things to say, but not like that. so there are blanks, gaps, you really can assess all the emotion."
"in these moments so strong and complete..."
hm...

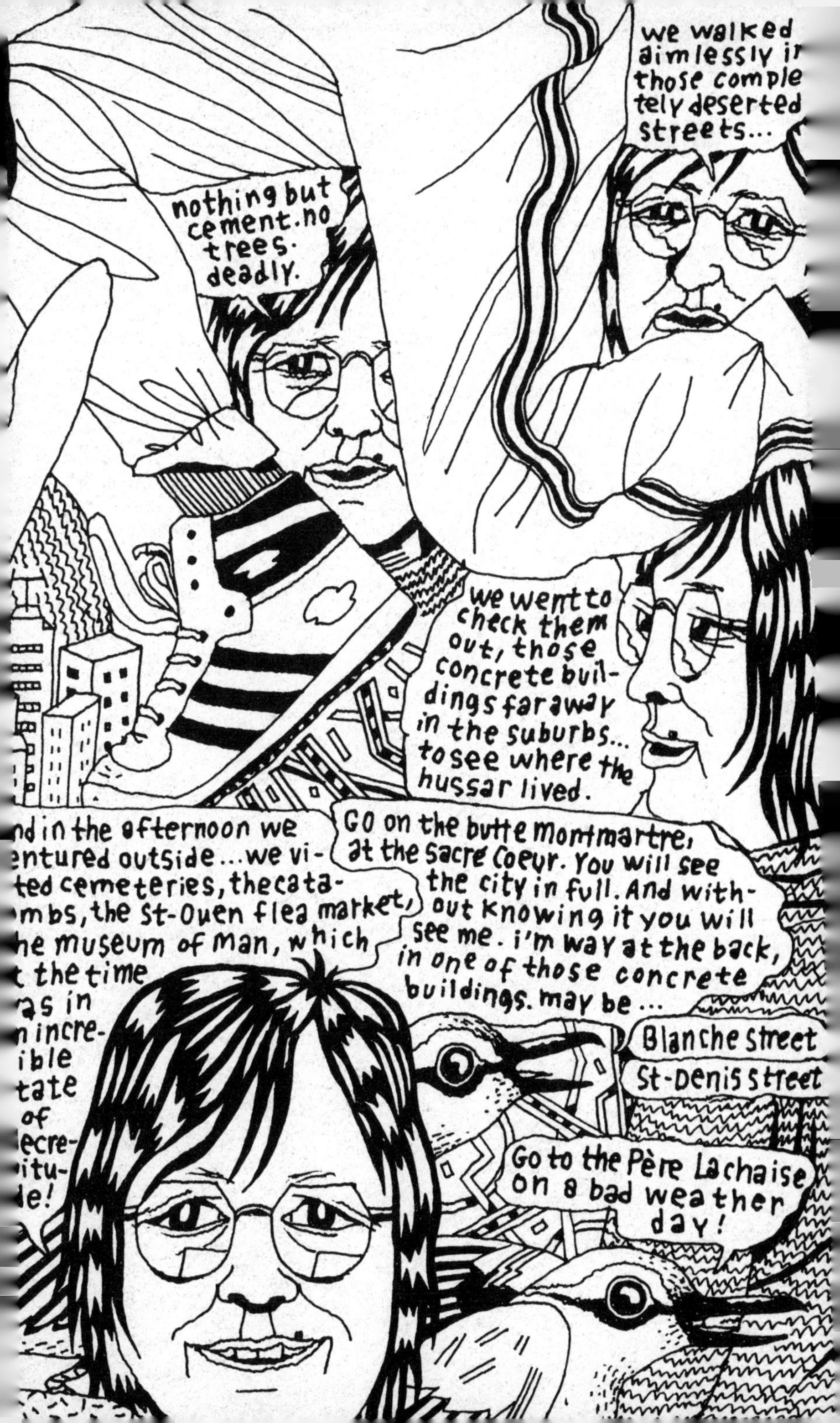

we walked aimlessly in those completely deserted streets...
nothing but cement. no trees. deadly.
we went to check them out, those concrete buildings far away in the suburbs... to see where the hussar lived.
nd in the afternoon we entured outside... we visited cemeteries, the catacombs, the St-Ouen flea market, he museum of man, which t the time as in n incredible tate of ecrepitude!
GO on the butte montmartre, at the sacre Coeur. You will see the city in full. And without knowing it you will see me. i'm way at the back, in one of those concrete buildings. may be...
Blanche Street
St-Denis Street
Go to the Père Lachaise on a bad weather day!

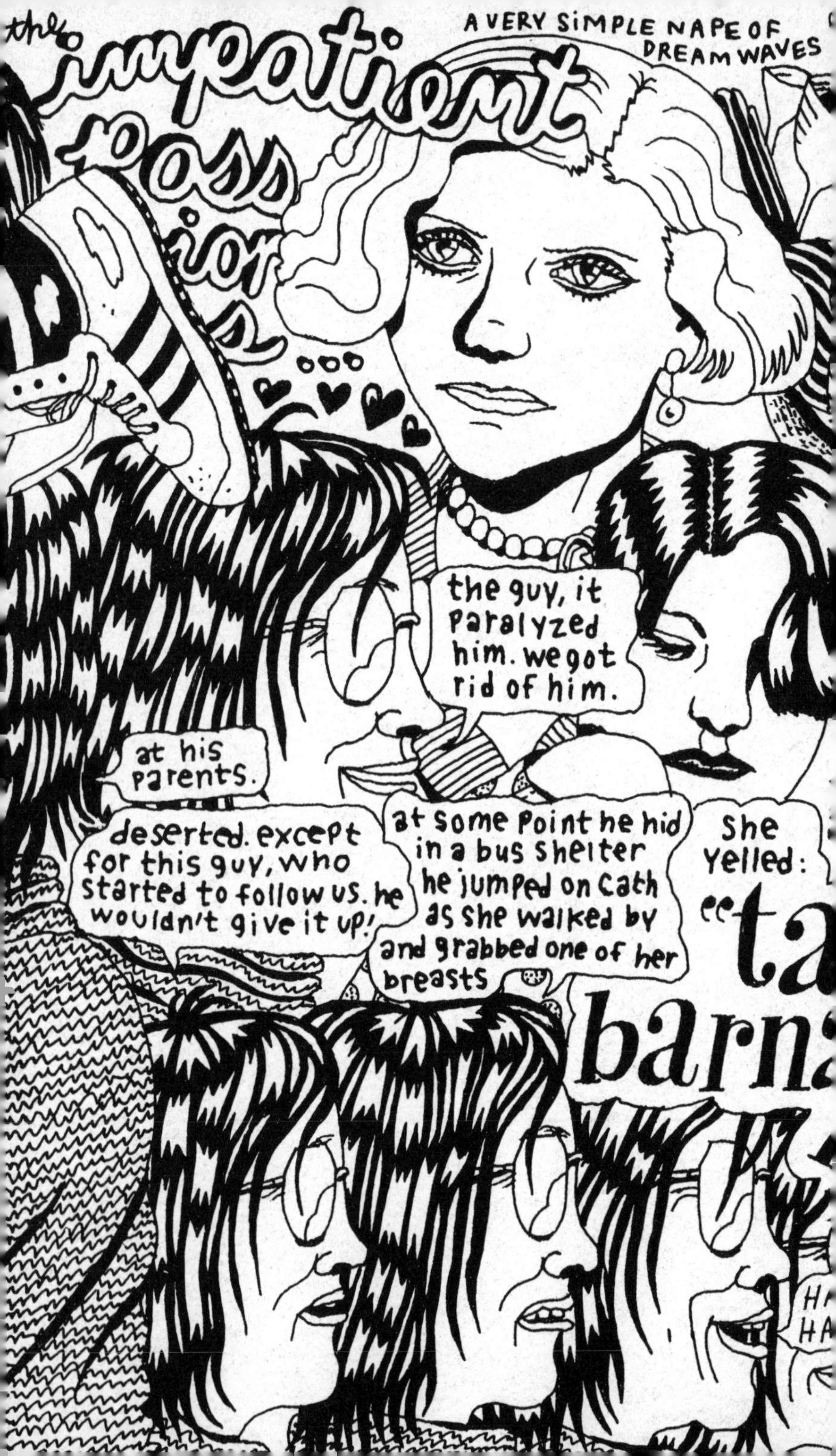

the impatient passions
A VERY SIMPLE NAPE OF DREAM WAVES
the guy, it paralyzed him. we got rid of him.
at his parents.
deserted. except for this guy, who started to follow us. he wouldn't give it up!
at some point he hid in a bus shelter he jumped on cath as she walked by and grabbed one of her breasts
she yelled:

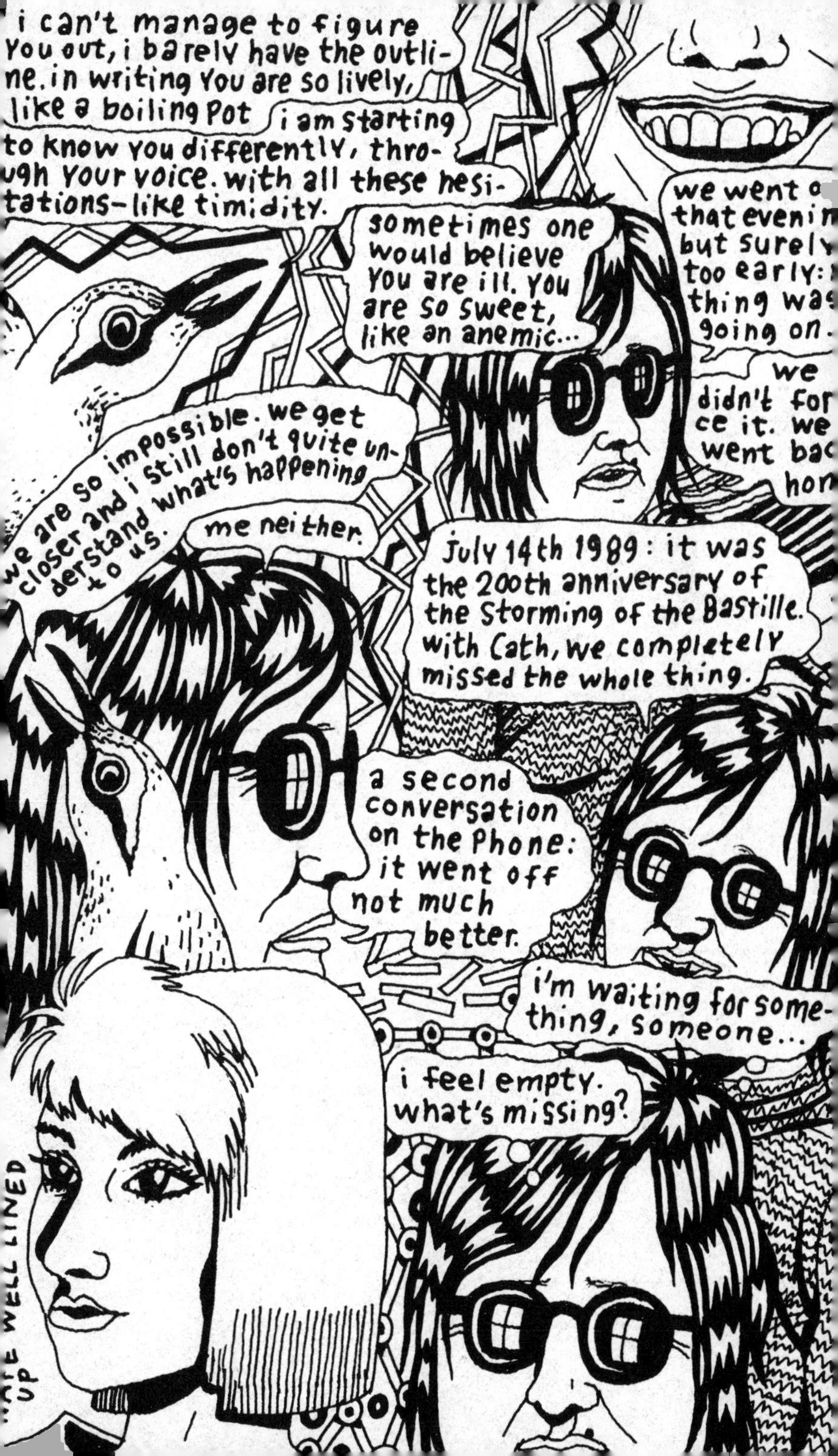
i can't manage to figure you out, i barely have the outline. in writing you are so lively, like a boiling pot
i am starting to know you differently, through your voice. with all these hesitations—like timidity.
sometimes one would believe you are ill. you are so sweet, like an anemic...
we went o that evenin but surely too early: thing was going on.
we didn't force it. we went ba hon
we are so impossible. we get closer and i still don't quite understand what's happening to us.
me neither.
July 14th 1989: it was the 200th anniversary of the Storming of the Bastille. with Cath, we completely missed the whole thing.
a second conversation on the phone: it went off not much better.
i'm waiting for something, someone...
i feel empty. what's missing?
WELL LINED UP

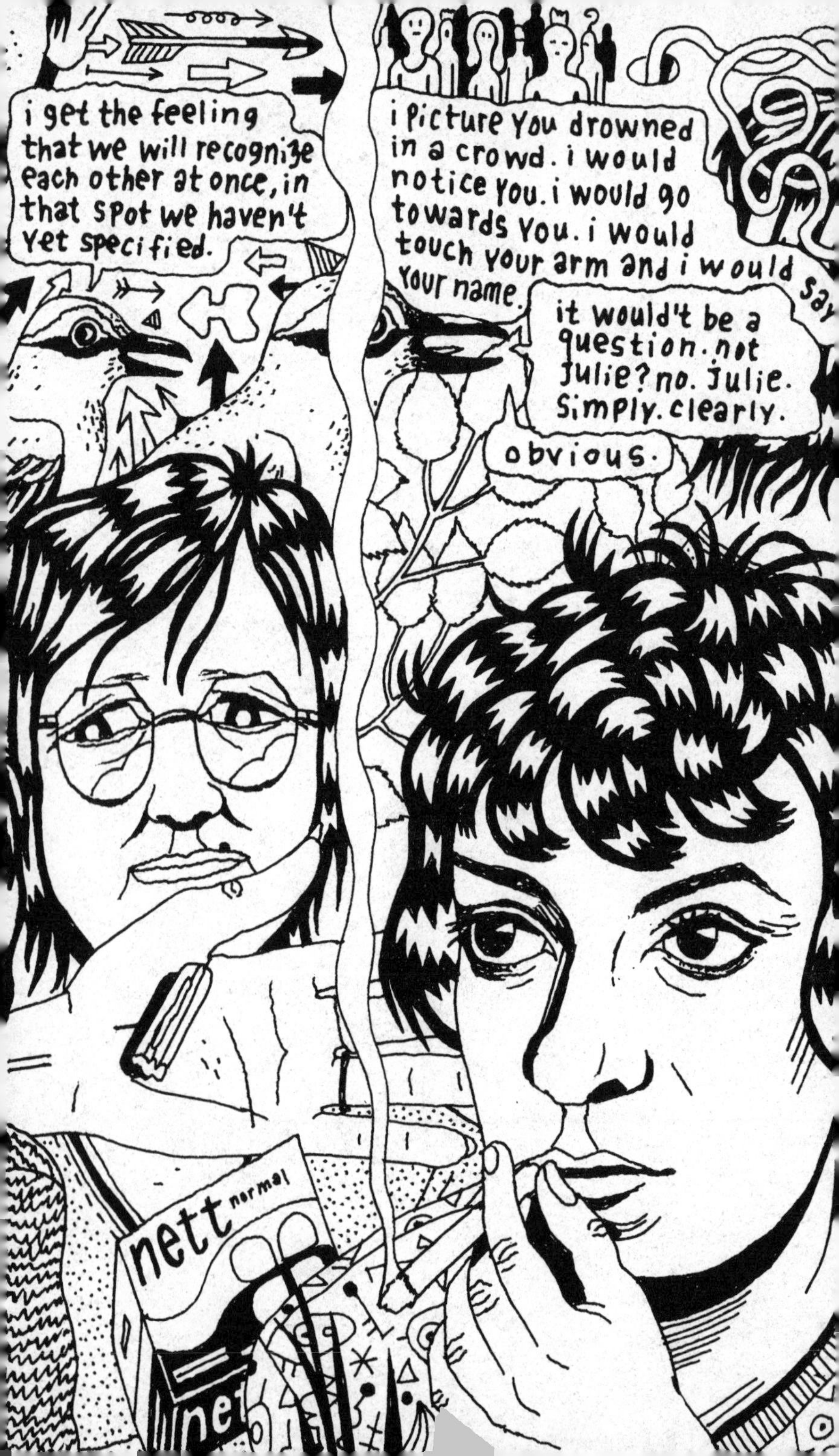
i get the feeling that we will recognize each other at once, in that spot we haven't yet specified.
i picture you drowned in a crowd. i would notice you. i would go towards you. i would touch your arm and i would say your name.
it would't be a question. not julie? no. julie. simply. clearly.
obvious.
nett normal

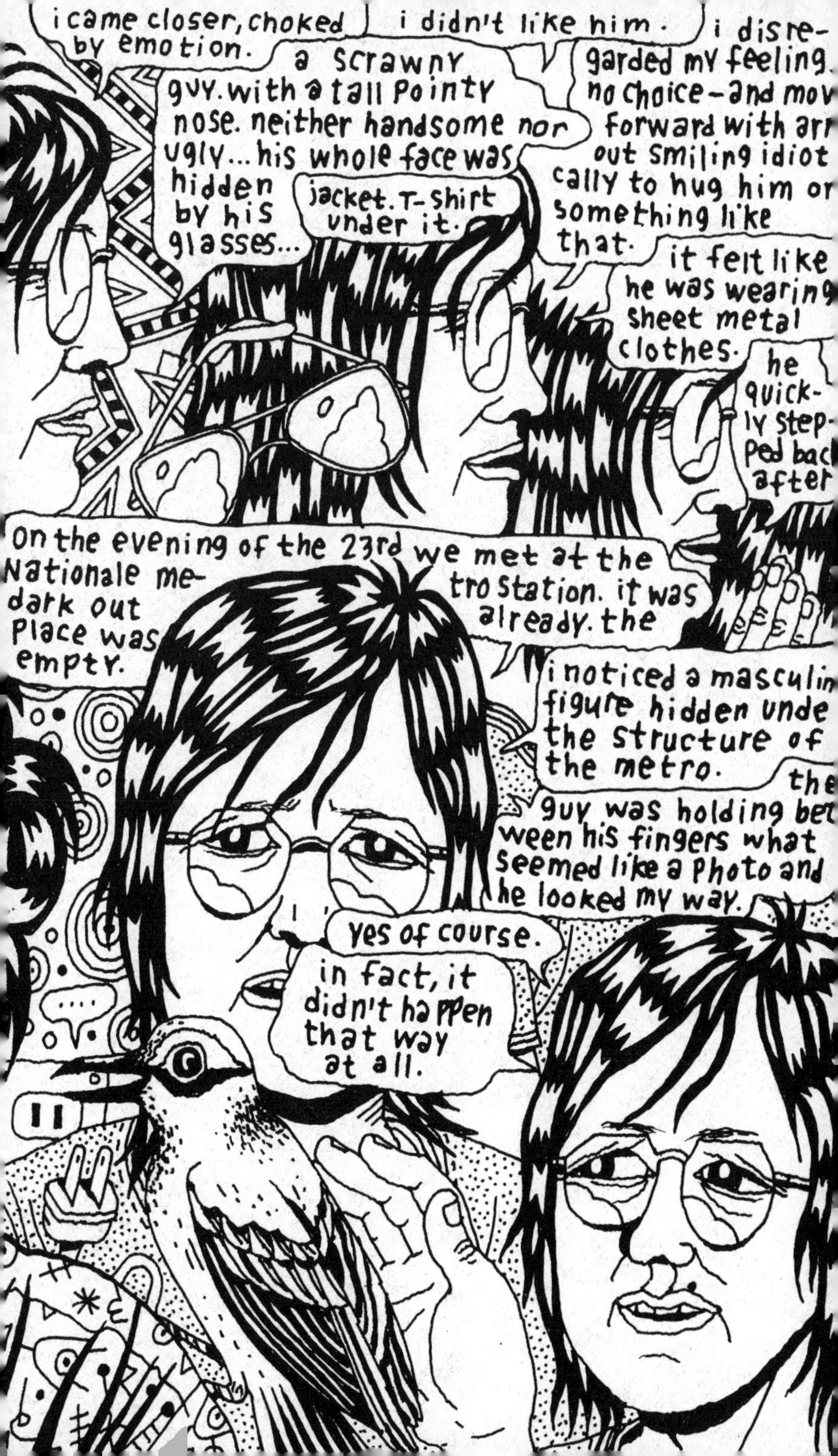
i came closer, choked by emotion.
i didn't like him.
a scrawny guy. with a tall pointy nose. neither handsome nor ugly... his whole face was hidden by his glasses...
jacket. T-shirt under it.
i disregarded my feeling. no choice—and mov forward with arr out smiling idiotcally to hug him or something like that.
it felt like he was wearing sheet metal clothes.
he quickly stepped bac after
on the evening of the 23rd we met at the Nationale metro station. it was already dark out. the place was empty.
i noticed a masculin figure hidden unde the structure of the metro.
the guy was holding bet ween his fingers what seemed like a photo and he looked my way.
yes of course.
in fact, it didn't happen that way at all.
....

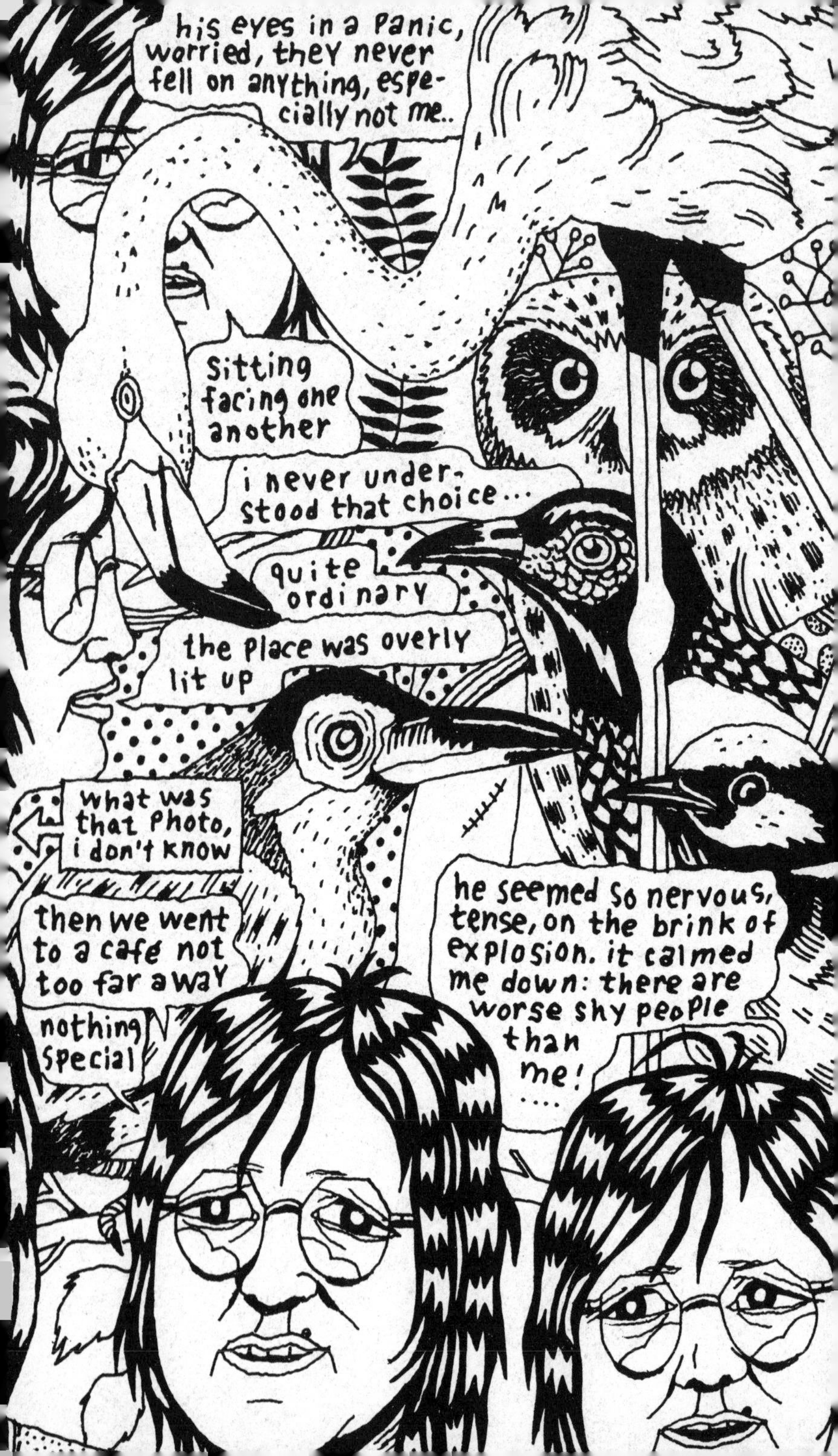
his eyes in a panic, worried, they never fell on anything, especially not me..
sitting facing one another
i never understood that choice...
quite ordinary
the place was overly lit up
what was that photo, i don't know
then we went to a cafe not too far away
nothing special
he seemed so nervous, tense, on the brink of explosion. it calmed me down: there are worse shy people than me! ....

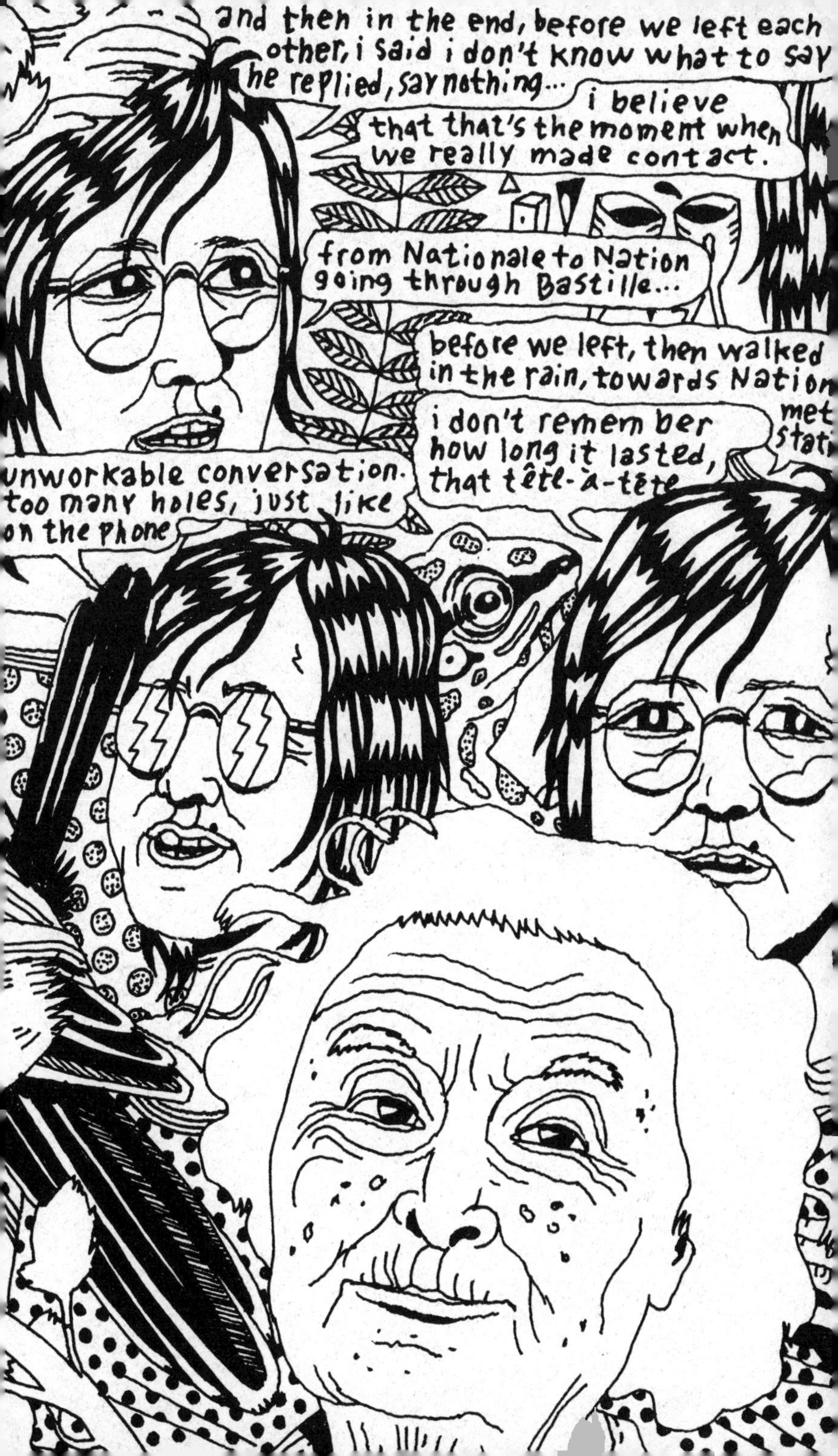
and then in the end, before we left each other, i said i don't know what to say he replied, say nothing...
i believe that that's the moment when we really made contact.
from Nationale to Nation going through Bastille...
before we left, then walked in the rain, towards Nation
i don't remember how long it lasted, that tête-à-tête
unworkable conversation. too many holes, just like on the phone

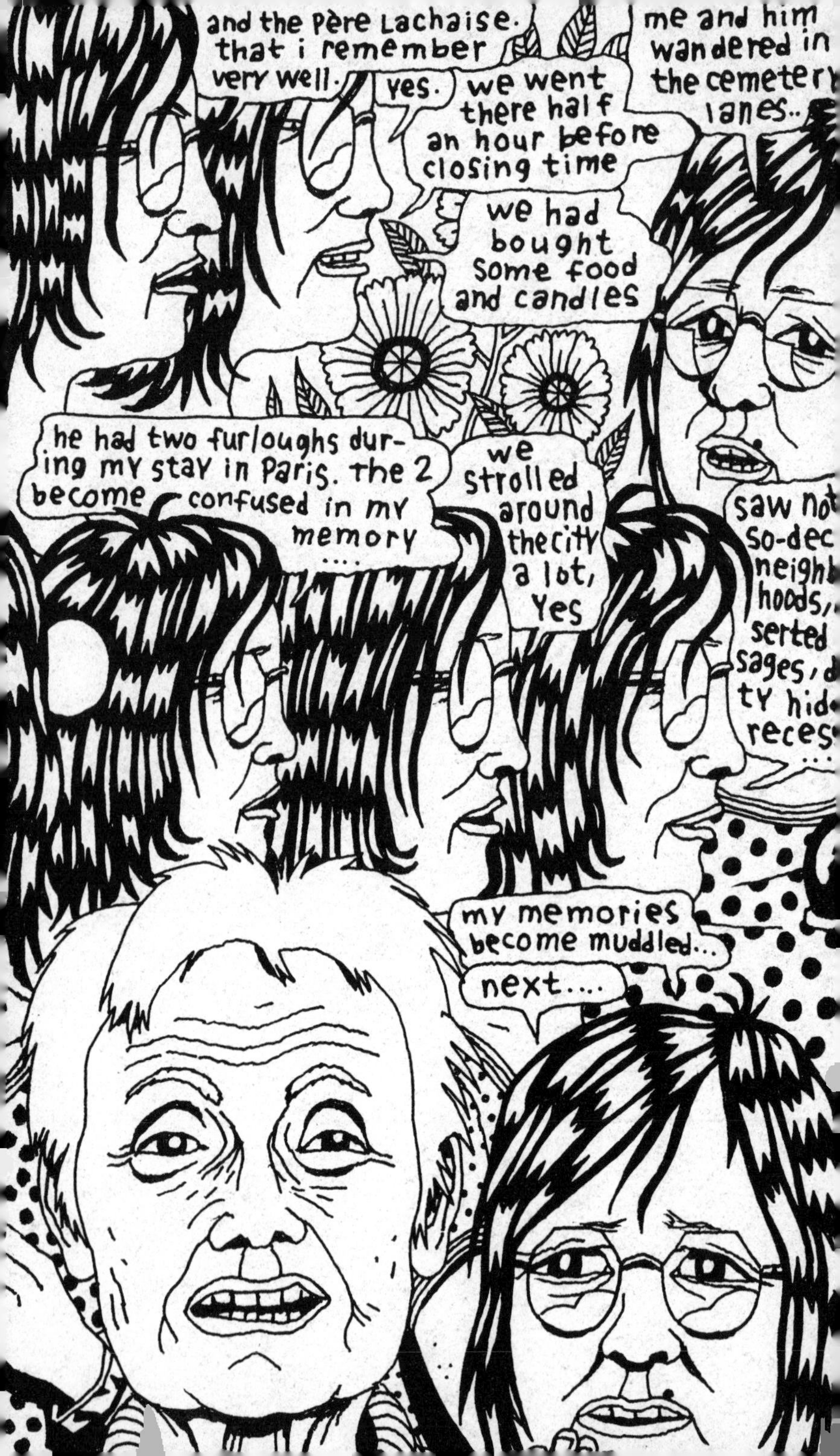
and the père Lachaise. that i remember very well.
yes.
we went there half an hour before closing time
we had bought some food and candles
me and him wandered in the cemetery lanes..
he had two furloughs during my stay in Paris. the 2 become confused in my memory ....
we strolled around the city a lot, yes
saw no so-dec neigh hoods, serted sages, ty hid reces ...
my memories become muddled...
next....

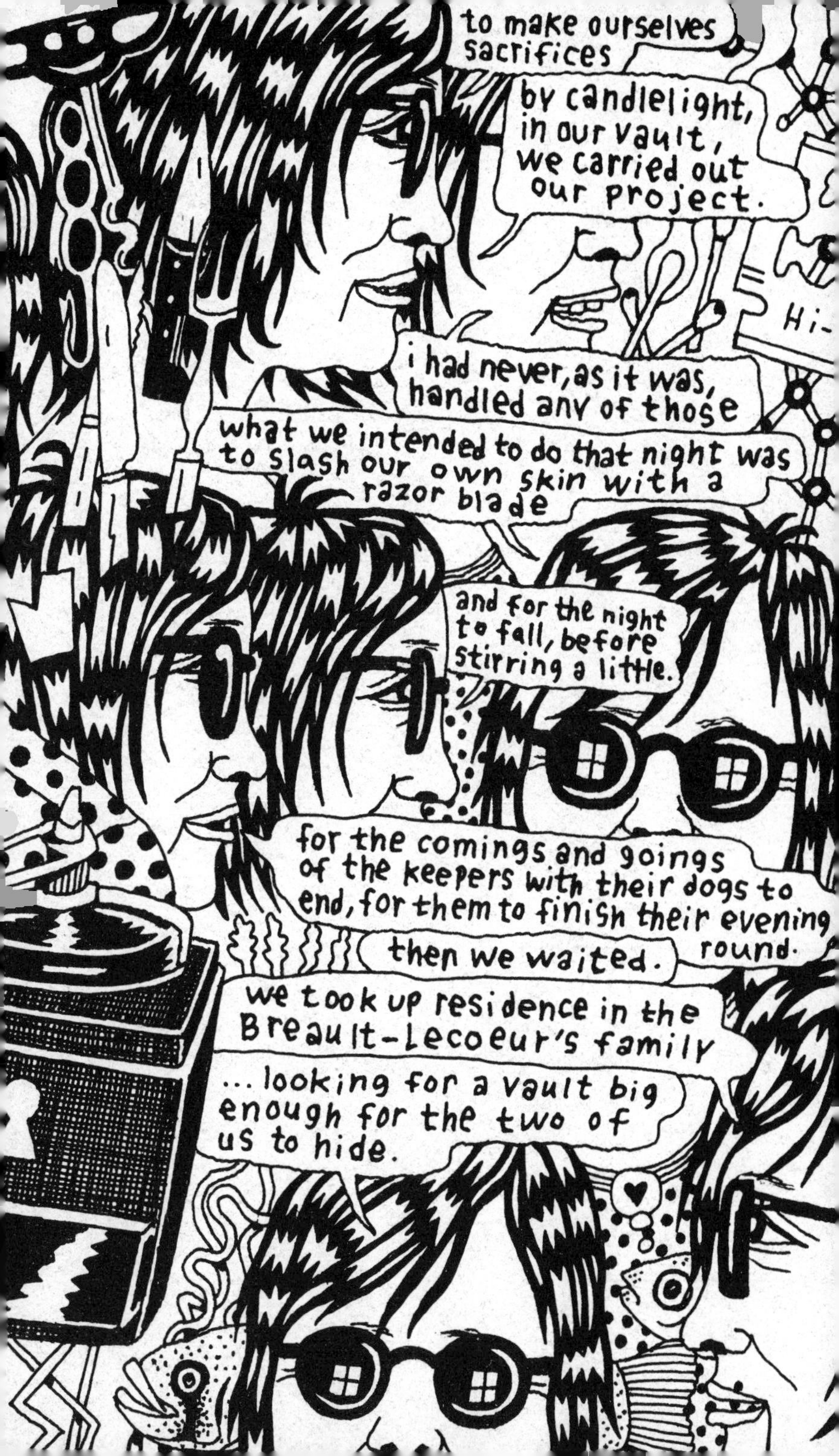
to make ourselves sacrifices
by candlelight, in our vault, we carried out our project.
Hi-
i had never, as it was, handled any of those
what we intended to do that night was to slash our own skin with a razor blade
and for the night to fall, before stirring a little.
for the comings and goings of the keepers with their dogs to end, for them to finish their evening round.
then we waited.
we took up residence in the Breault-Lecoeur's family
...looking for a vault big enough for the two of us to hide.

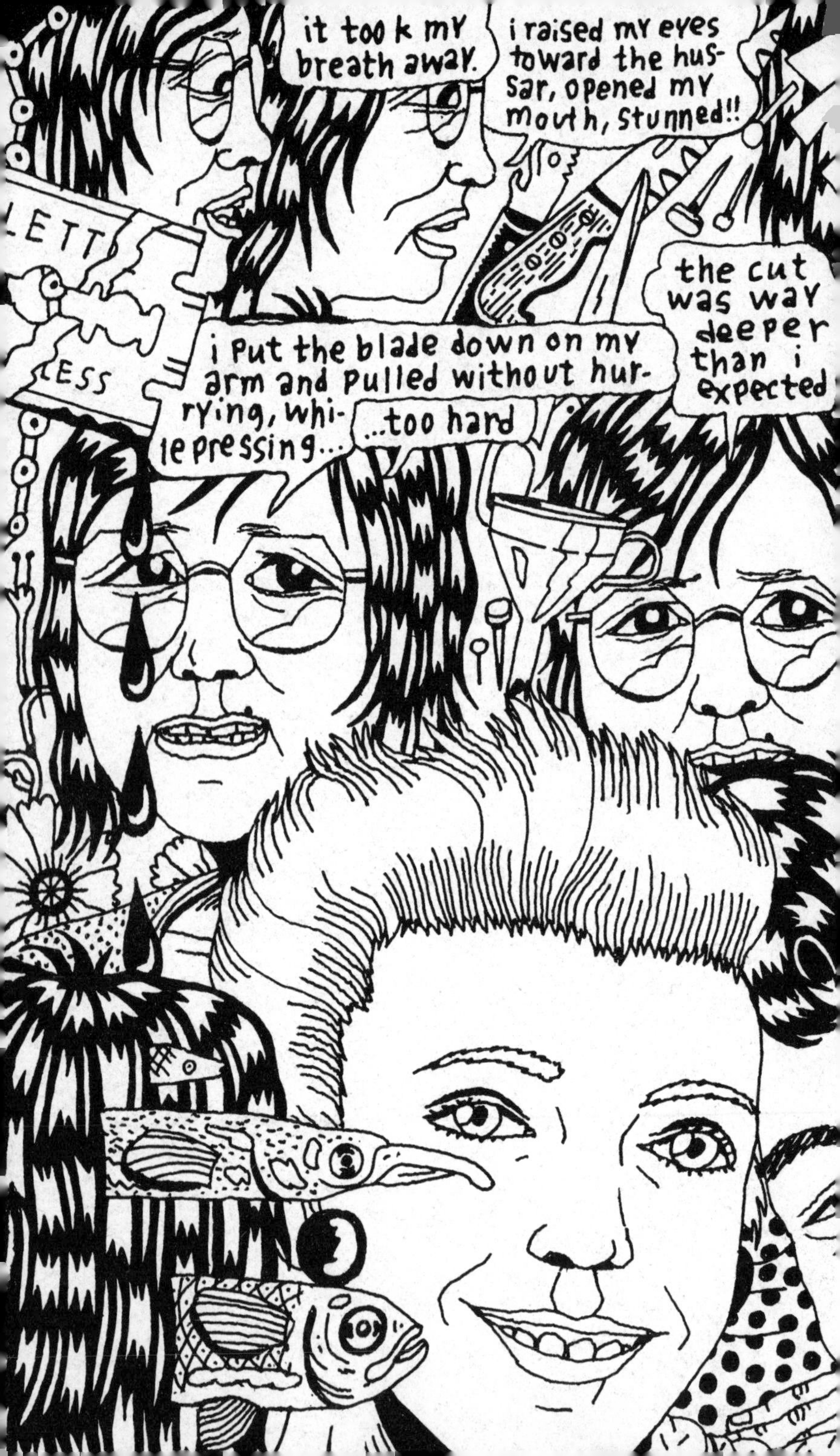
it took my breath away.
i raised my eyes toward the hussar, opened my mouth, stunned!!
i put the blade down on my arm and pulled without hurrying, while pressing...
...too hard
the cut was way deeper than i expected
LETT
LESS

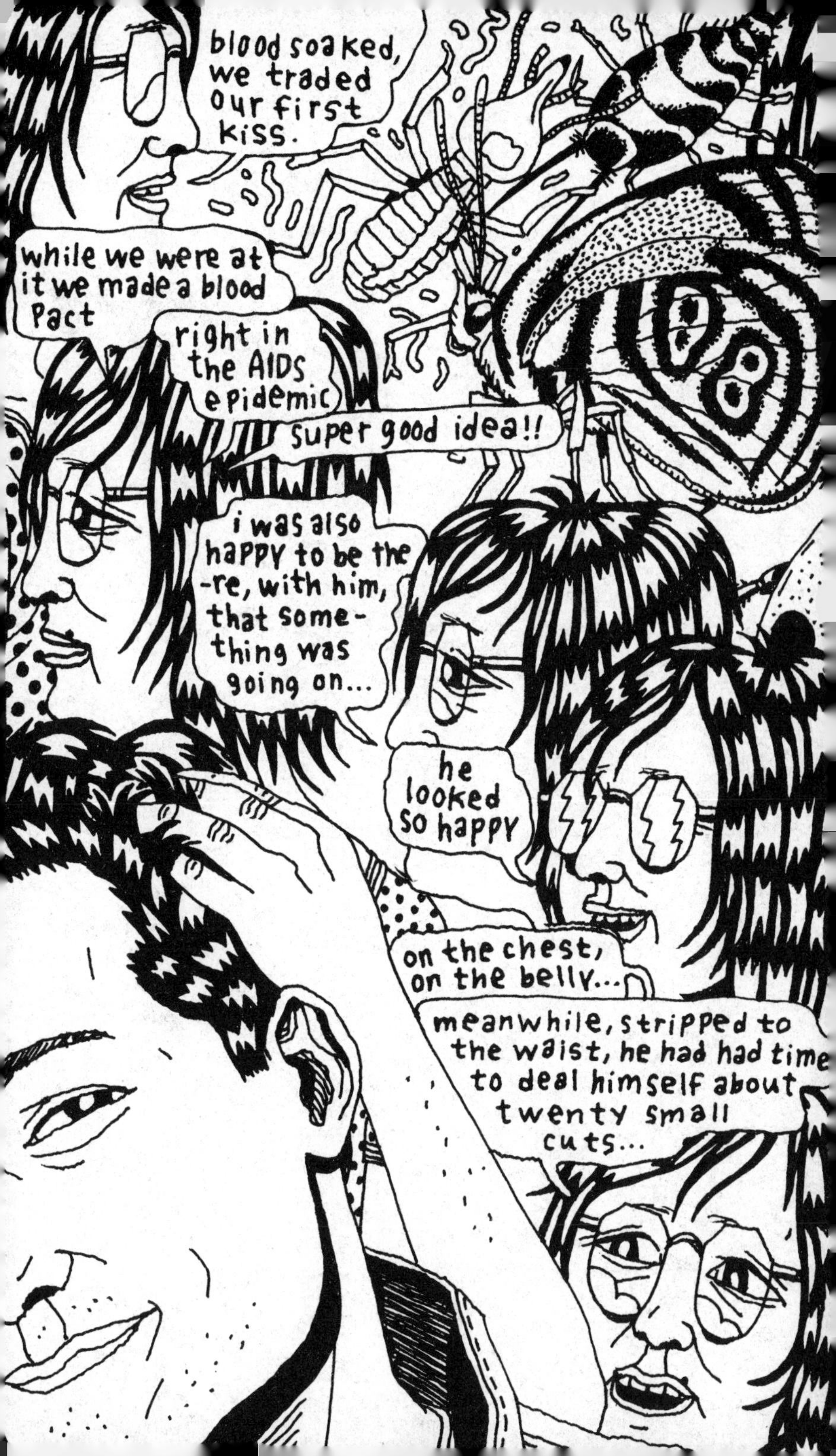
blood soaked, we traded our first kiss.
while we were at it we made a blood pact
right in the AIDS epidemic
super good idea!!
i was also happy to be the -re, with him, that some-thing was going on...
he looked so happy
on the chest, on the belly...
meanwhile, stripped to the waist, he had had time to deal himself about twenty small cuts...

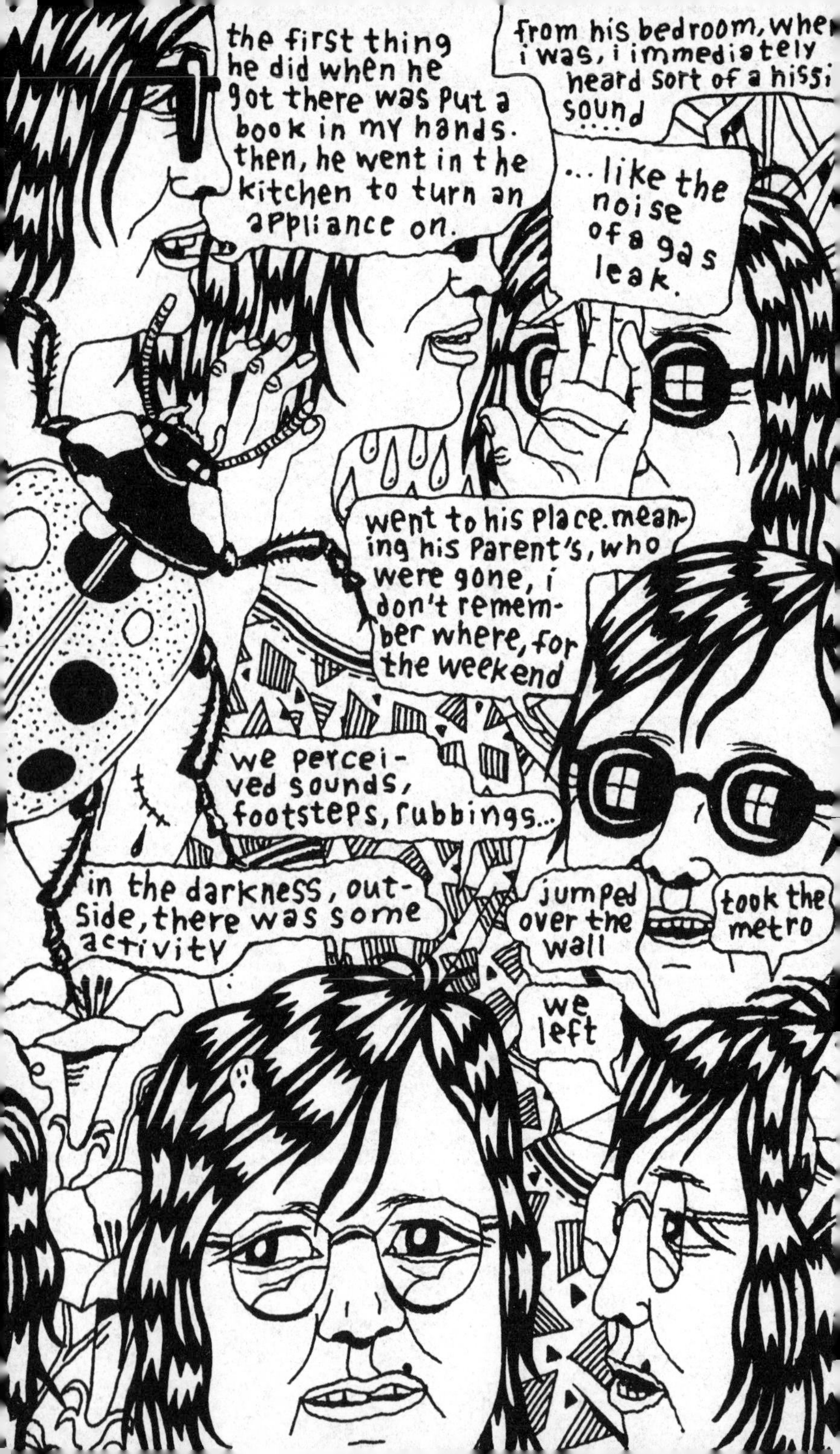
the first thing he did when he got there was put a book in my hands. then, he went in the kitchen to turn an appliance on.
from his bedroom, wher i was, i immediately heard sort of a hissi sound....
...like the noise of a gas leak.
went to his place. meaning his parent's, who were gone, i don't remember where, for the weekend
we perceived sounds, footsteps, rubbings...
in the darkness, outside, there was some activity
jumped over the wall
took the metro
we left

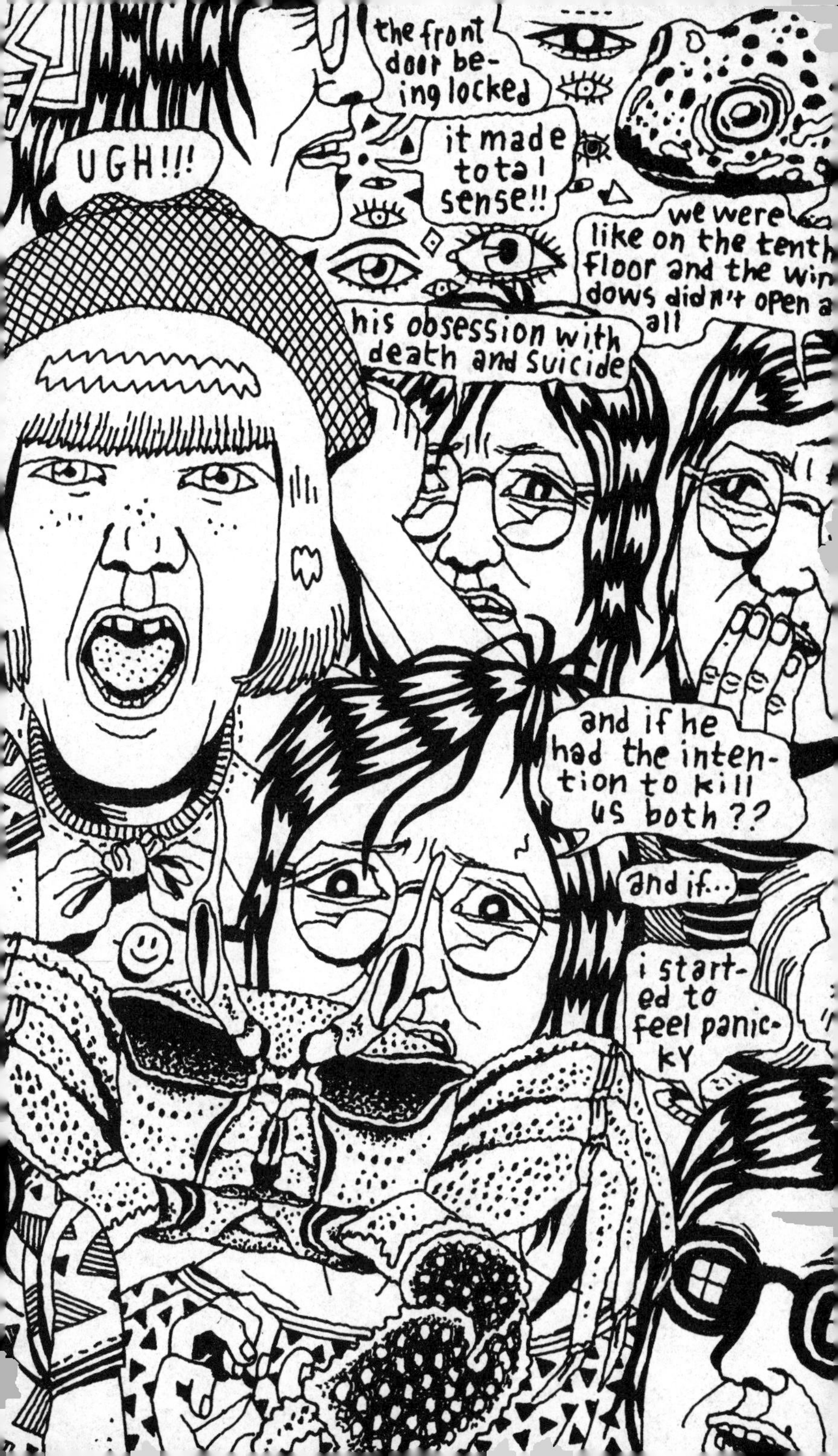
the front door being locked
UGH!!!
it made total sense!!
we were like on the tenth floor and the windows didn't open at all
his obsession with death and suicide
and if he had the intention to kill us both??
and if...
i started to feel panicky

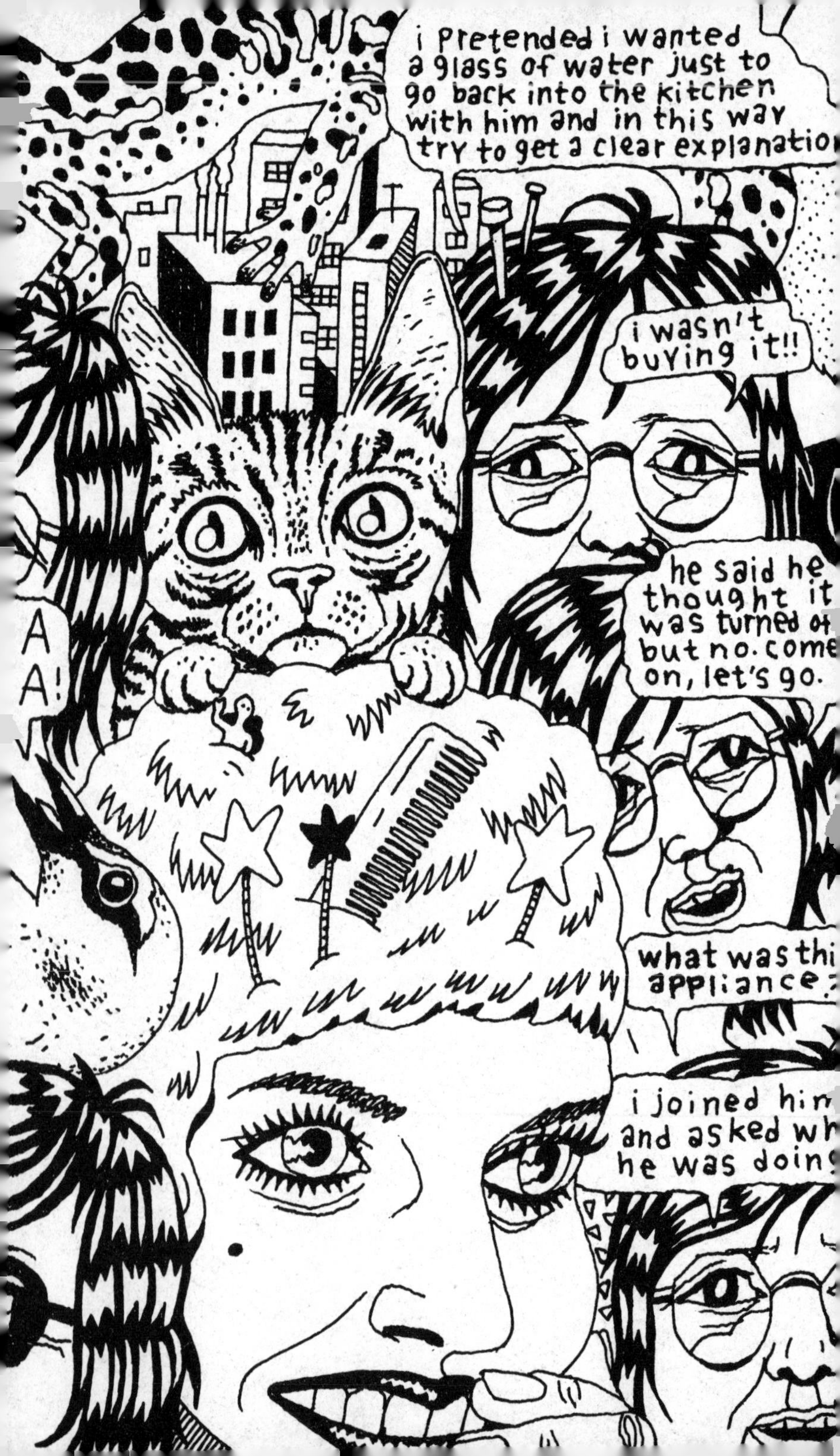
i pretended i wanted a glass of water just to go back into the kitchen with him and in this way try to get a clear explanatio
i wasn't buying it!!
he said he thought it was turned of but no. come on, let's go.
AA!
what was thi appliance
i joined hi and asked wh he was doin

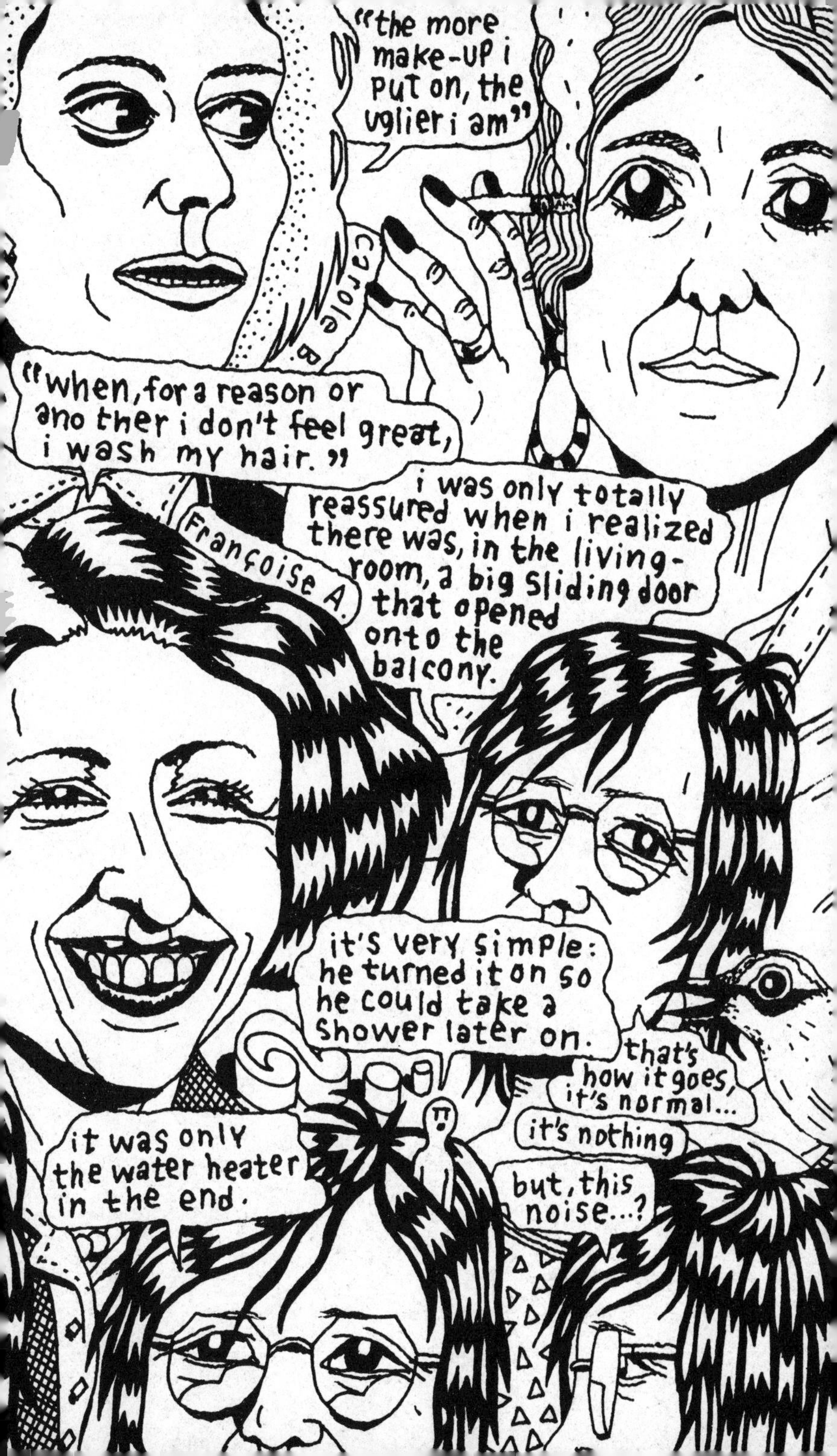
"the more make-up i put on, the uglier i am"
Carole B.
"when, for a reason or another i don't feel great, i wash my hair."
Françoise A.
i was only totally reassured when i realized there was, in the living-room, a big sliding door that opened onto the balcony.
it's very simple: he turned it on so he could take a shower later on.
that's how it goes, it's normal...
it's nothing
it was only the water heater in the end.
but, this noise...?

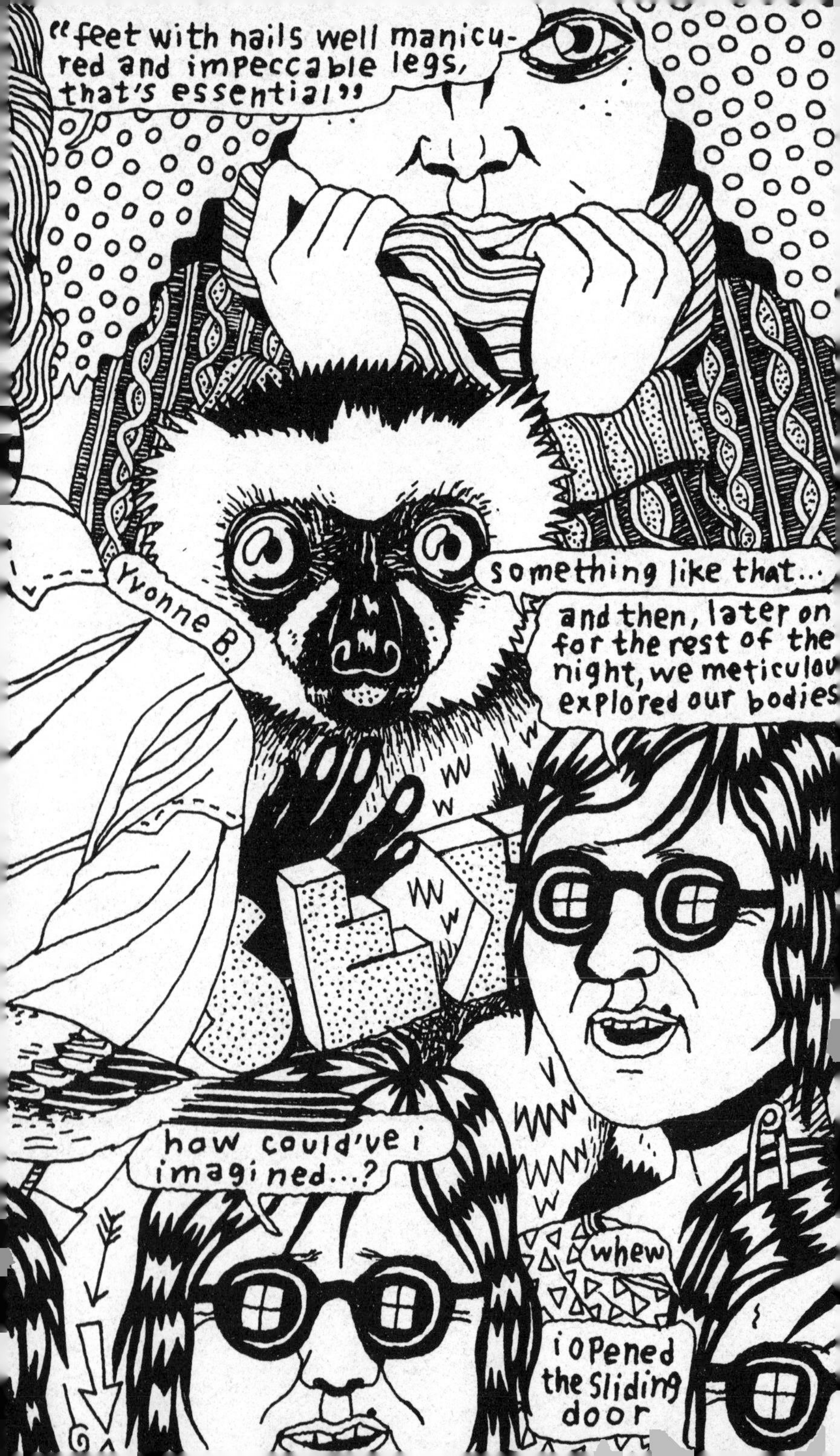
"feet with nails well manicu-red and impeccable legs, that's essential"
Yvonne B.
something like that...
and then, later on for the rest of the night, we meticulou explored our bodies
how could've i imagined...?
whew
i opened the sliding door

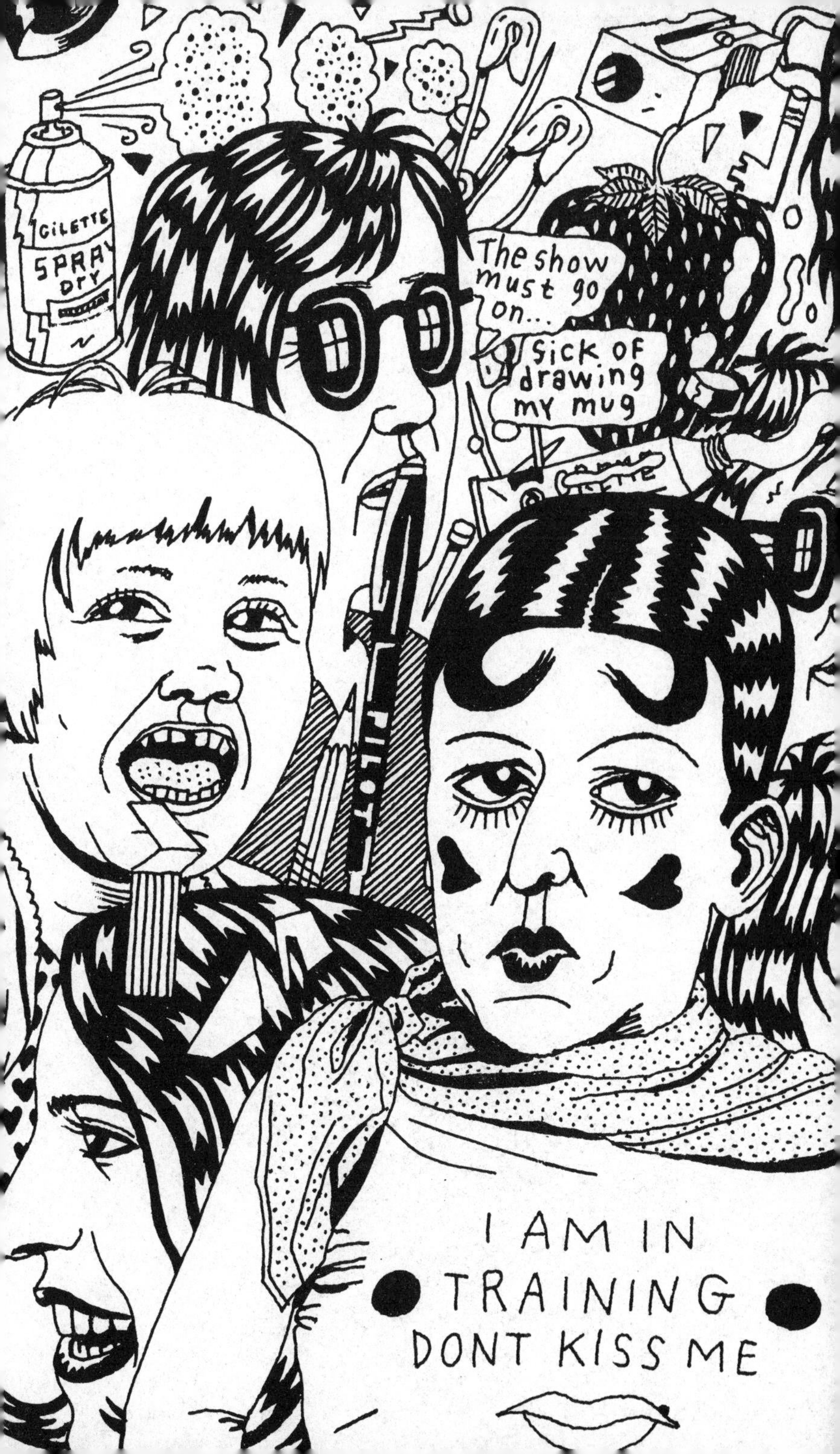
GILETTE
SPRAY
DRY
The show must go on...
sick of drawing my mug
PILOT
I AM IN TRAINING DONT KISS ME

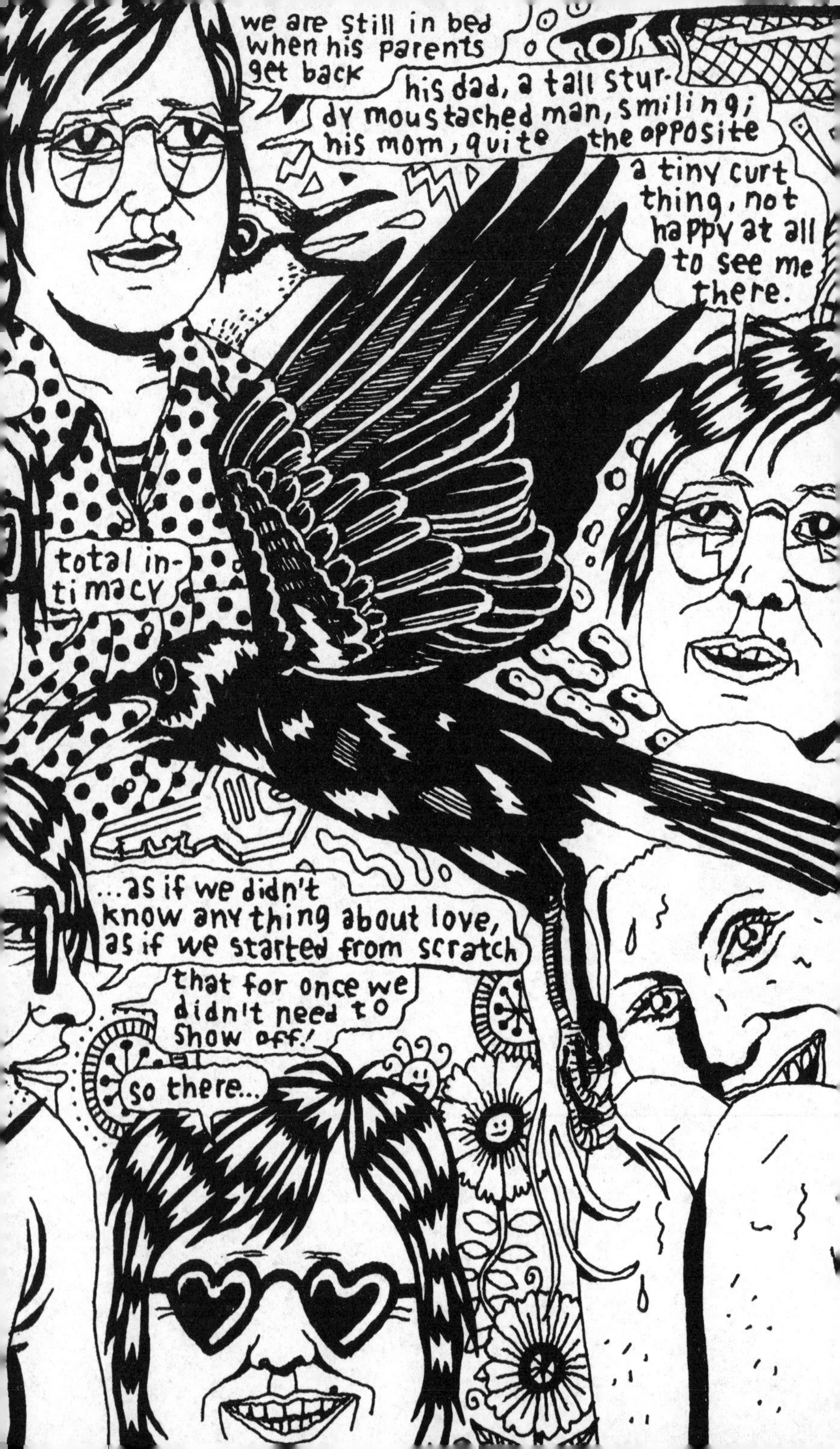
we are still in bed when his parents get back
his dad, a tall sturdy moustached man, smiling; his mom, quite the opposite
a tiny curt thing, not happy at all to see me there.
total intimacy
...as if we didn't know any thing about love, as if we started from scratch
that for once we didn't need to show off!
so there...

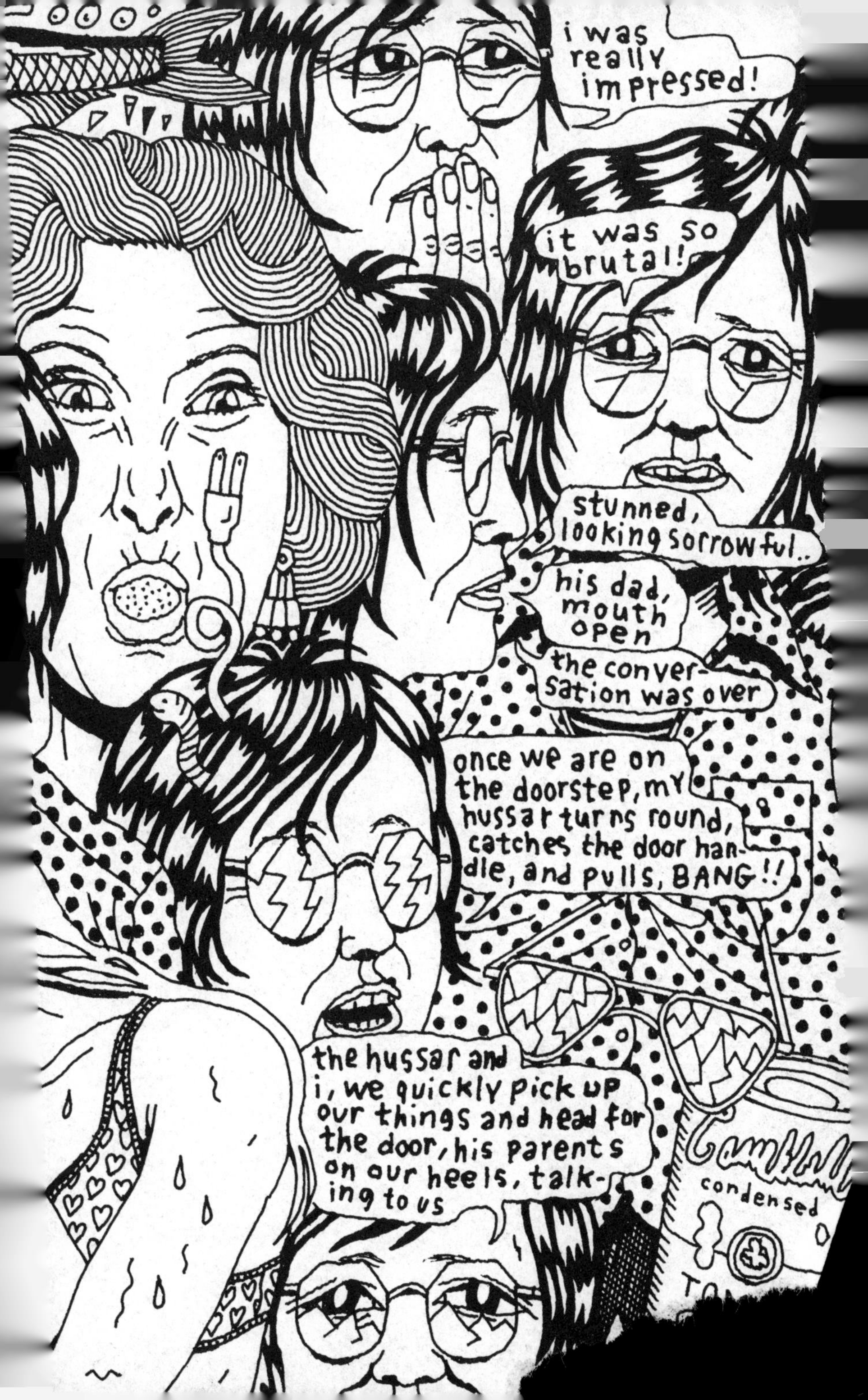
i was really impressed!
it was so brutal!
stunned, looking sorrowful..
his dad, mouth open
the conversation was over
once we are on the doorstep, my hussar turns round, catches the door handle, and pulls, BANG!!
the hussar and i, we quickly pick up our things and head for the door, his parents on our heels, talking to us
condensed

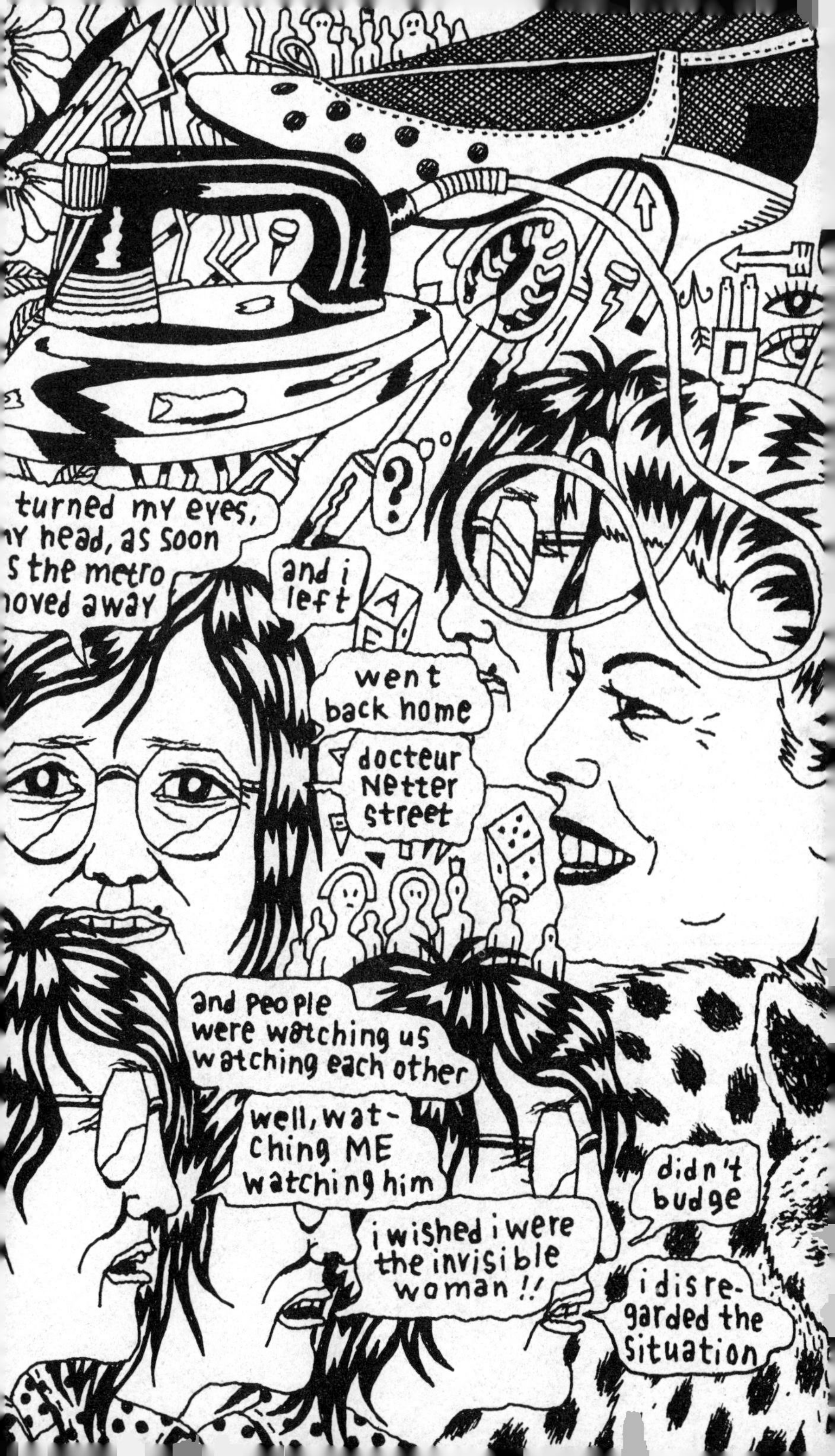
turned my eyes, my head, as soon as the metro moved away
and i left
?
went back home
docteur Netter street
and people were watching us watching each other
well, watching ME watching him
didn't budge
i wished i were the invisible woman !!
i disregarded the situation

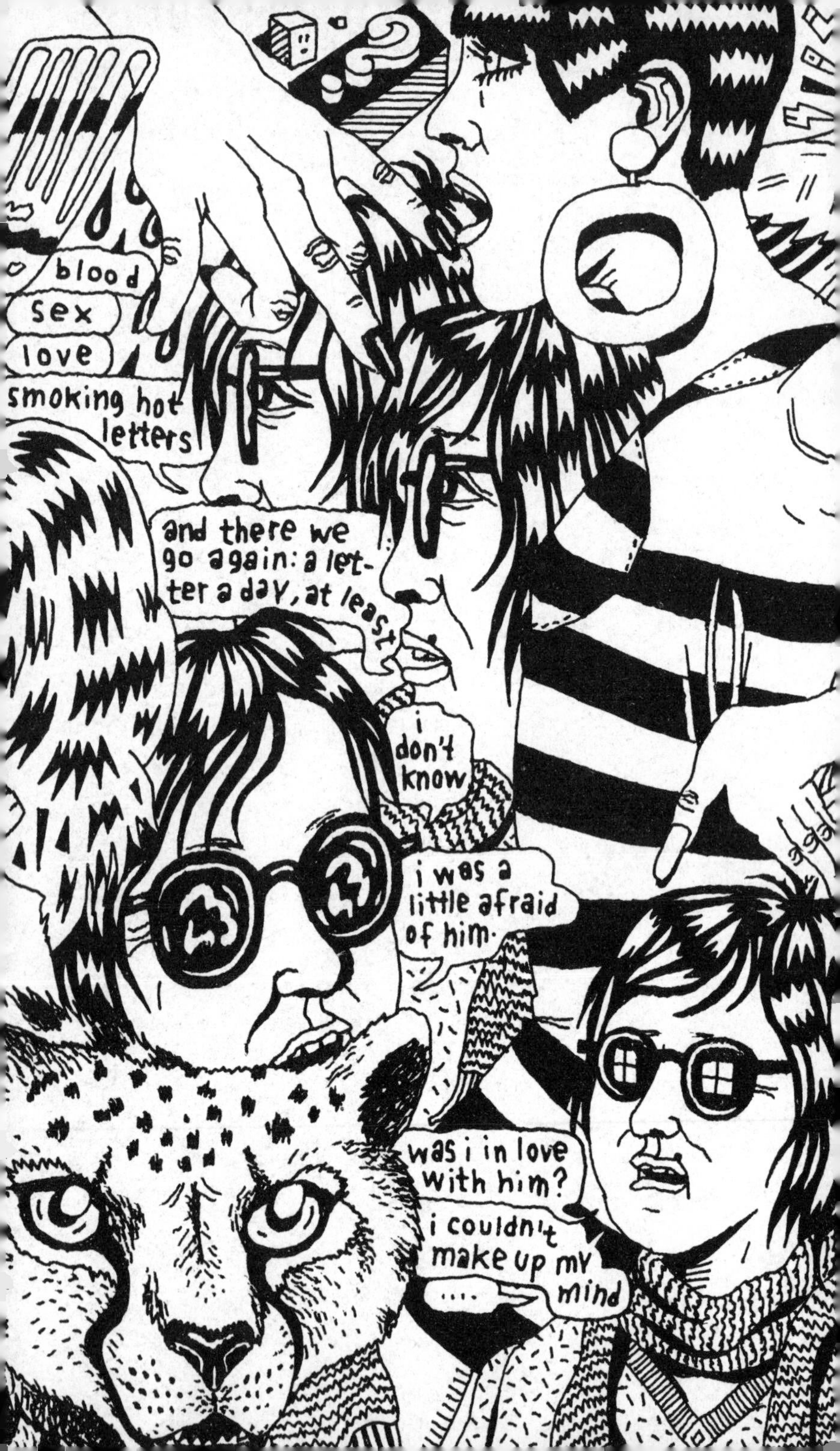
blood
sex
love
smoking hot letters
and there we go again: a letter a day, at least
i don't know
i was a little afraid of him.
was i in love with him?
i couldn't make up my mind
....

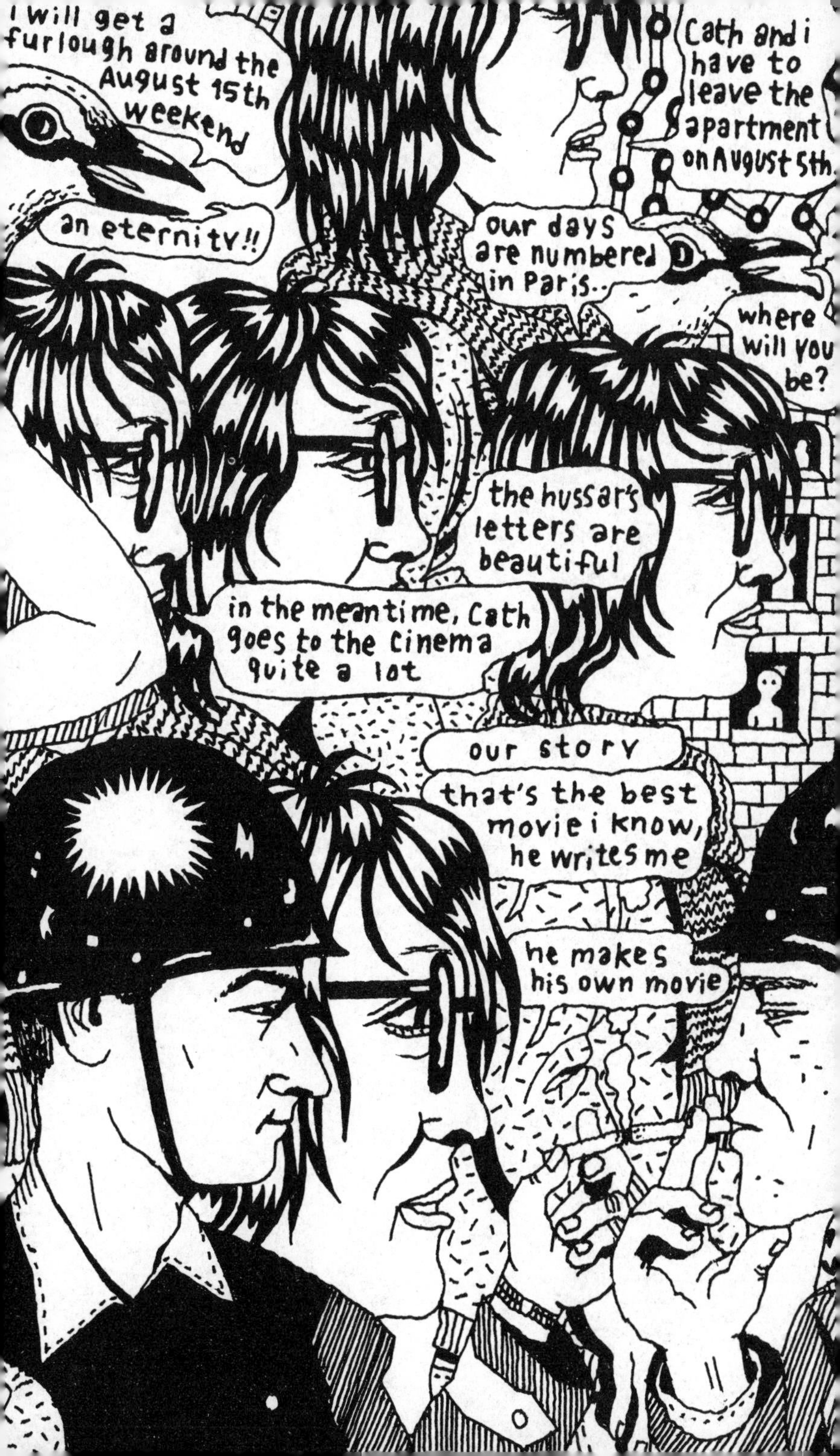
i will get a furlough around the August 15th weekend
Cath and i have to leave the apartment on August 5th.
an eternity!!
our days are numbered in Paris..
where will you be?
the hussar's letters are beautiful
in the meantime, Cath goes to the cinema quite a lot
our story
that's the best movie i know, he writes me
he makes his own movie

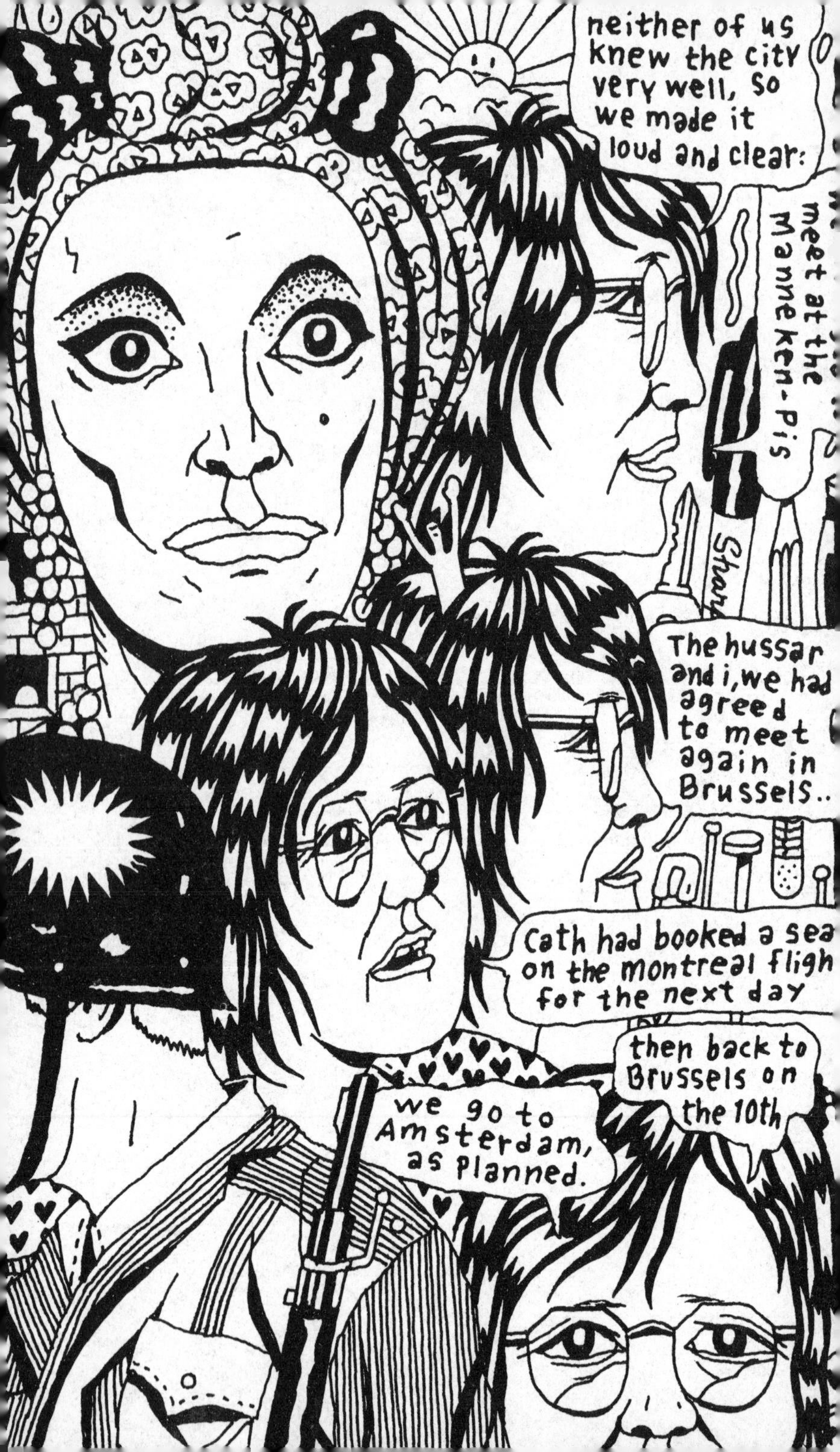
neither of us knew the city very well, so we made it loud and clear:
meet at the Manneken-Pis
The hussar and i, we had agreed to meet again in Brussels..
Cath had booked a sea on the montreal fligh for the next day
we go to Amsterdam, as planned.
then back to Brussels on the 10th

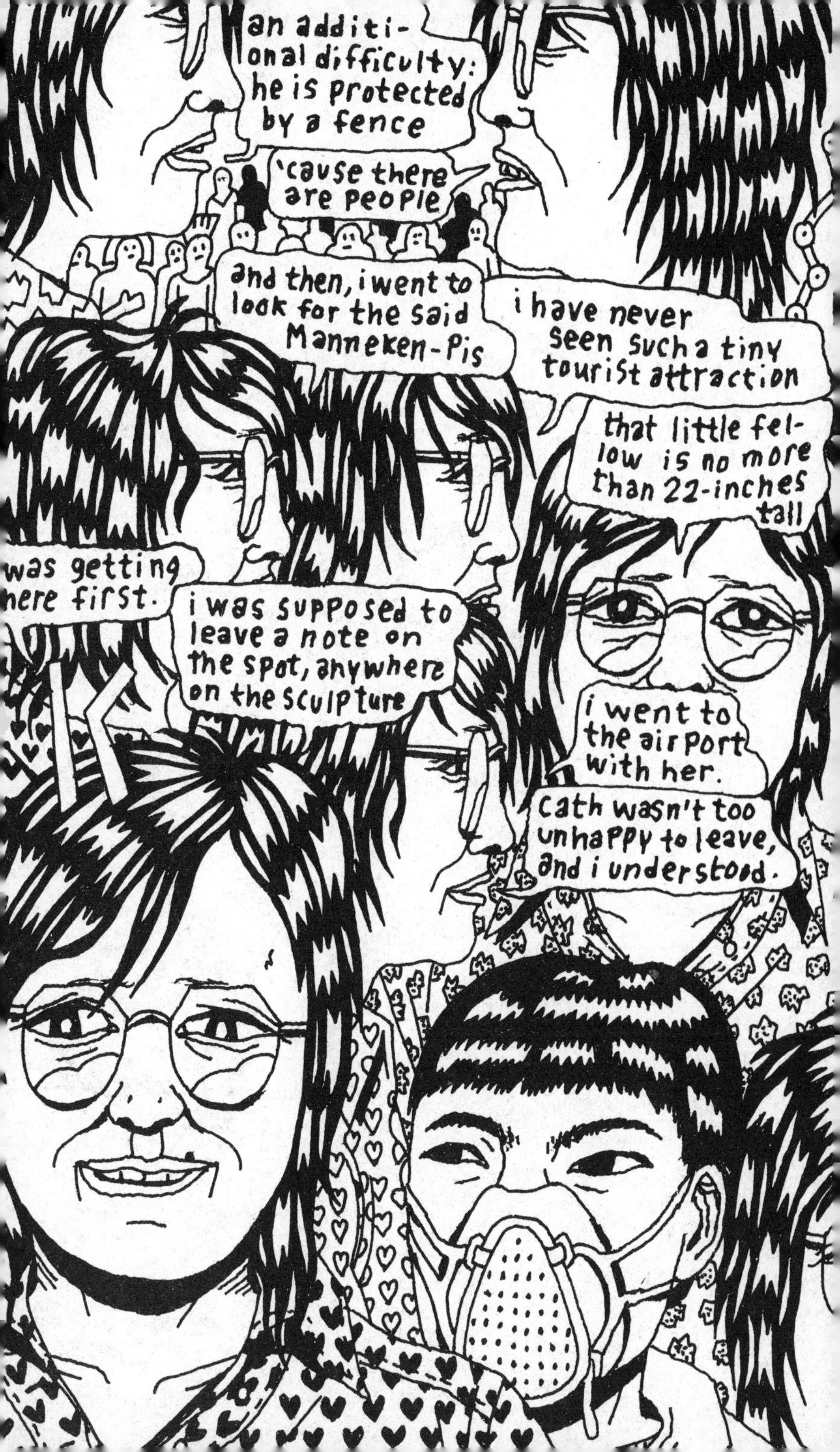
an additi-onal difficulty: he is protected by a fence
'cause there are people
and then, i went to look for the said Manneken-Pis
i have never seen such a tiny tourist attraction
that little fel-low is no more than 22-inches tall
was getting here first.
i was supposed to leave a note on the spot, anywhere on the sculpture
i went to the airport with her.
cath wasn't too unhappy to leave, and i understood.

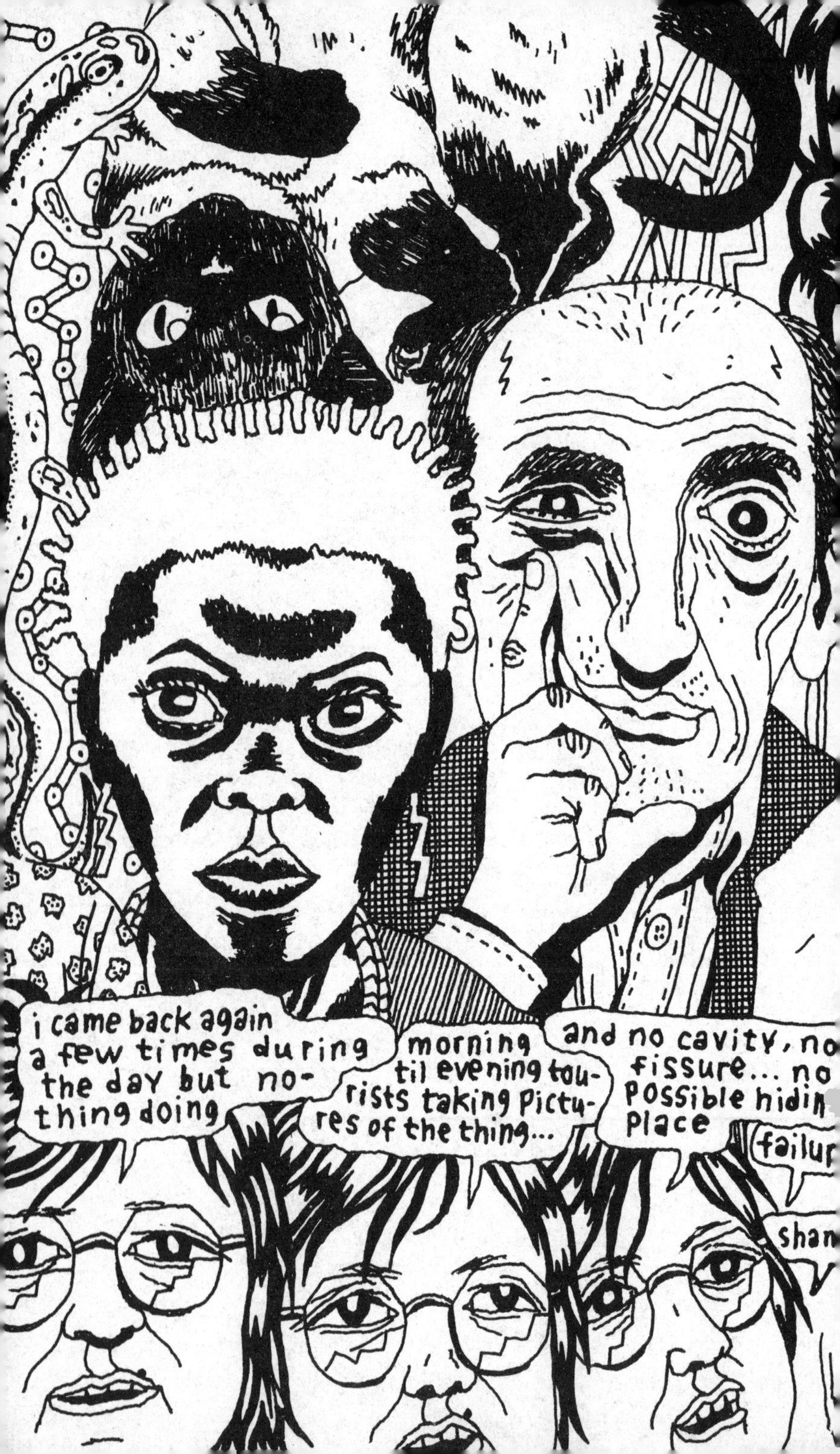
i came back again a few times during the day but nothing doing
morning til evening tourists taking pictures of the thing...
and no cavity, no fissure... no possible hidin place
failur
shan

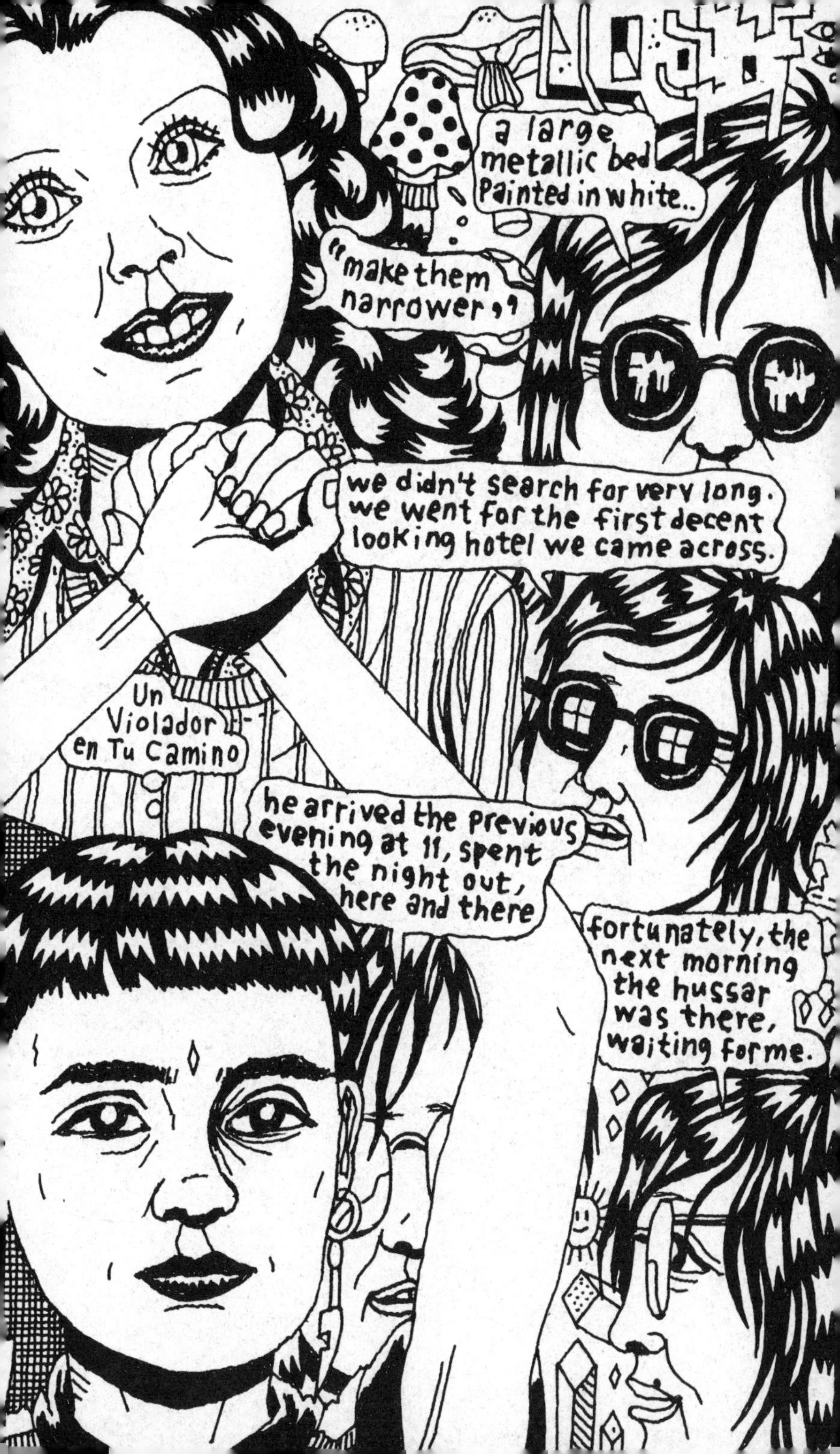
a large metallic bed Painted in white..
"make them narrower,"
we didn't search for very long. we went for the first decent looking hotel we came across.
Un Violador en Tu Camino
he arrived the previous evening at 11, spent the night out, here and there
fortunately, the next morning the hussar was there, waiting for me.

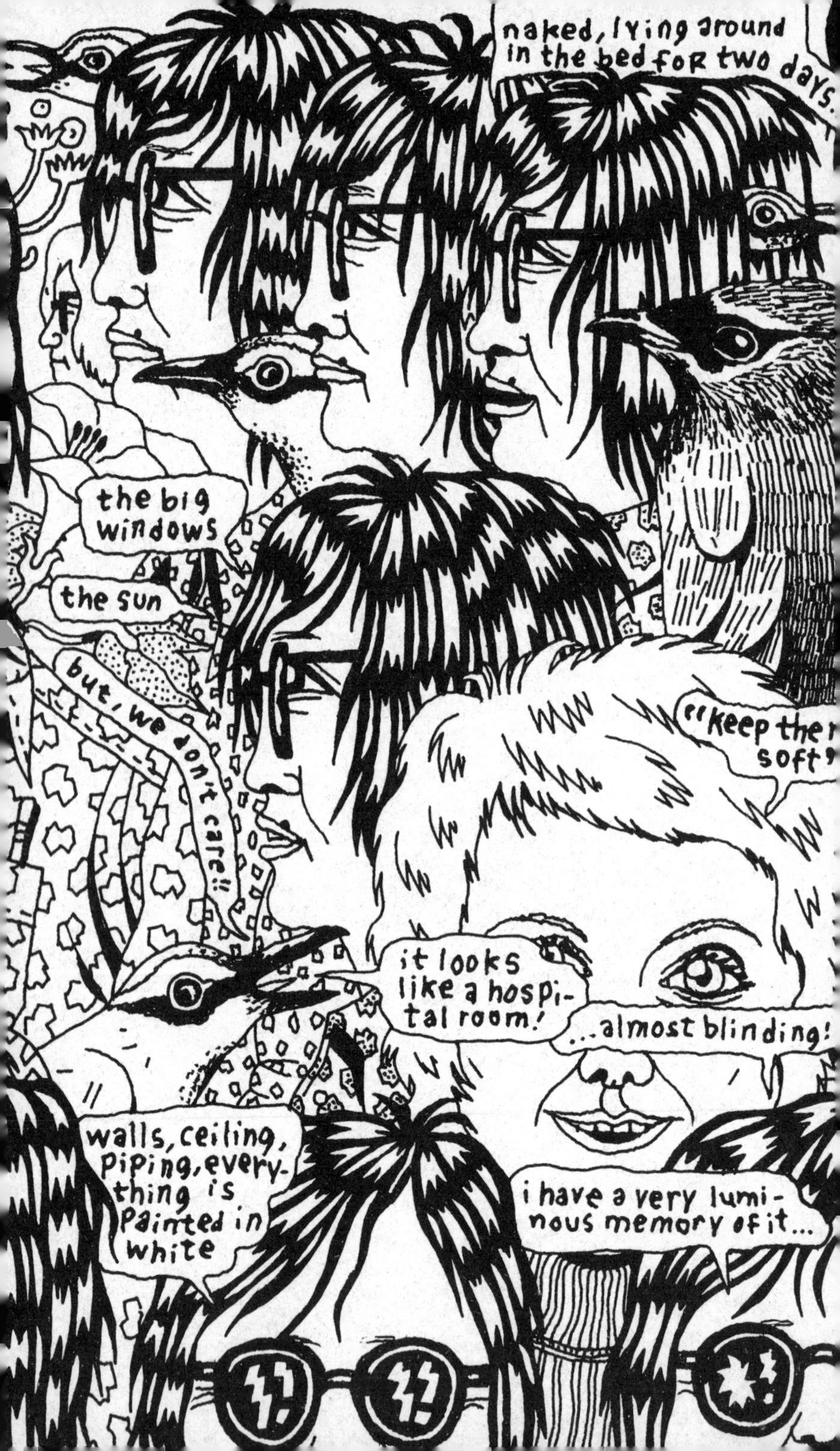
naked, lying around in the bed for two days.
the big windows
the sun
but, we don't care!!
"keep the r soft"
it looks like a hospital room!
...almost blinding!
walls, ceiling, piping, everything is painted in white
i have a very luminous memory of it...

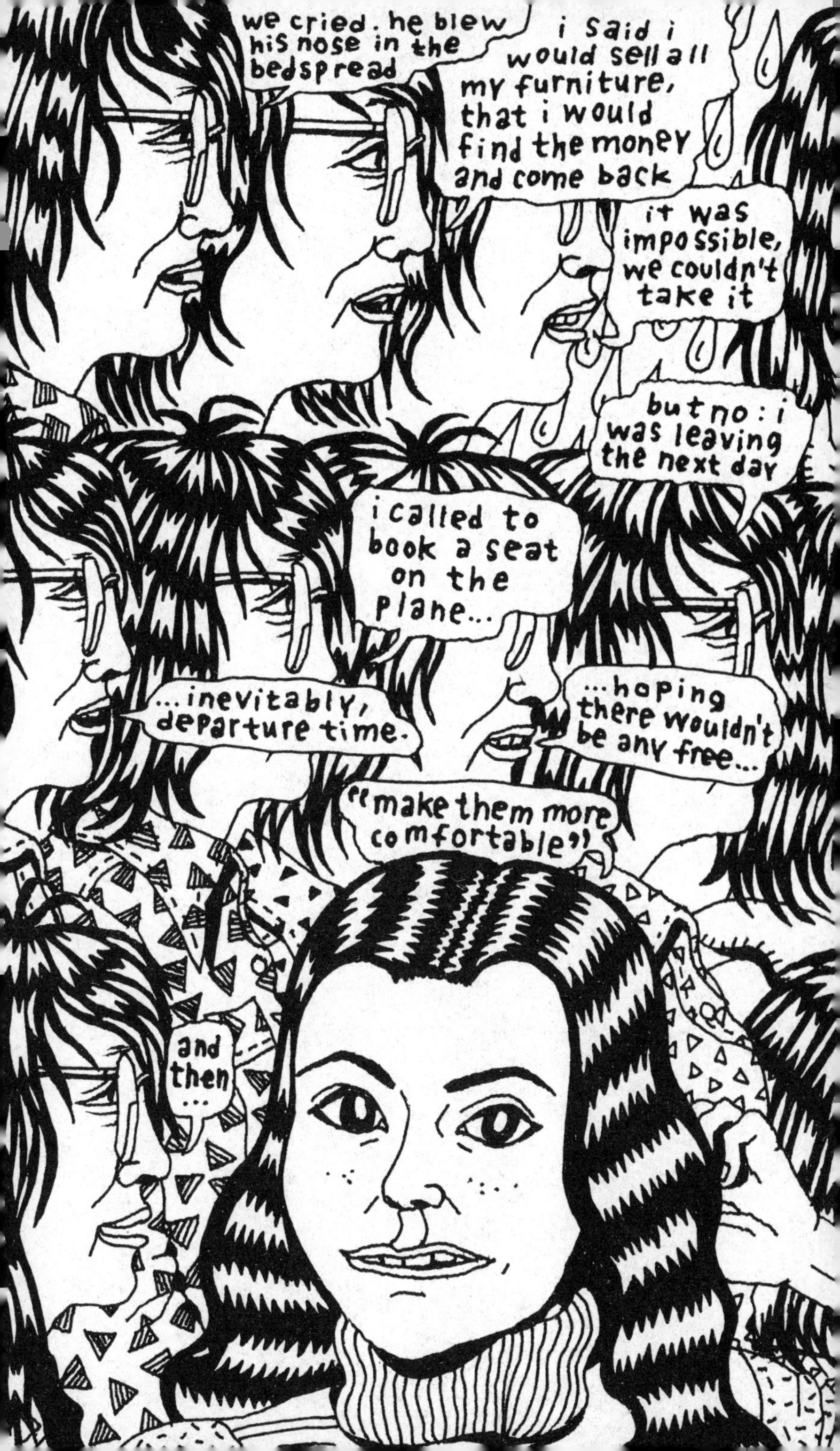
we cried. he blew his nose in the bedspread
i said i would sell all my furniture, that i would find the money and come back
it was impossible, we couldn't take it
but no: i was leaving the next day
i called to book a seat on the plane...
...hoping there wouldn't be any free...
...inevitably, departure time.
"make them more comfortable"
and then ...

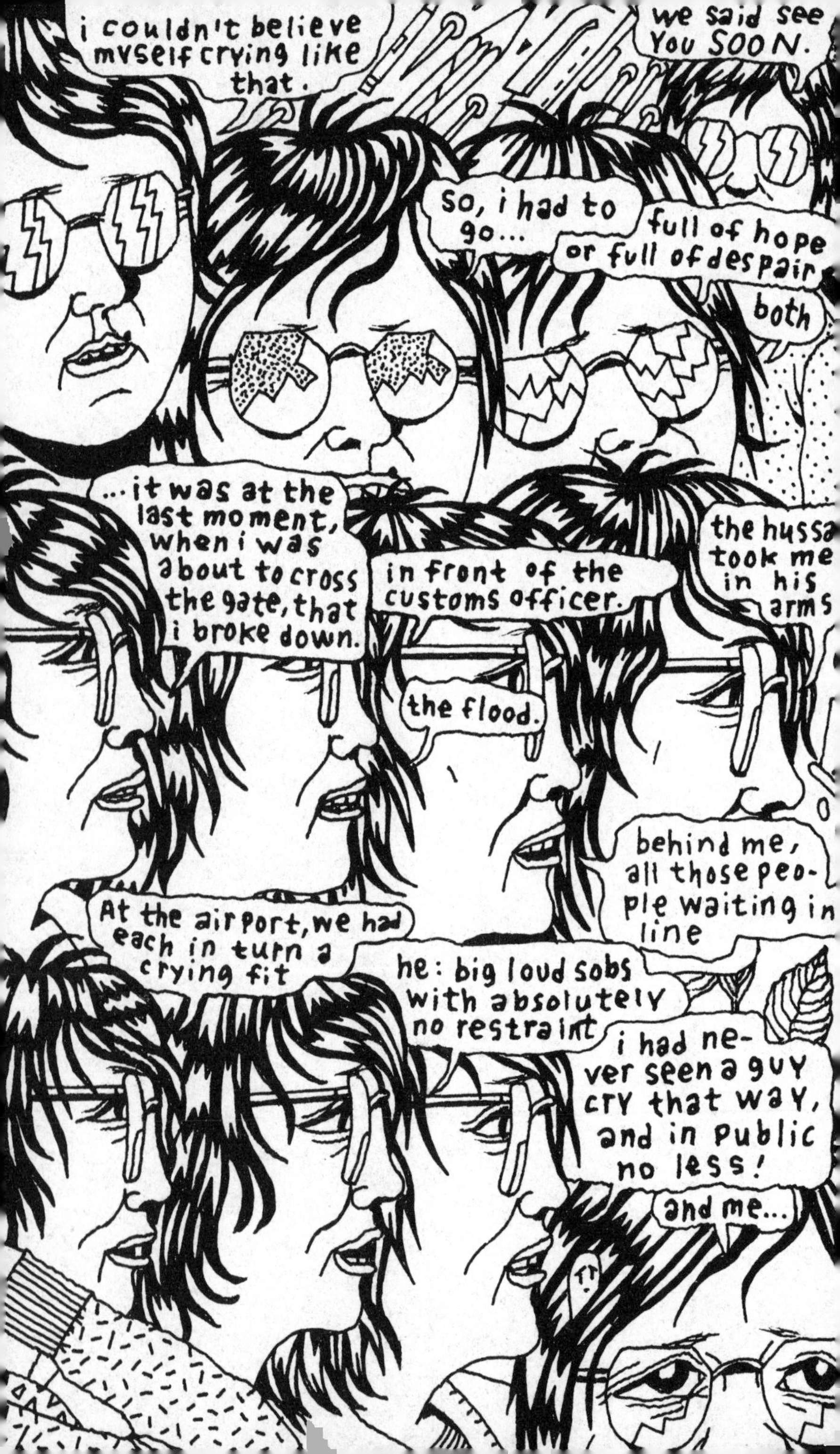
i couldn't believe myself crying like that.
we said see you SOON.
so, i had to go...
full of hope or full of despair
both
...it was at the last moment, when i was about to cross the gate, that i broke down.
in front of the customs officer.
the hussa took me in his arms
the flood.
behind me, all those people waiting in line
At the airport, we had each in turn a crying fit
he: big loud sobs with absolutely no restraint
i had never seen a guy cry that way, and in public no less!
and me...

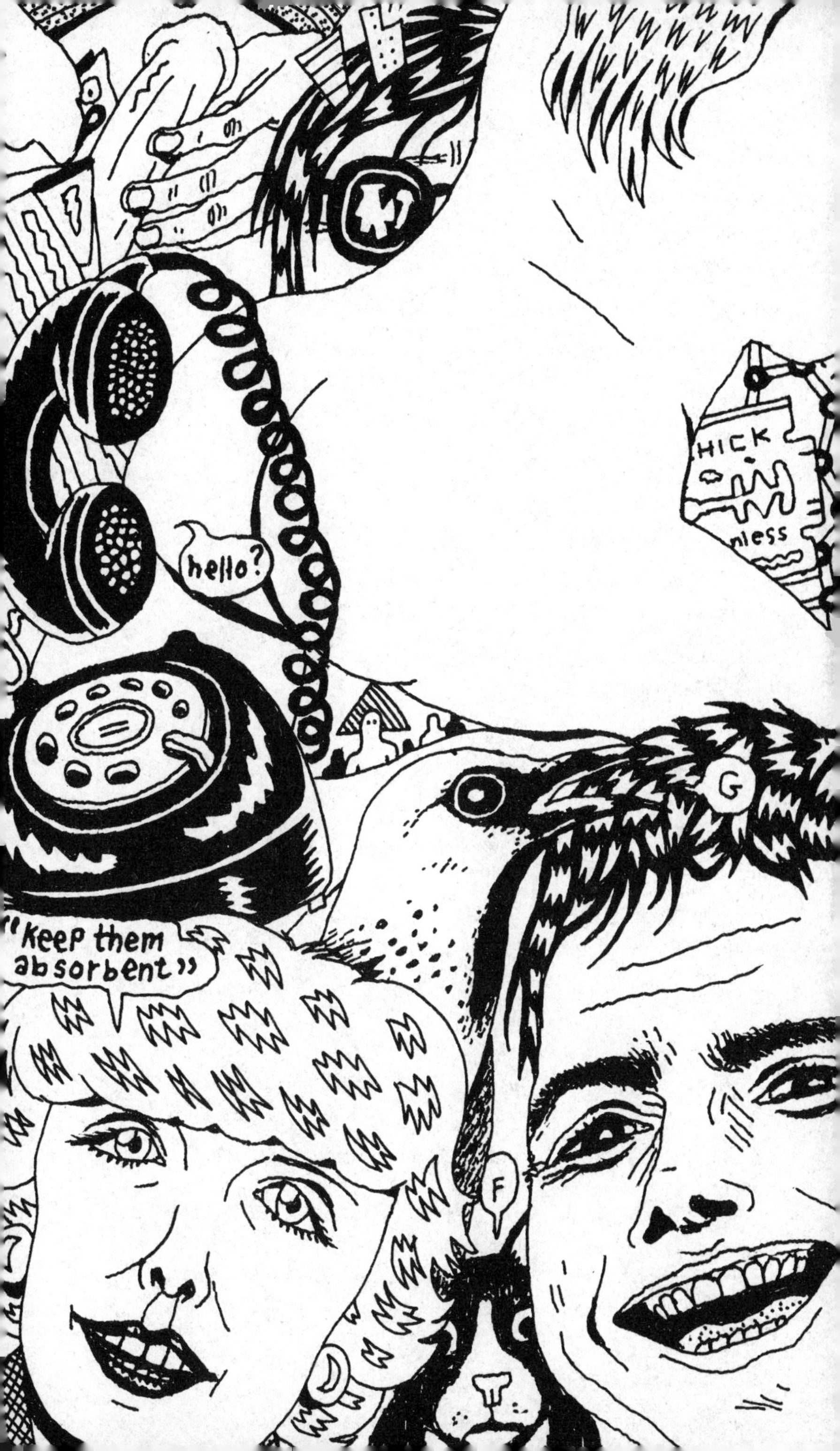

hello?
HICK
nless
G
"keep them absorbent"
F

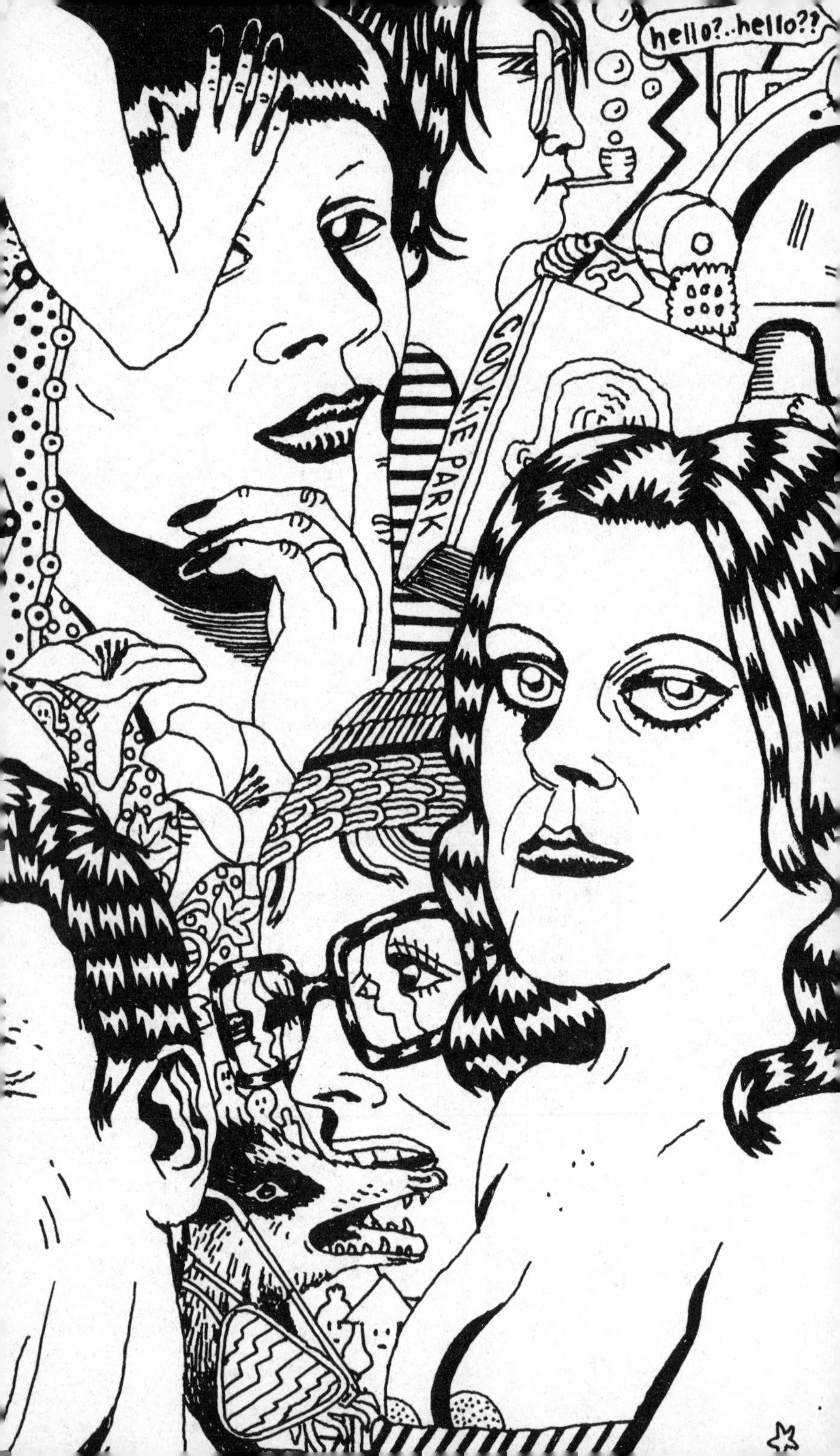
hello?..hello??
COOKIE PARK

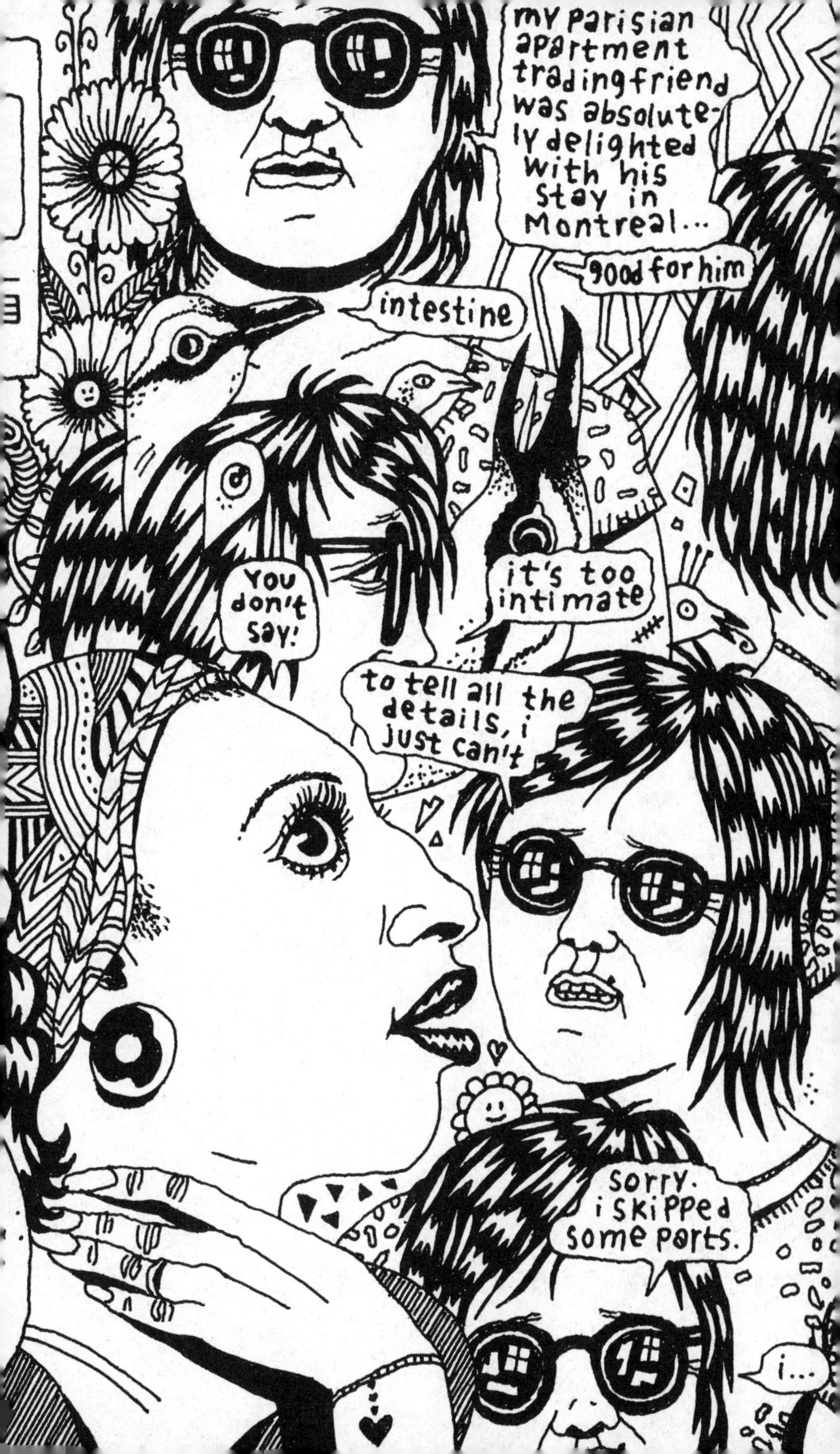
my parisian apartment tradingfriend was absolutely delighted with his stay in Montreal...
good for him
intestine
You don't say!
it's too intimate
to tell all the details, i just can't
sorry. i skipped some parts.
i...

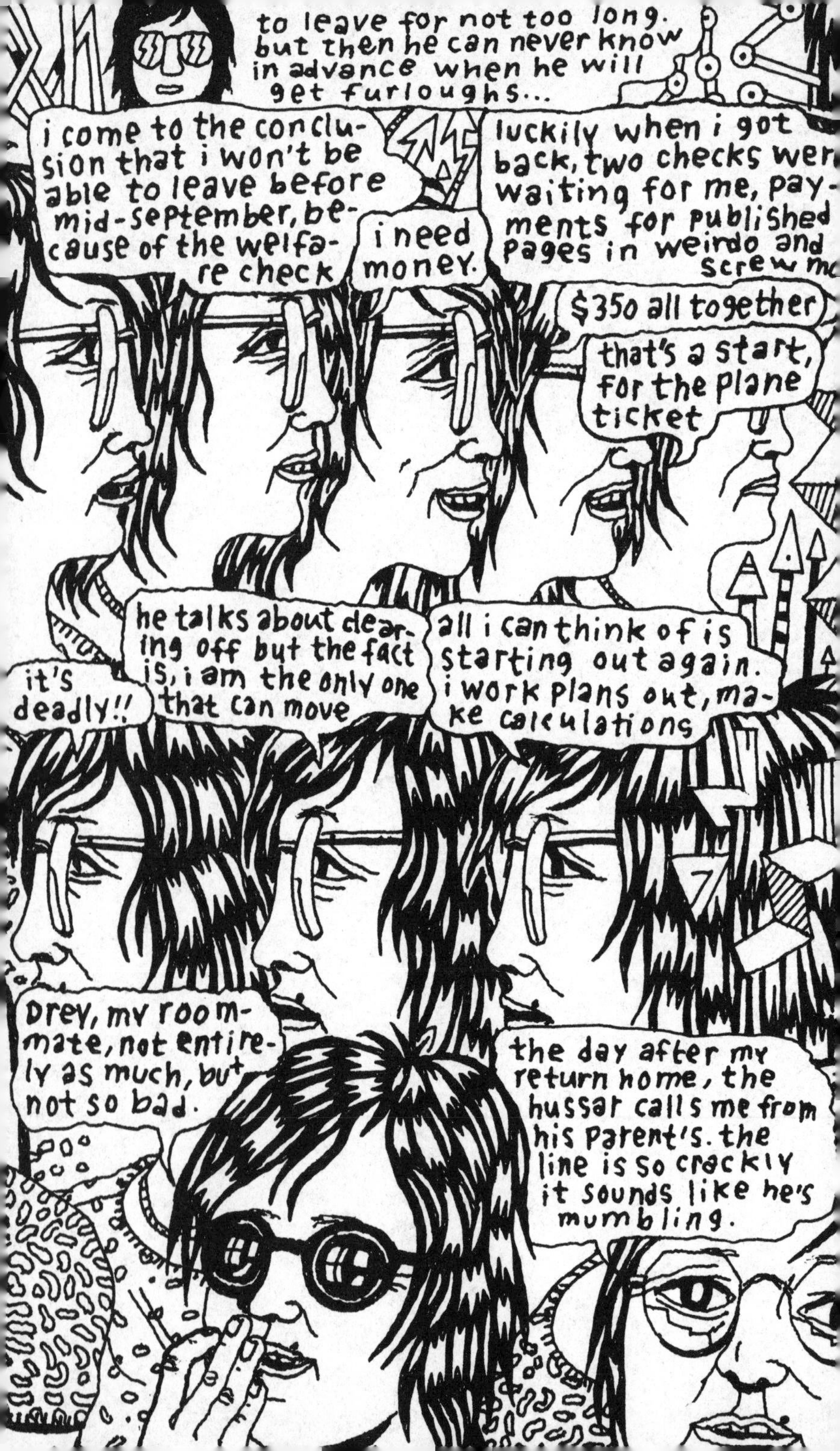
to leave for not too long. but then he can never know in advance when he will get furloughs...
i come to the conclusion that i won't be able to leave before mid-september, because of the welfare check
i need money.
luckily when i got back, two checks wer waiting for me, payments for published pages in weirdo and screw m
$350 all together
that's a start, for the plane ticket
he talks about clearing off but the fact is, i am the only one that can move
all i can think of is starting out again. i work plans out, make calculations
it's deadly!!
drey, my roommate, not entirely as much, but not so bad.
the day after my return home, the hussar calls me from his parent's. the line is so crackly it sounds like he's mumbling.

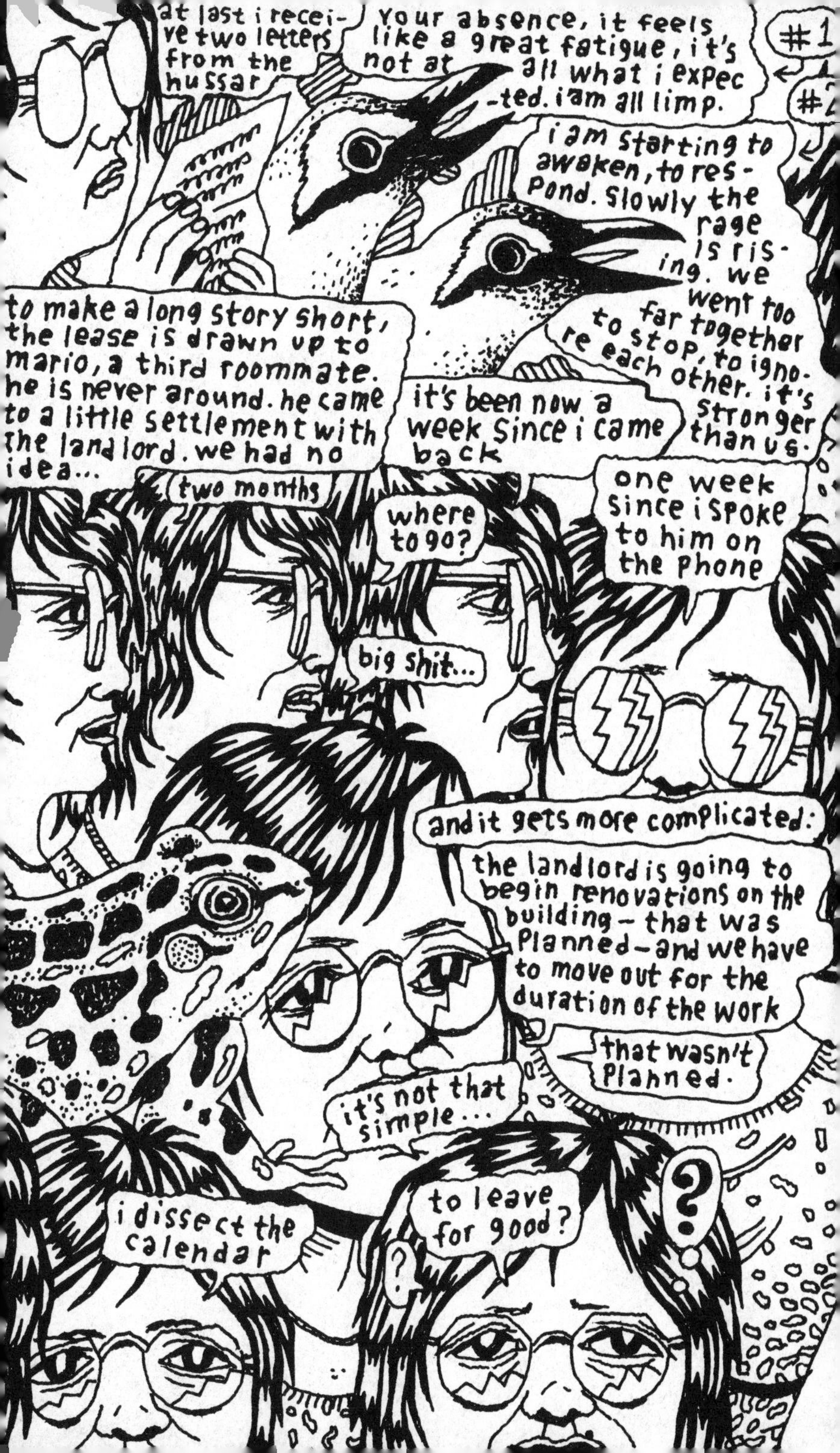

at last i receive two letters from the hussar
your absence, it feels like a great fatigue, it's not at all what i expected. i am all limp.
#1
#2
i am starting to awaken, to respond. slowly the rage is rising. we went too far together to stop, to ignore each other. it's stronger than us.
to make a long story short, the lease is drawn up to mario, a third roommate. he is never around. he came to a little settlement with the landlord. we had no idea...
it's been now a week since i came back
two months
where to go?
one week since i spoke to him on the phone
big shit...
and it gets more complicated:
the landlord is going to begin renovations on the building – that was planned – and we have to move out for the duration of the work
that wasn't planned.
it's not that simple...
i dissect the calendar
to leave for good?

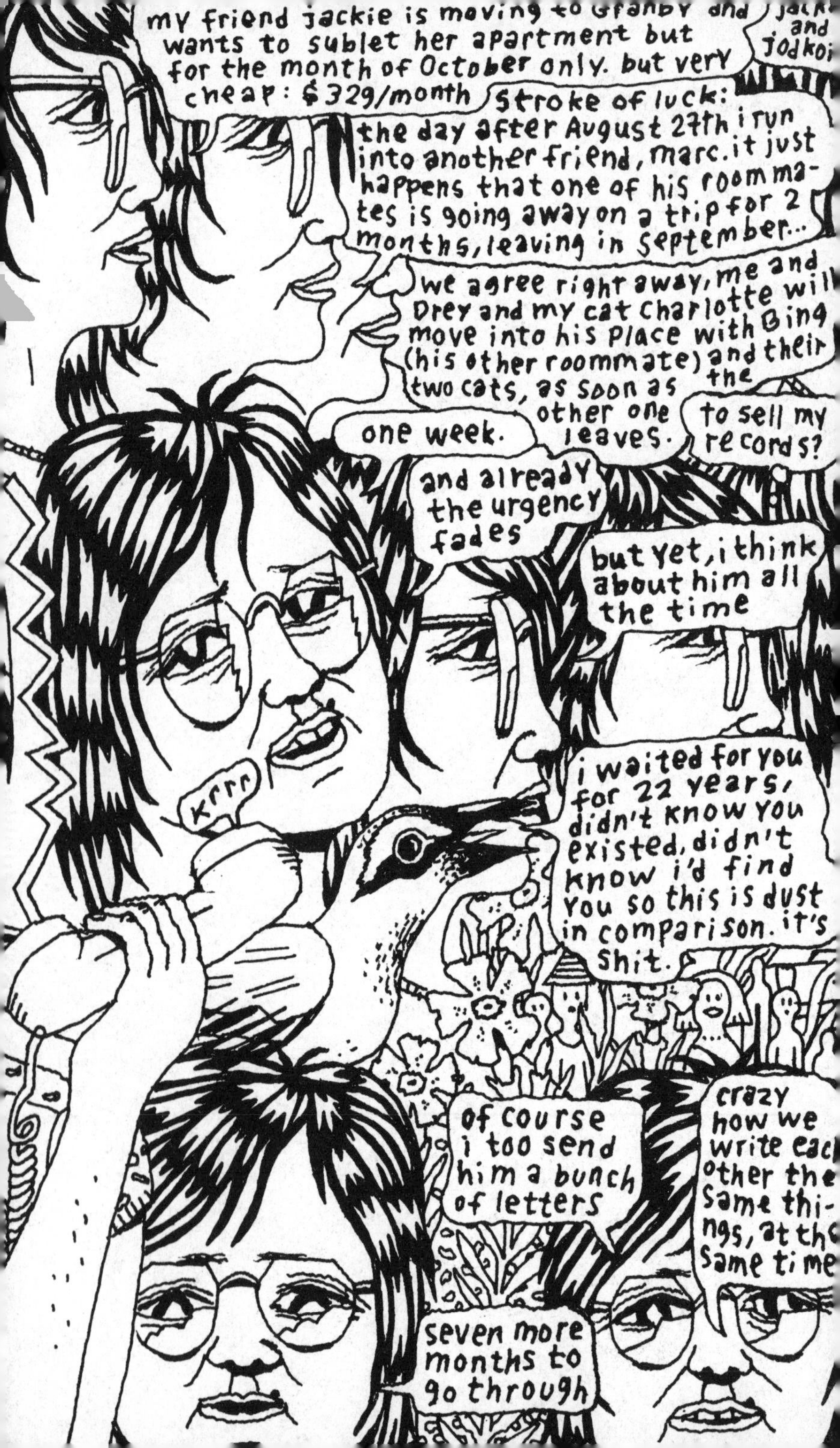
my friend jackie is moving to Granby and wants to sublet her apartment but for the month of October only. but very cheap: $329/month
jackie and
stroke of luck: the day after August 27th i run into another friend, marc. it just happens that one of his roommates is going away on a trip for 2 months, leaving in september...
we agree right away, me and Drey and my cat Charlotte will move into his place with Bing (his other roommate) and their two cats, as soon as the other one leaves.
one week.
to sell my records?
and already the urgency fades
but yet, i think about him all the time
krrr
i waited for you for 22 years, didn't know you existed, didn't know i'd find you so this is dust in comparison. it's shit.
of course i too send him a bunch of letters
crazy how we write each other the same things, at the same time
seven more months to go through

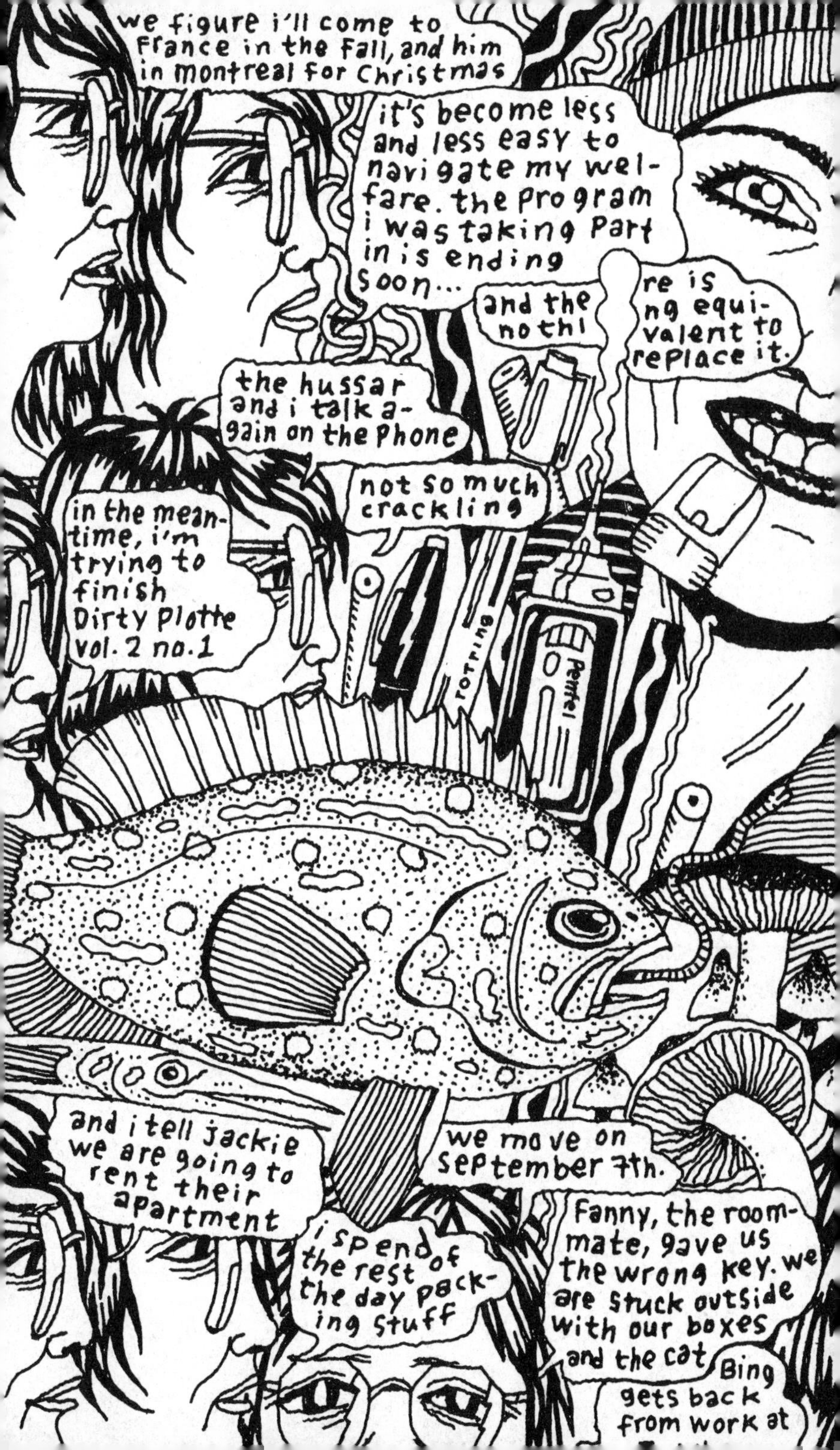
we figure i'll come to France in the Fall, and him in montreal for Christmas
it's become less and less easy to navigate my welfare. the program i was taking Part in is ending soon...
and the no thi
re is ng equivalent to replace it.
the hussar and i talk again on the Phone
not so much crackling
in the meantime, i'm trying to finish Dirty plotte vol. 2 no. 1
rotring
Pentel
and i tell Jackie we are going to rent their apartment
we move on September 7th.
i spend the rest of the day packing stuff
Fanny, the roommate, gave us the wrong key. we are stuck outside with our boxes and the cat
Bing gets back from work at

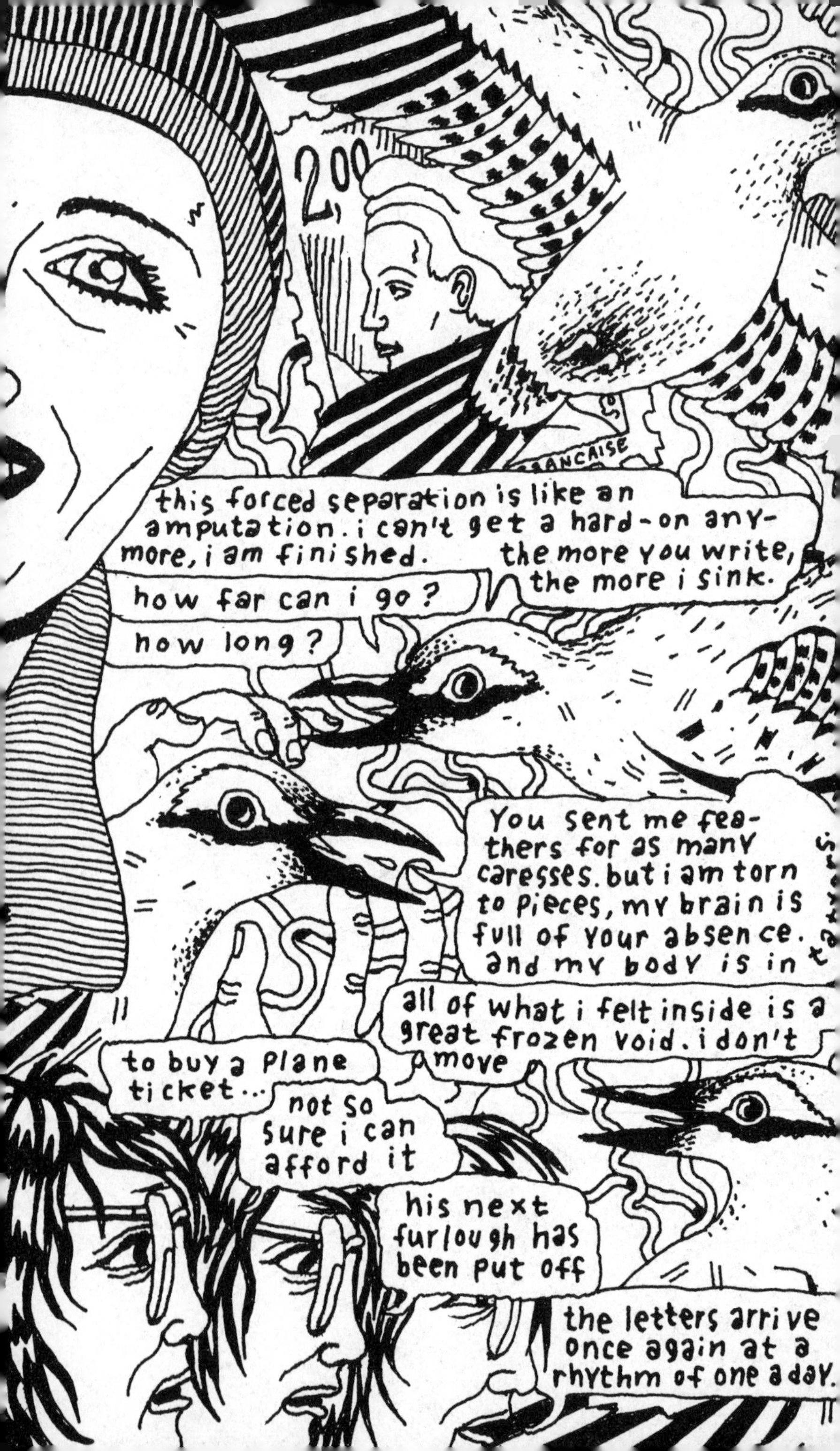
2,00
this forced separation is like an amputation. i can't get a hard-on any-more, i am finished.
the more you write, the more i sink.
how far can i go?
how long?
You sent me fea-thers for as many caresses. but i am torn to pieces, my brain is full of your absence. and my body is in
all of what i felt inside is a great frozen void. i don't move
to buy a plane ticket...
not so sure i can afford it
his next furlough has been put off
the letters arrive once again at a rhythm of one a day.

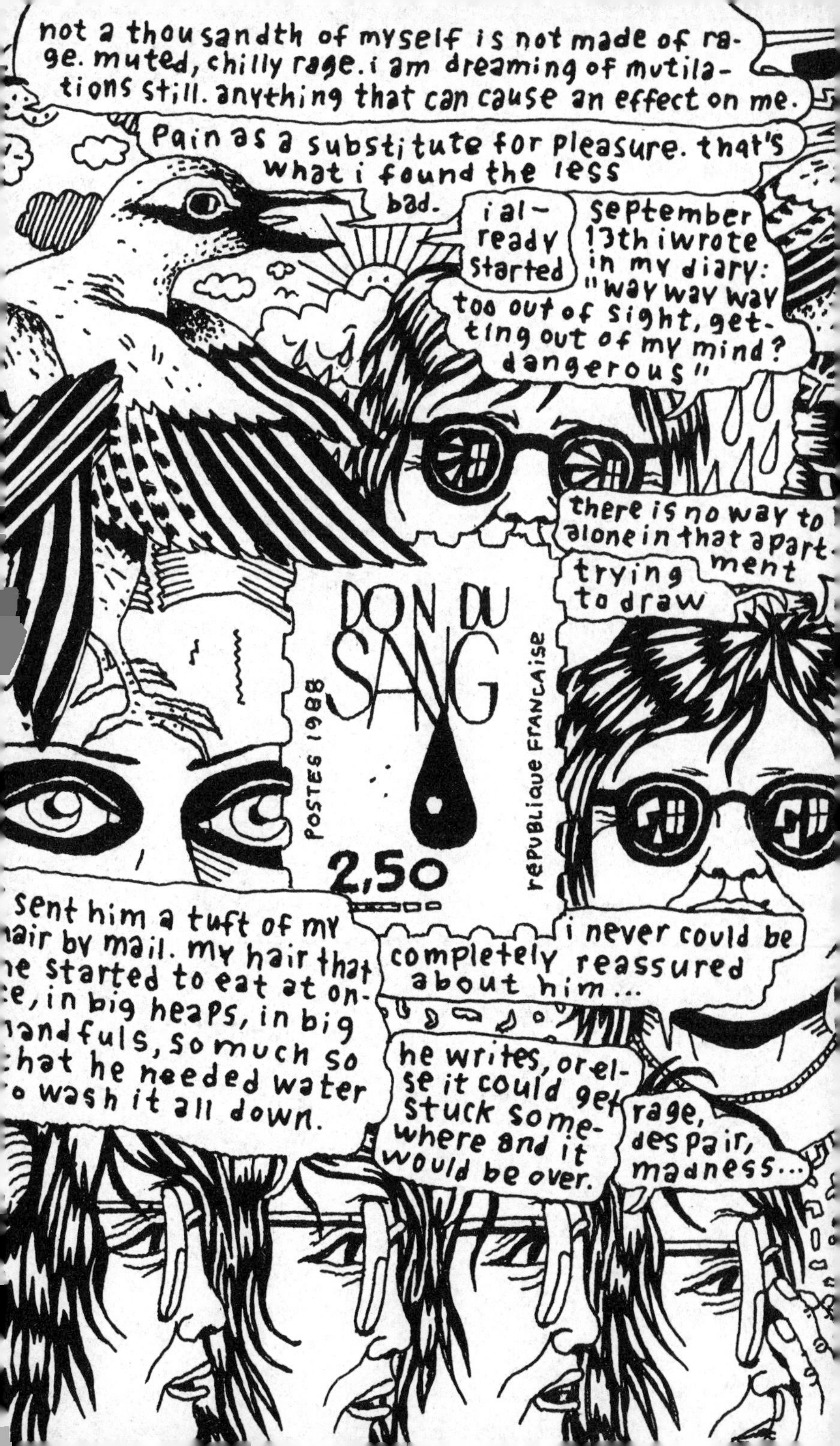
not a thousandth of myself is not made of rage. muted, chilly rage. i am dreaming of mutilations still. anything that can cause an effect on me.
pain as a substitute for pleasure. that's what i found the less bad.
i already started
september 13th i wrote in my diary: "way way way too out of sight, getting out of my mind? dangerous"
there is no way to alone in that apartment
trying to draw
DON DU SANG
POSTES 1988
RÉPUBLIQUE FRANÇAISE
2,50
sent him a tuft of my hair by mail. my hair that he started to eat at once, in big heaps, in big handfuls, so much so that he needed water to wash it all down.
i never could be completely reassured about him...
he writes, or else it could get stuck somewhere and it would be over.
rage, despair, madness...

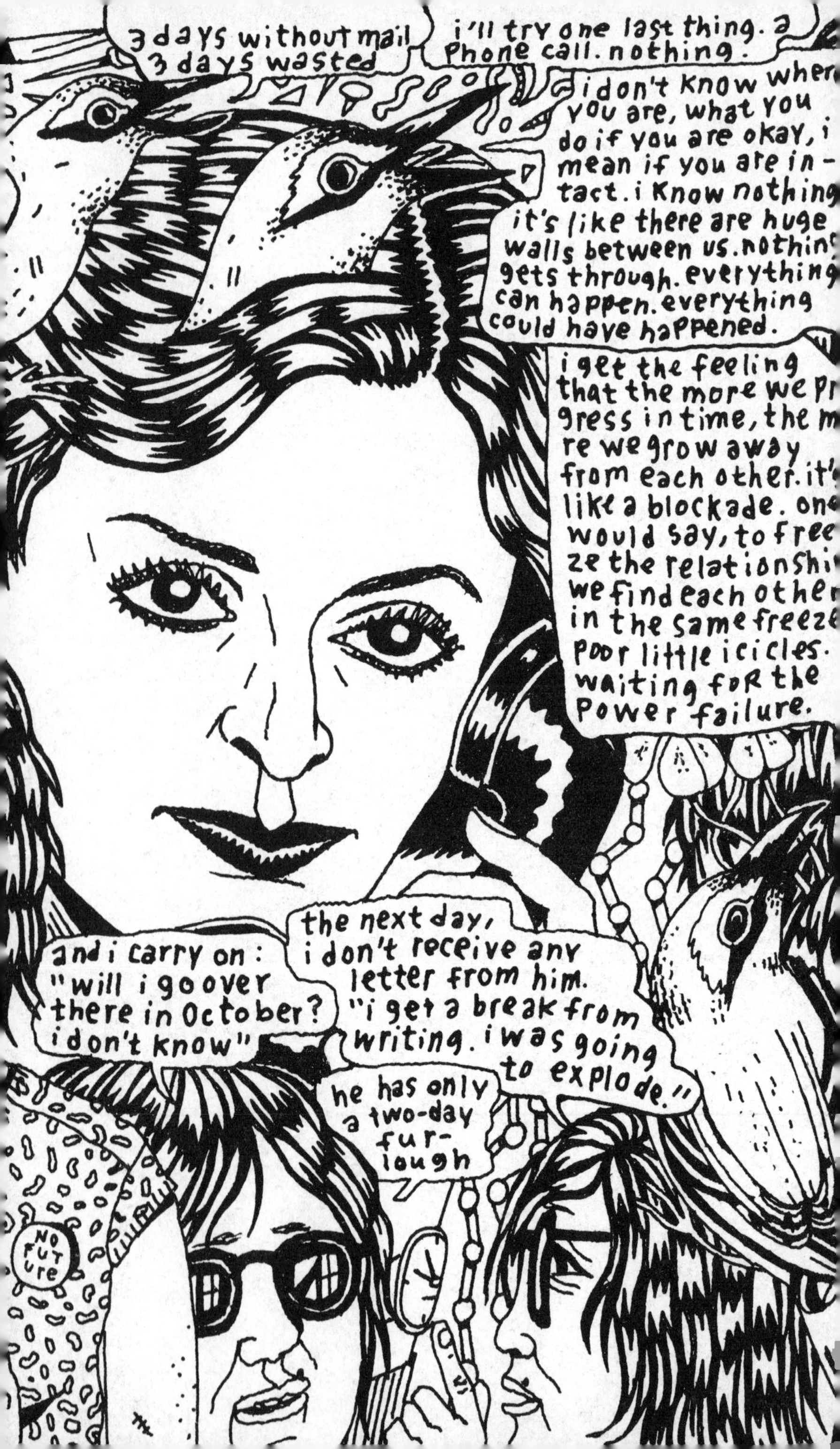
3 days without mail
3 days wasted
i'll try one last thing. a phone call. nothing.
i don't know where you are, what you do if you are okay, i mean if you are in-tact. i know nothing
it's like there are huge walls between us. nothing gets through. everything can happen. everything could have happened.
i get the feeling that the more we pr gress in time, the m re we grow away from each other. it's like a blockade. one would say, to free ze the relationshi we find each other in the same freeze poor little icicles. waiting for the power failure.
and i carry on: "will i go over there in October? i don't know"
the next day, i don't receive any letter from him. "i get a break from writing. i was going to explode."
he has only a two-day fur-lough
NO FUT URE

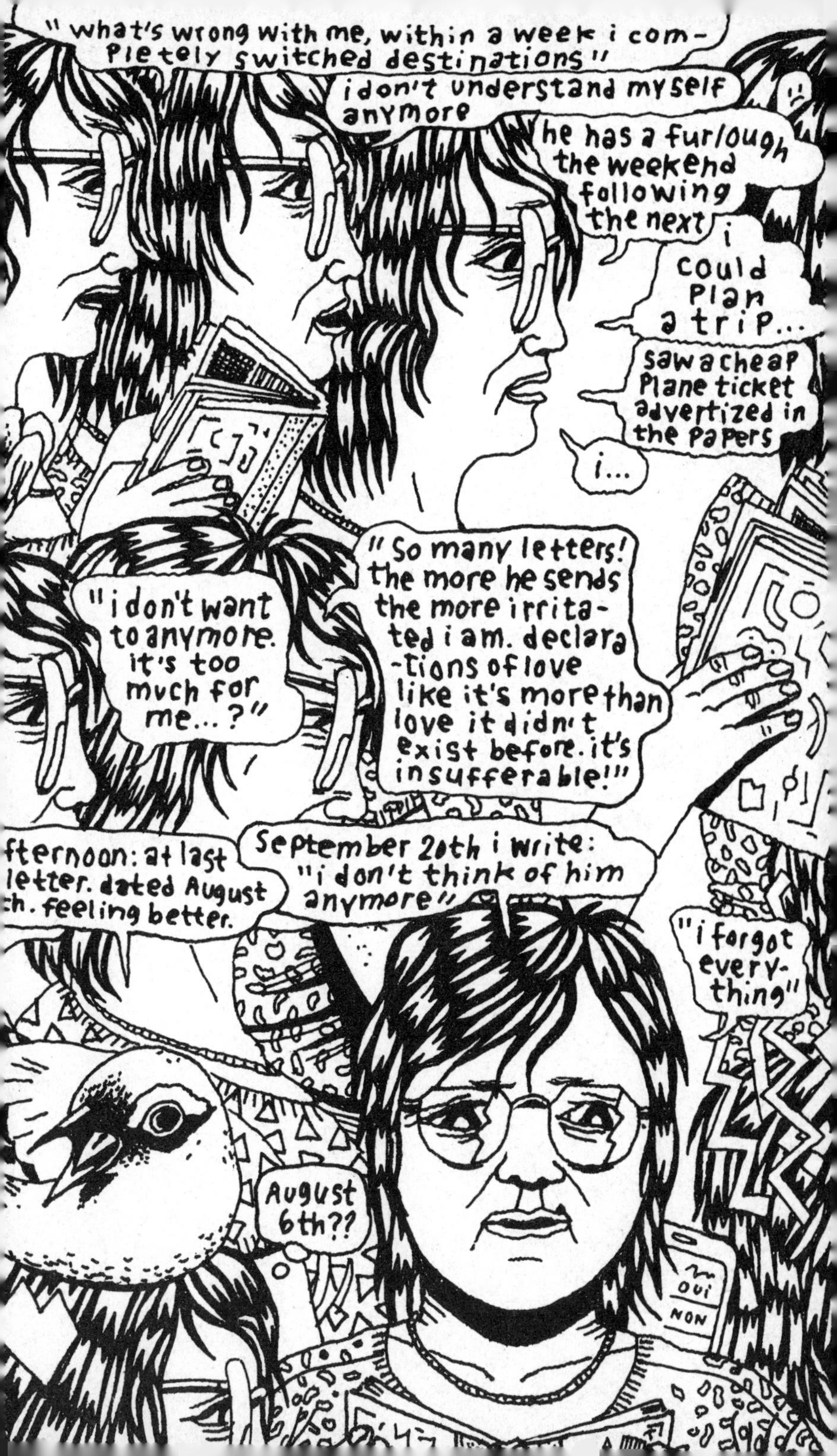
"what's wrong with me, within a week i completely switched destinations"
i don't understand myself anymore
he has a furlough the weekend following the next
i could plan a trip...
saw a cheap plane ticket advertized in the papers
i...
"i don't want to anymore. it's too much for me...?"
"So many letters! the more he sends the more irritated i am. declarations of love like it's more than love it didn't exist before. it's insufferable!"
fternoon: at last letter. dated August h. feeling better.
September 20th i write: "i don't think of him anymore"
"i forgot everything"
August 6th??
OUI
NON

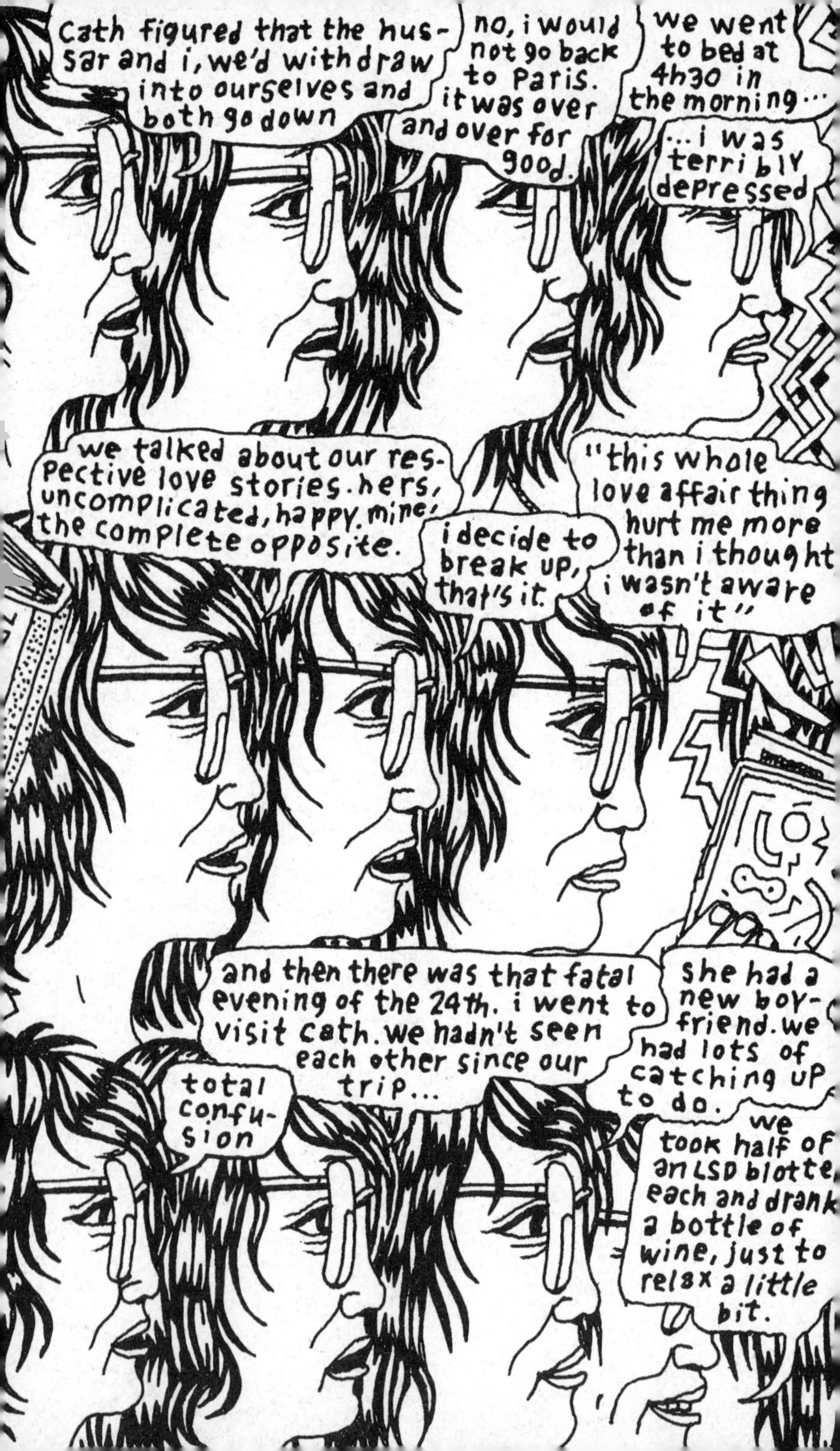
cath figured that the hussar and i, we'd withdraw into ourselves and both go down
no, i would not go back to Paris. it was over and over for good.
we went to bed at 4h30 in the morning...
...i was terribly depressed
we talked about our respective love stories. hers, uncomplicated, happy. mine, the complete opposite.
i decide to break up, that's it.
"this whole love affair thing hurt me more than i thought i wasn't aware of it"
and then there was that fatal evening of the 24th. i went to visit cath. we hadn't seen each other since our trip...
she had a new boyfriend. we had lots of catching up to do.
total confusion
we took half of an LSD blotte each and drank a bottle of wine, just to relax a little bit.

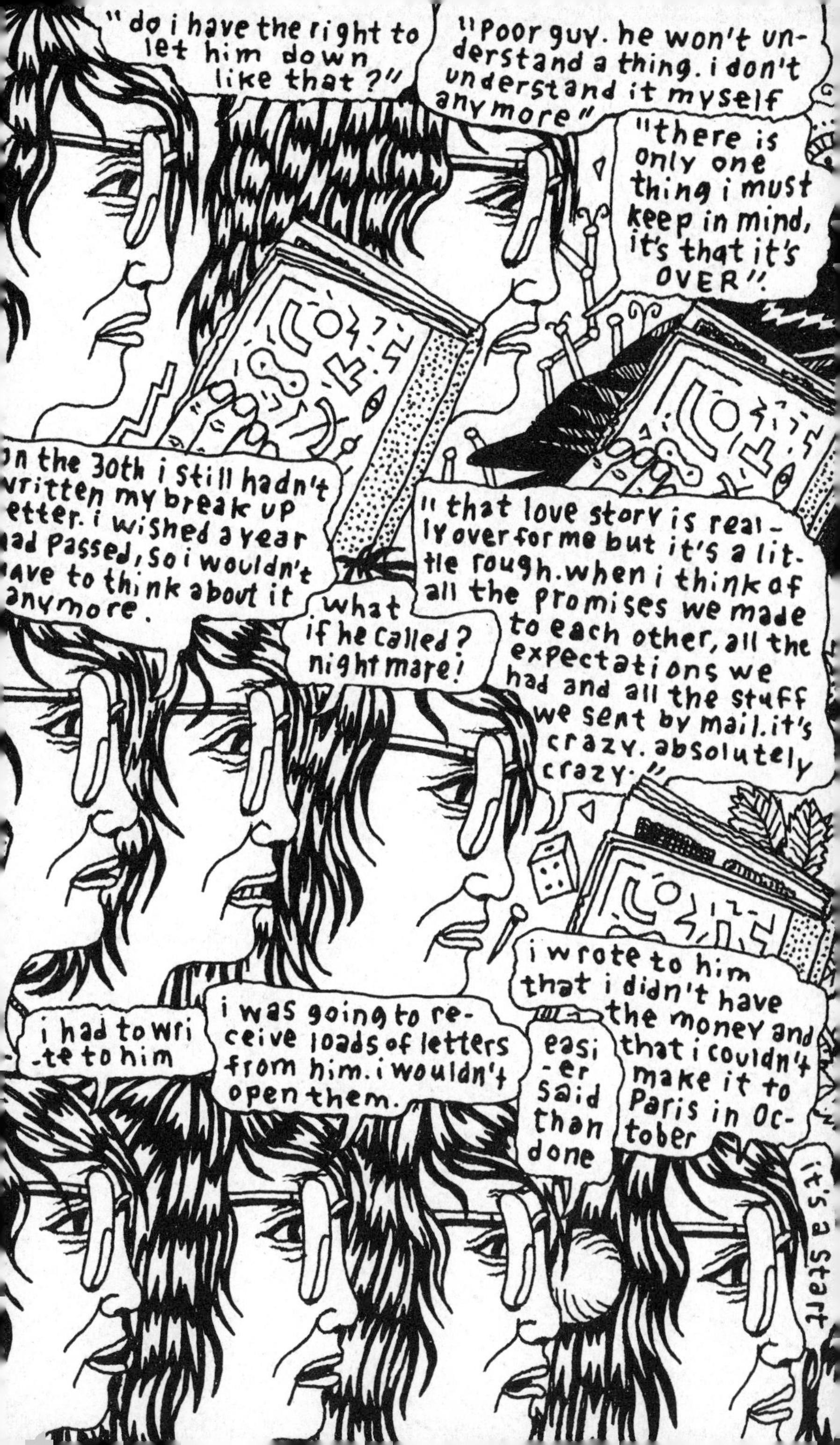
"do i have the right to let him down like that?"
"poor guy. he won't understand a thing. i don't understand it myself anymore"
"there is only one thing i must keep in mind, it's that it's OVER".
on the 30th i still hadn't written my break up letter. i wished a year had passed, so i wouldn't have to think about it anymore.
"that love story is really over for me but it's a little rough. when i think of all the promises we made to each other, all the expectations we had and all the stuff we sent by mail. it's crazy. absolutely crazy."
what if he called? nightmare!
i had to write to him
i was going to receive loads of letters from him. i wouldn't open them.
i wrote to him that i didn't have the money and that i couldn't make it to Paris in October
easier said than done
it's a start

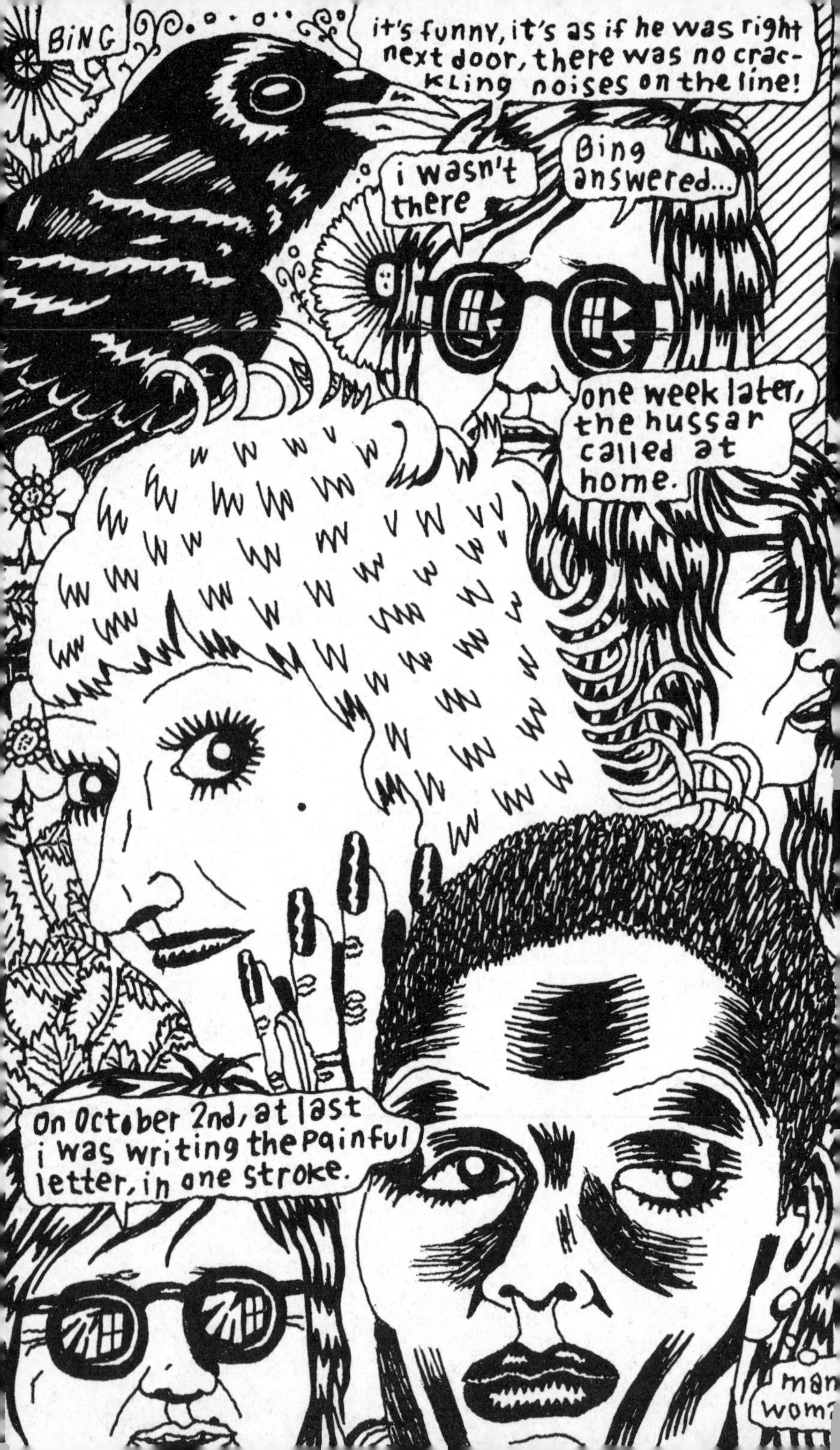
BiNG
it's funny, it's as if he was right next door, there was no crac-kling noises on the line!
Bing answered...
i wasn't there
one week later, the hussar called at home.
On October 2nd, at last i was writing the painful letter, in one stroke.
man
wom

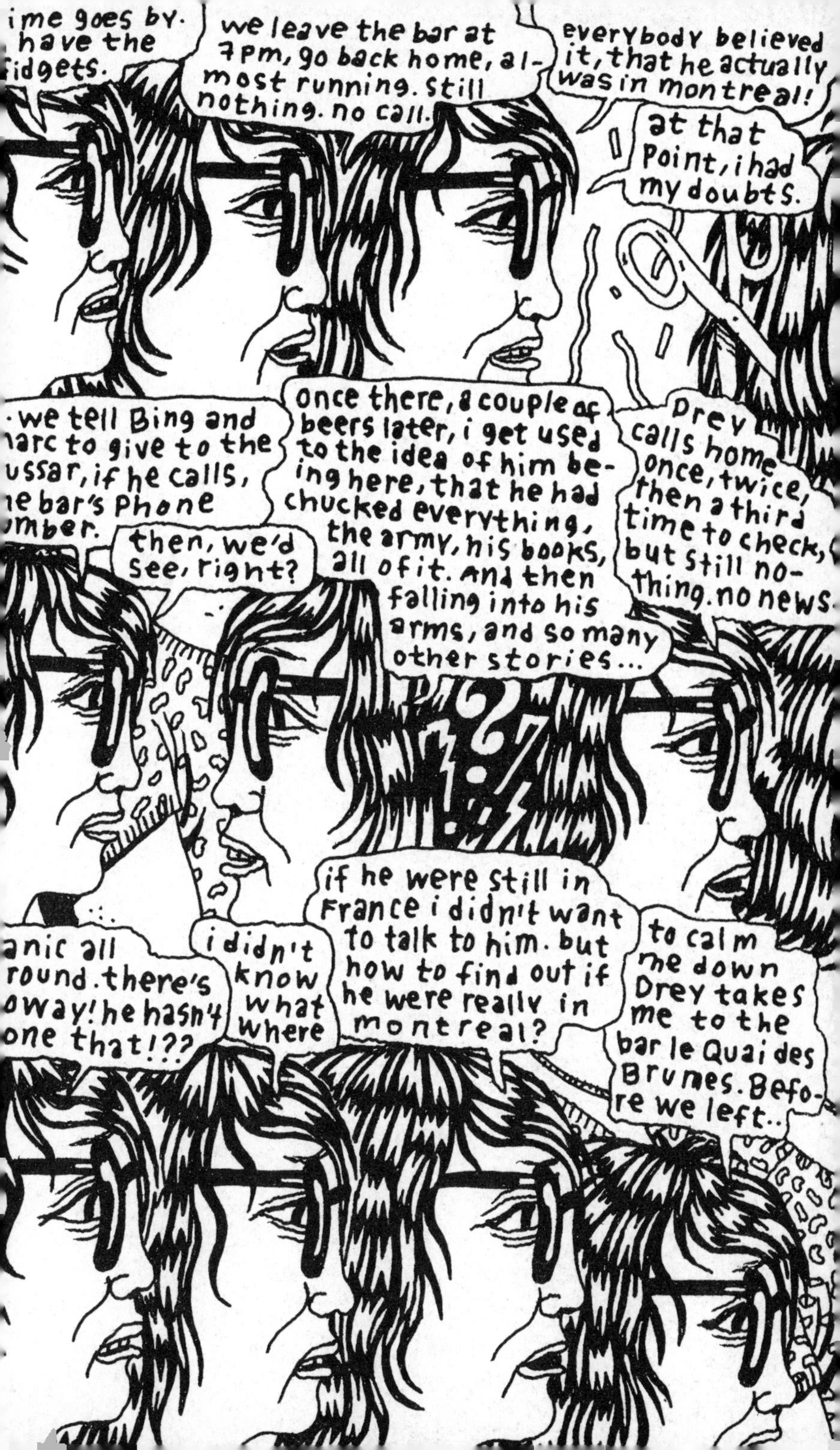
ime goes by. have the fidgets.
we leave the bar at 7pm, go back home, almost running. still nothing. no call.
everybody believed it, that he actually was in montreal!
at that point, i had my doubts.
we tell Bing and marc to give to the ussar, if he calls, the bar's phone umber.
then, we'd see, right?
once there, a couple of beers later, i get used to the idea of him being here, that he had chucked everything, the army, his books, all of it. and then falling into his arms, and so many other stories...
Drey calls home once, twice, then a third time to check, but still nothing. no news.
anic all round. there's o way! he hasn't one that!??
i didn't know what where
if he were still in France i didn't want to talk to him. but how to find out if he were really in montreal?
to calm me down Drey takes me to the bar le Quai des Brunes. Before we left...

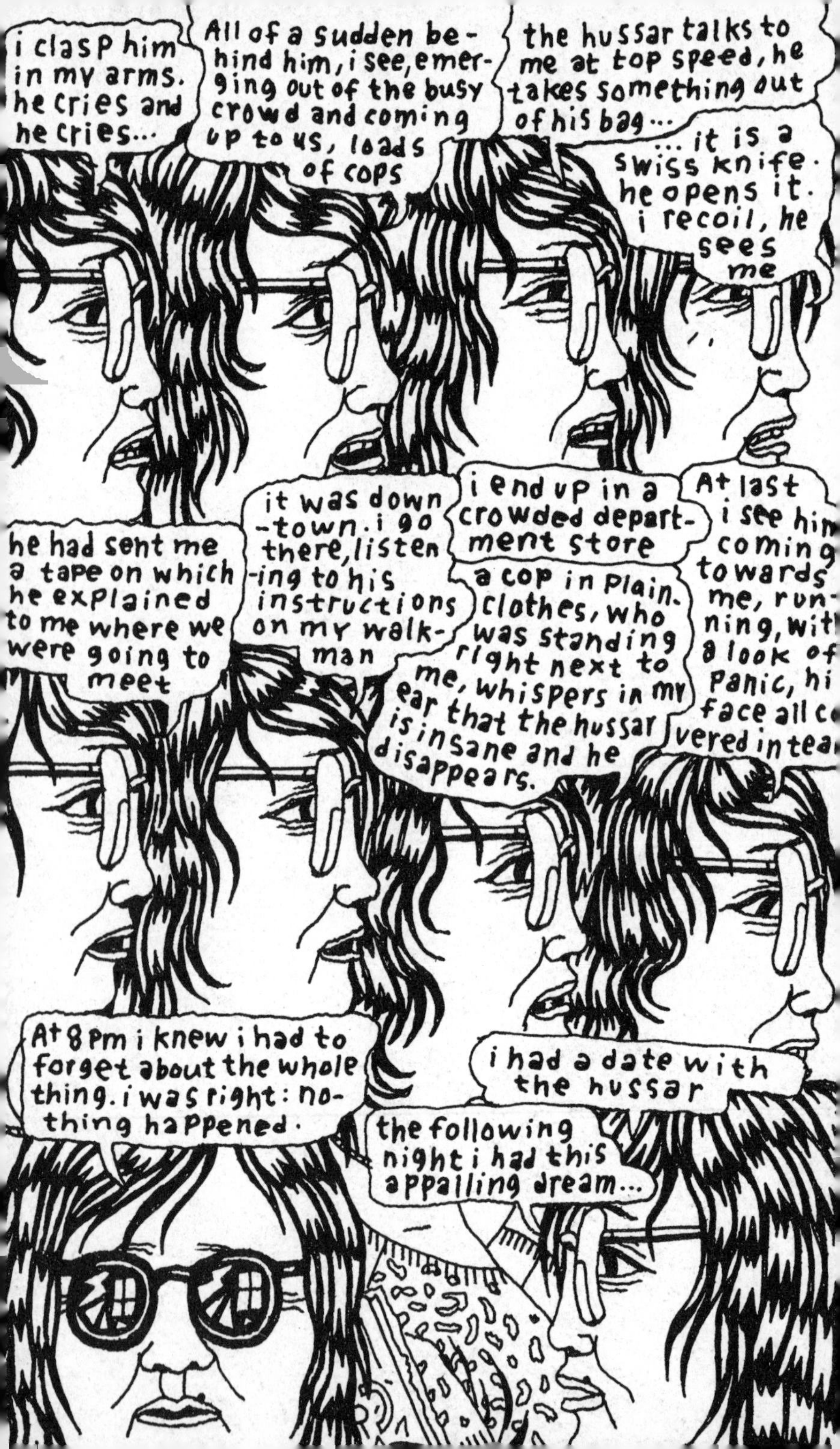
i had a date with the hussar
At 8 pm i knew i had to forget about the whole thing. i was right: nothing happened.
the following night i had this appalling dream...
he had sent me a tape on which he explained to me where we were going to meet
it was down-town. i go there, listen-ing to his instructions on my walk-man
i end up in a crowded depart-ment store
a cop in plain-clothes, who was standing right next to me, whispers in my ear that the hussar is insane and he disappears.
At last i see hi coming towards me, run-ning, wit a look of panic, hi face all c vered in tea
i clasp him in my arms. he cries and he cries...
All of a sudden be-hind him, i see, emer-ging out of the busy crowd and coming up to us, loads of cops
the hussar talks to me at top speed, he takes something out of his bag...
... it is a swiss knife. he opens it. i recoil, he sees me

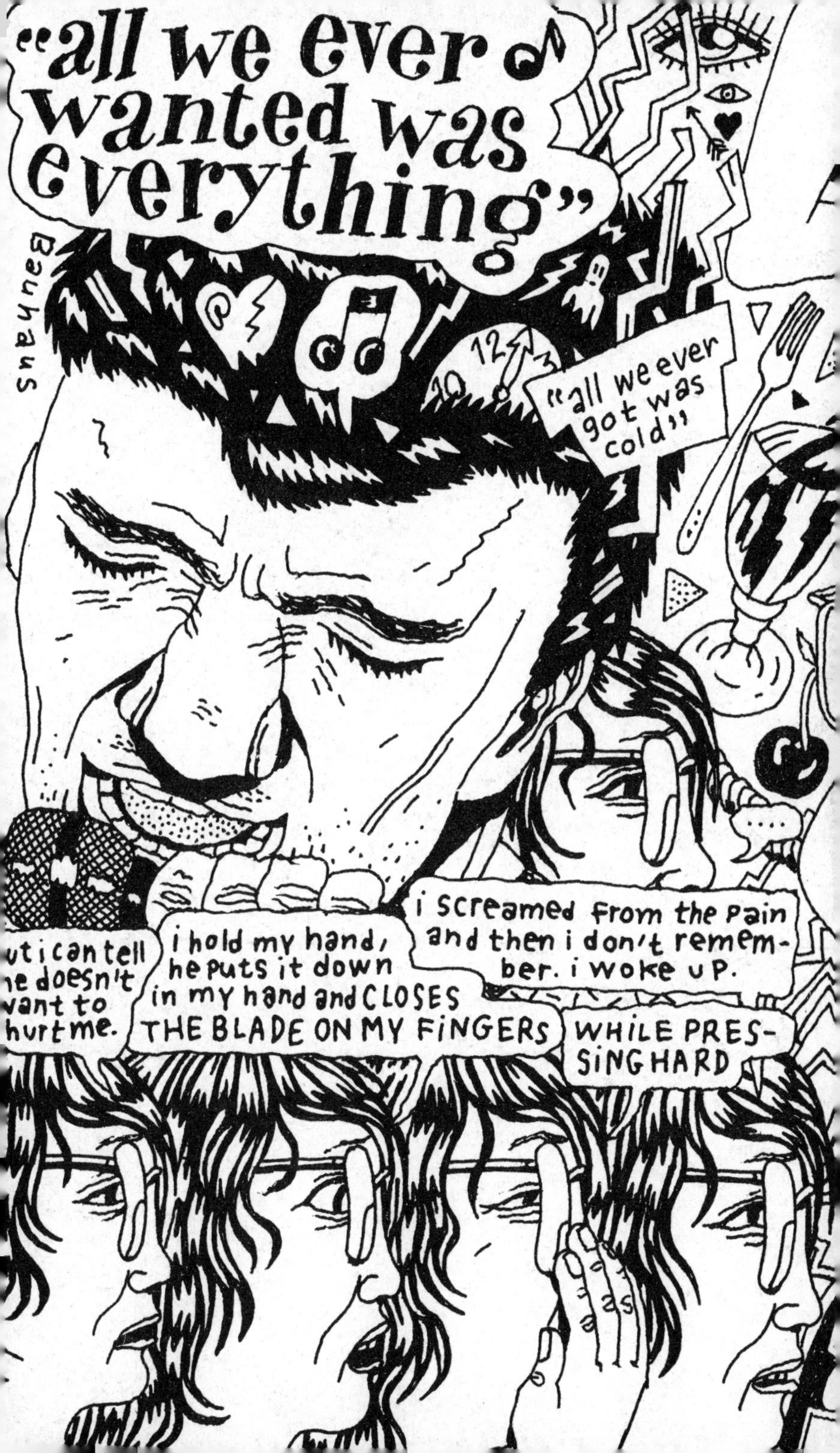
"all we ever wanted was everything"
Bauhaus
"all we ever got was cold"
ut i can tell
e doesn't
vant to
hurt me.
i hold my hand, he puts it down in my hand and CLOSES THE BLADE ON MY FINGERS
WHILE PRES-SING HARD
i screamed from the pain and then i don't remem-ber. i woke up.

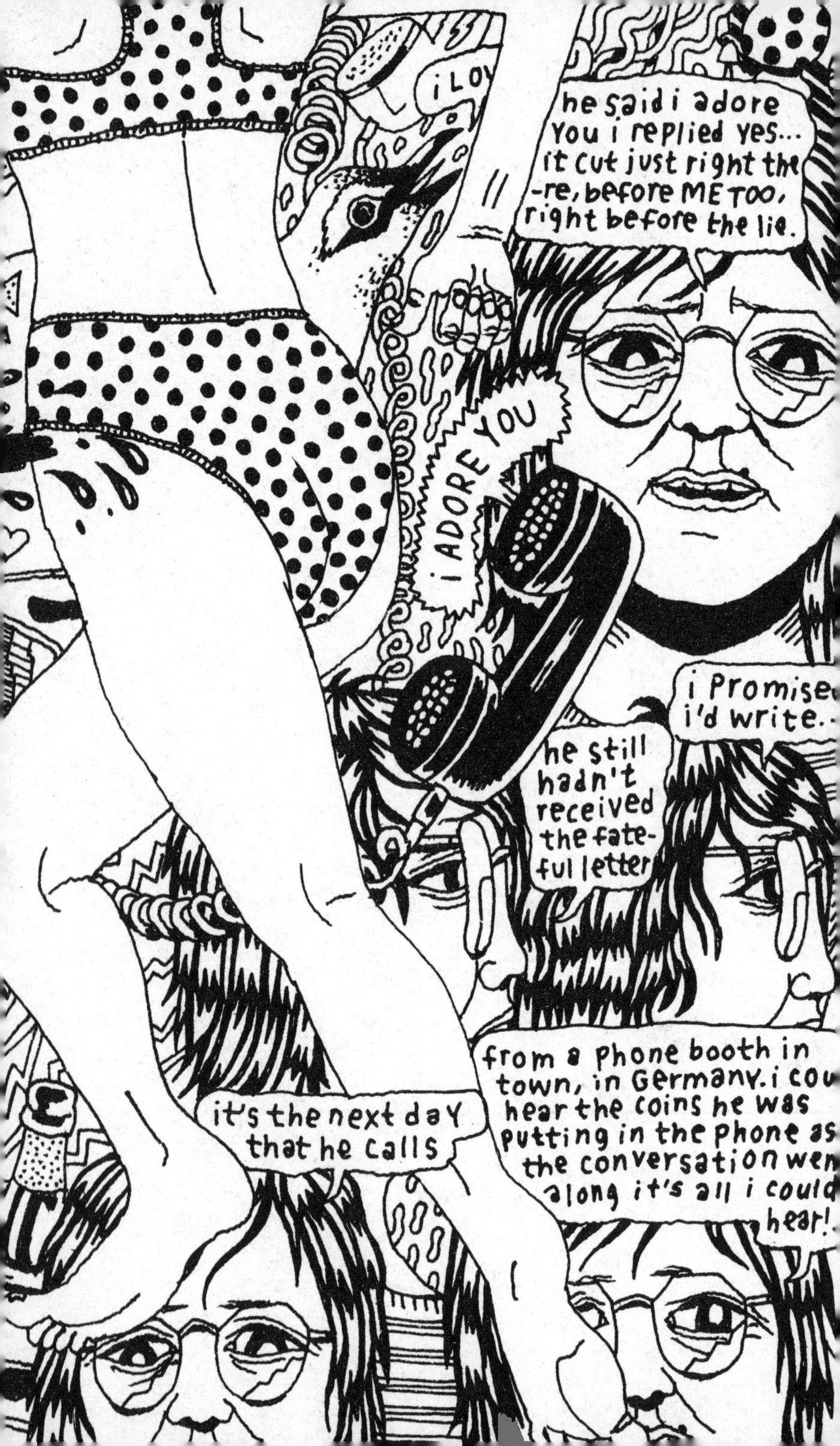
i LO
he said i adore you i replied yes... it cut just right the -re, before ME TOO, right before the lie.
i ADORE YOU
i Promise
i'd write..
he still hadn't received the fate-ful letter
from a phone booth in town, in Germany. i cou
hear the coins he was putting in the phone as the conversation wen along it's all i could hear!
it's the next day that he calls

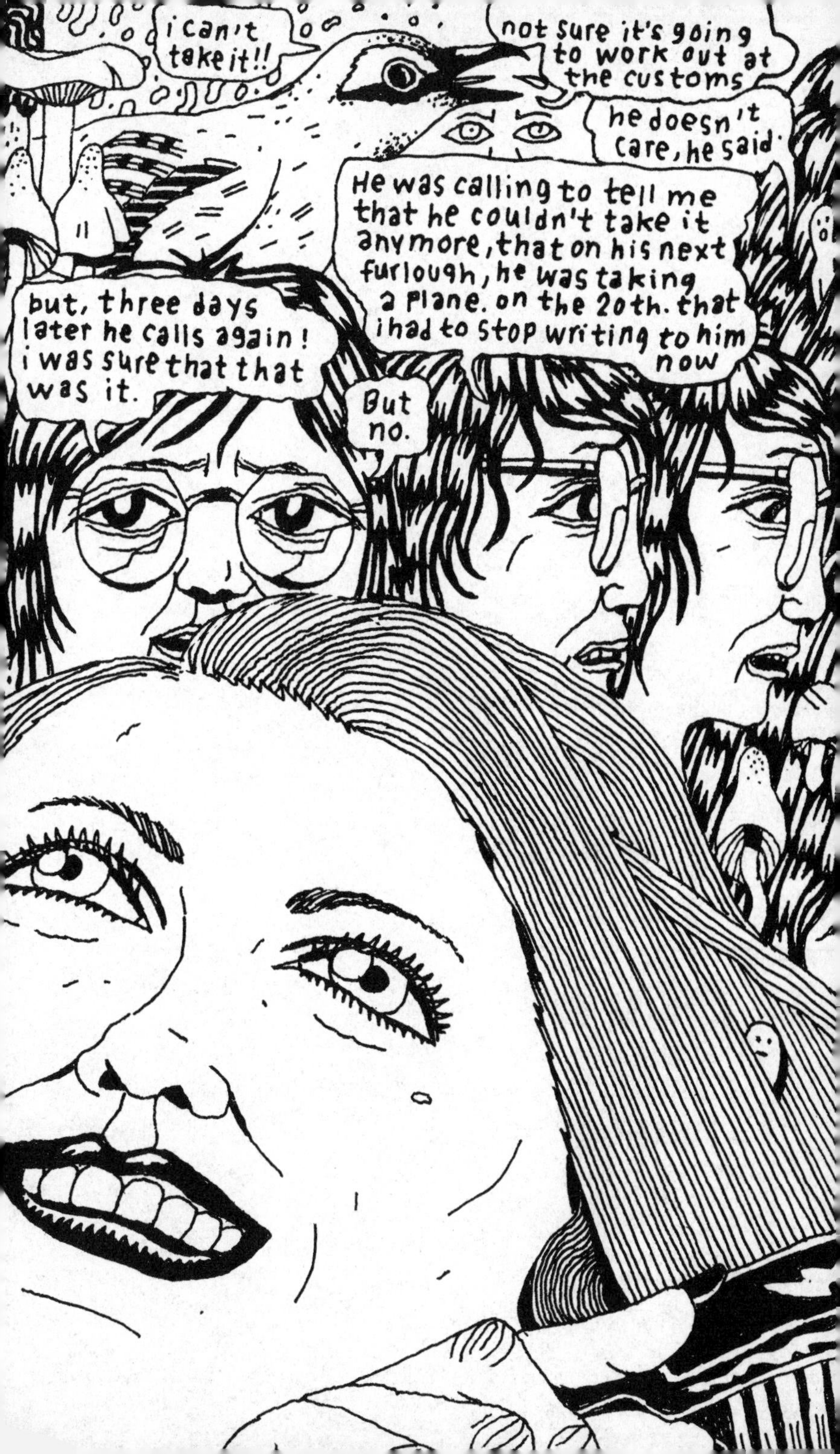
i can't take it!!
not sure it's going to work out at the customs
he doesn't care, he said
He was calling to tell me that he couldn't take it anymore, that on his next furlough, he was taking a plane. on the 20th. that i had to stop writing to him now
but, three days later he calls again! i was sure that that was it.
But no.

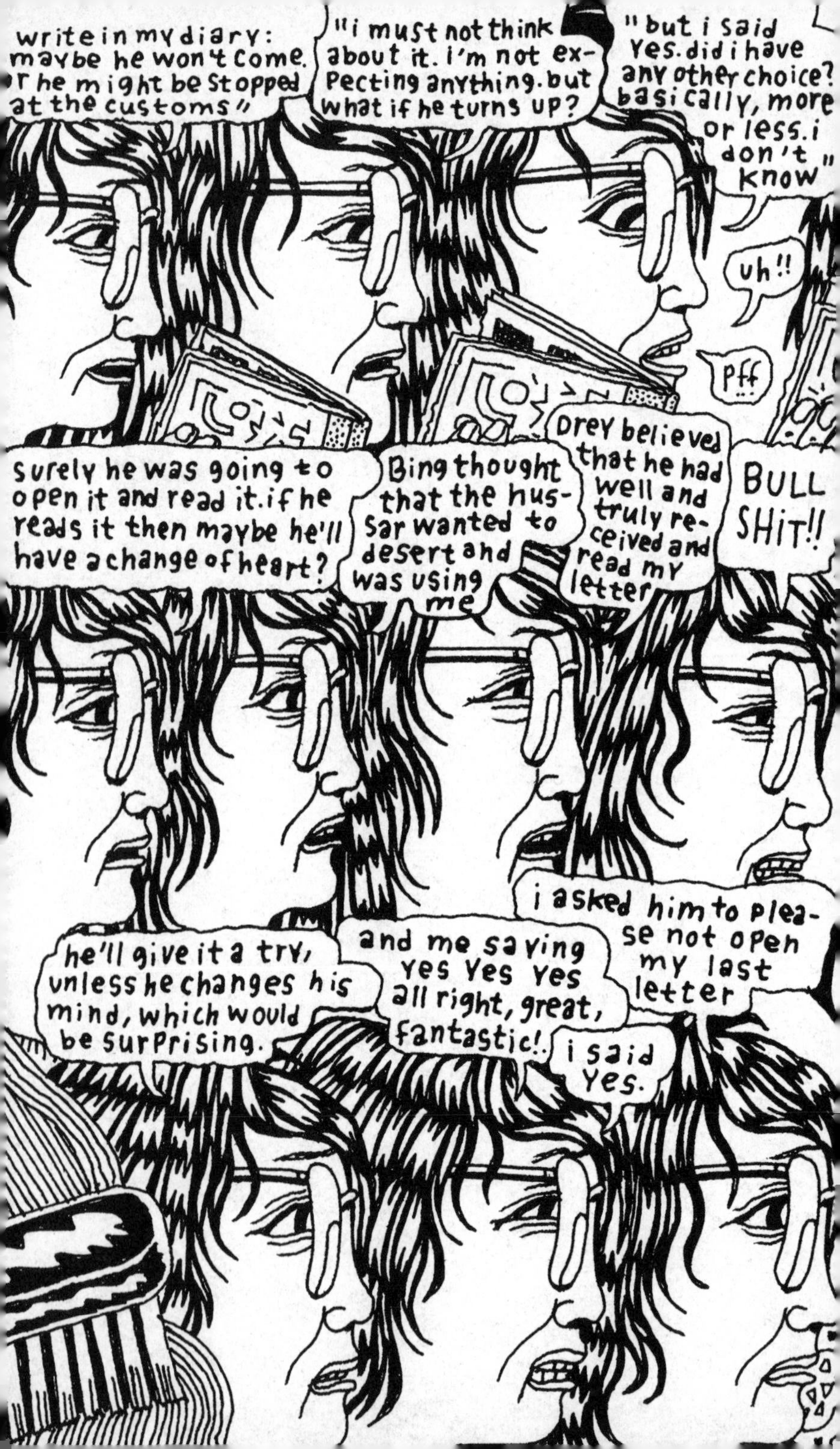
write in my diary: maybe he won't come. or he might be stopped at the customs"
"i must not think about it. i'm not expecting anything. but what if he turns up?
"but i said yes. did i have any other choice? basically, more or less. i don't know"
uh!!
pff...
surely he was going to open it and read it. if he reads it then maybe he'll have a change of heart?
Bing thought that the hussar wanted to desert and was using me
Drey believed that he had well and truly received and read my letter
BULL SHIT!!
he'll give it a try, unless he changes his mind, which would be surprising.
and me saying yes yes yes all right, great, fantastic!.
i asked him to please not open my last letter
i said yes.

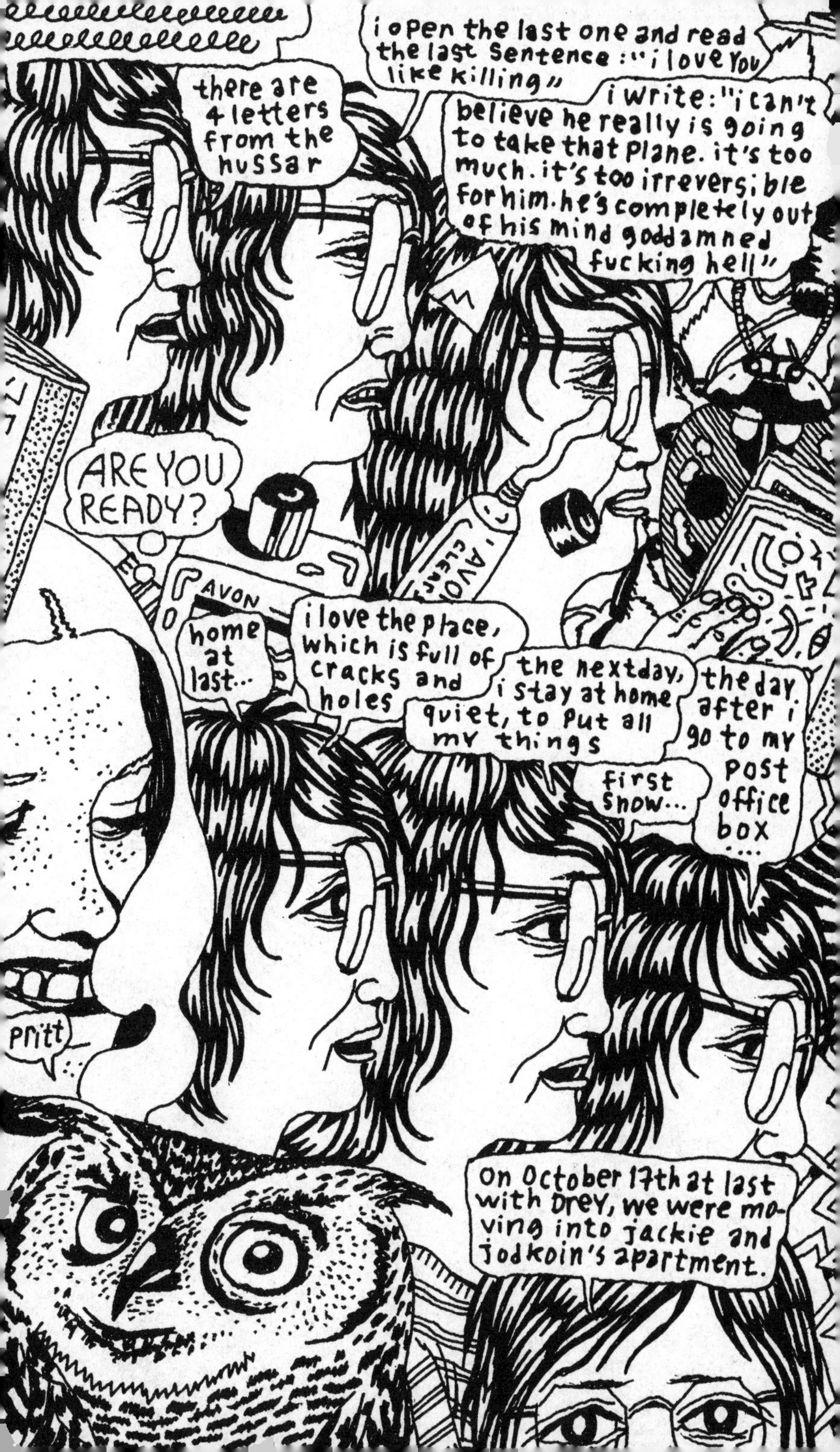
there are 4 letters from the hussar
i open the last one and read the last sentence : "i love you like killing"
i write: "i can't believe he really is going to take that plane. it's too much. it's too irreversible for him. he's completely out of his mind goddamned fucking hell"
ARE YOU READY?
AVON
AVON
home at last...
i love the place, which is full of cracks and holes
the nextday, i stay at home quiet, to put all my things
first snow...
the day after i go to my post office box ...
pritt
On October 17th at last with Drey, we were moving into jackie and Jodkoin's apartment.

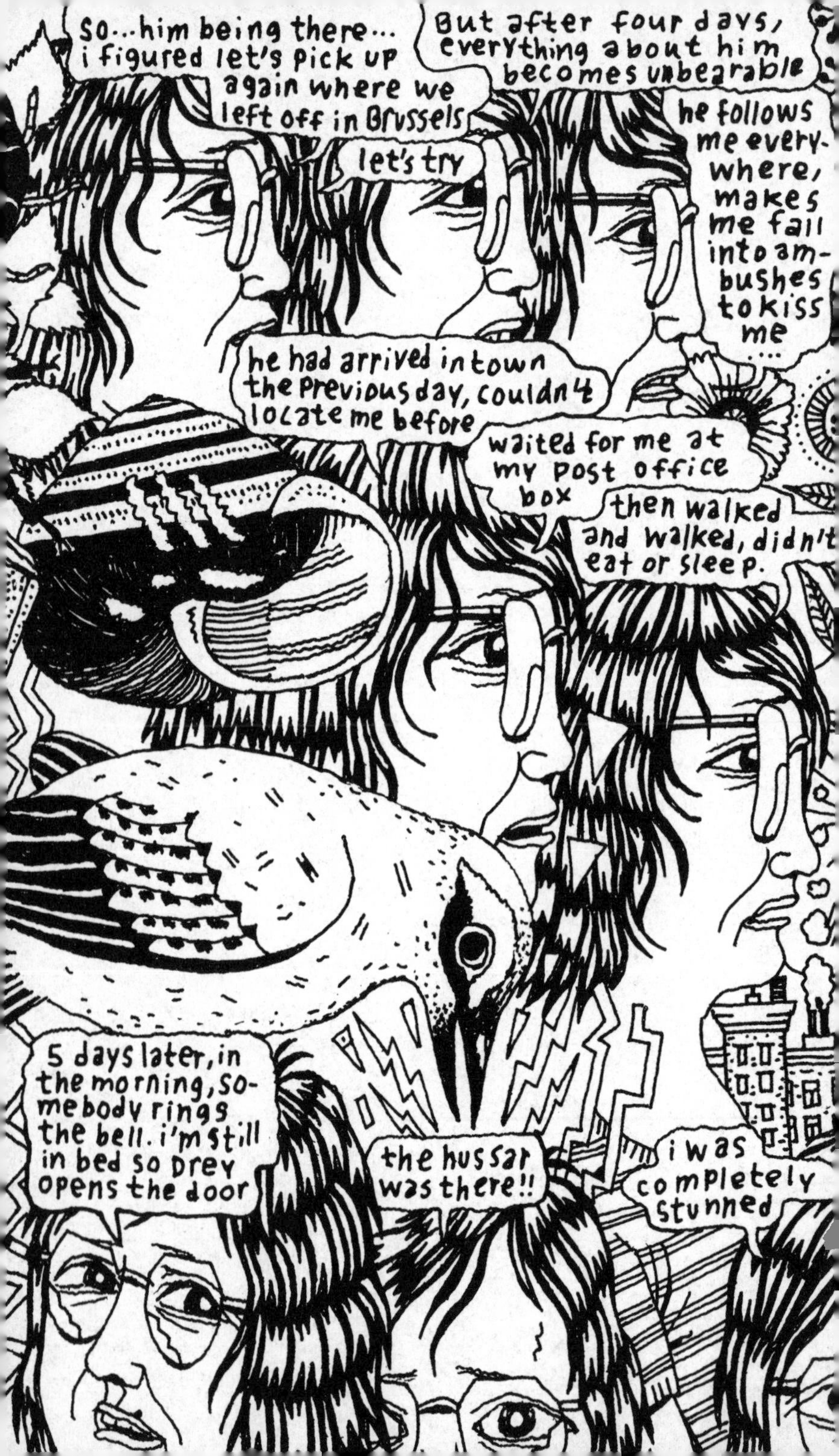
so...him being there... i figured let's pick up again where we left off in Brussels
let's try
But after four days, everything about him becomes unbearable
he follows me everywhere, makes me fall into ambushes to kiss me ...
he had arrived in town the previous day, couldn't locate me before
waited for me at my post office box
then walked and walked, didn't eat or sleep.
5 days later, in the morning, somebody rings the bell. i'm still in bed so Drey opens the door
the hussar was there!!
i was completely stunned

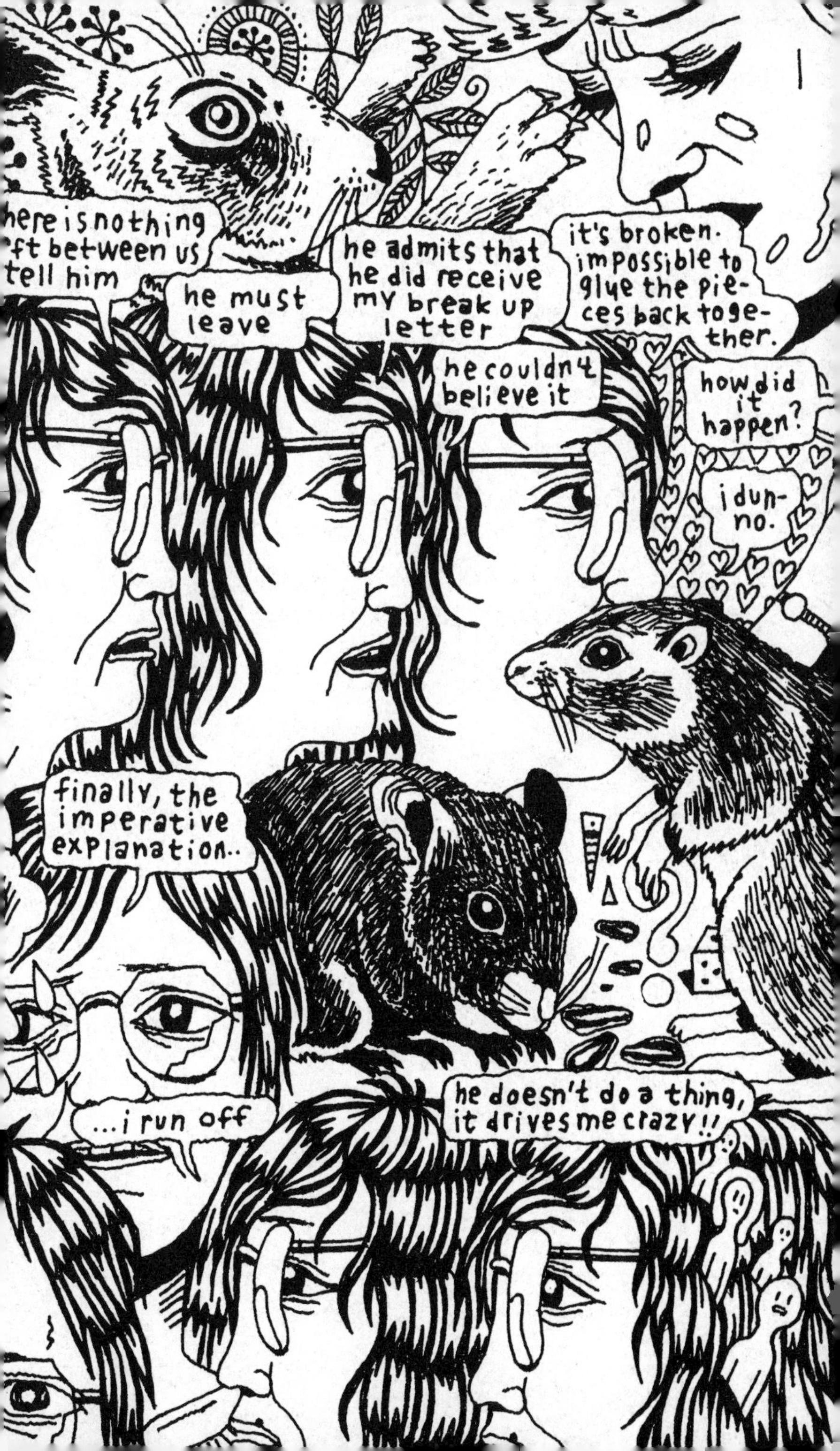
here is nothing
ft between us
tell him
he must leave
he admits that he did receive my break up letter
it's broken. impossible to glue the pieces back together.
he couldn't believe it
how did it happen?
i dunno.
finally, the imperative explanation..
...i run off
he doesn't do a thing, it drives me crazy!!

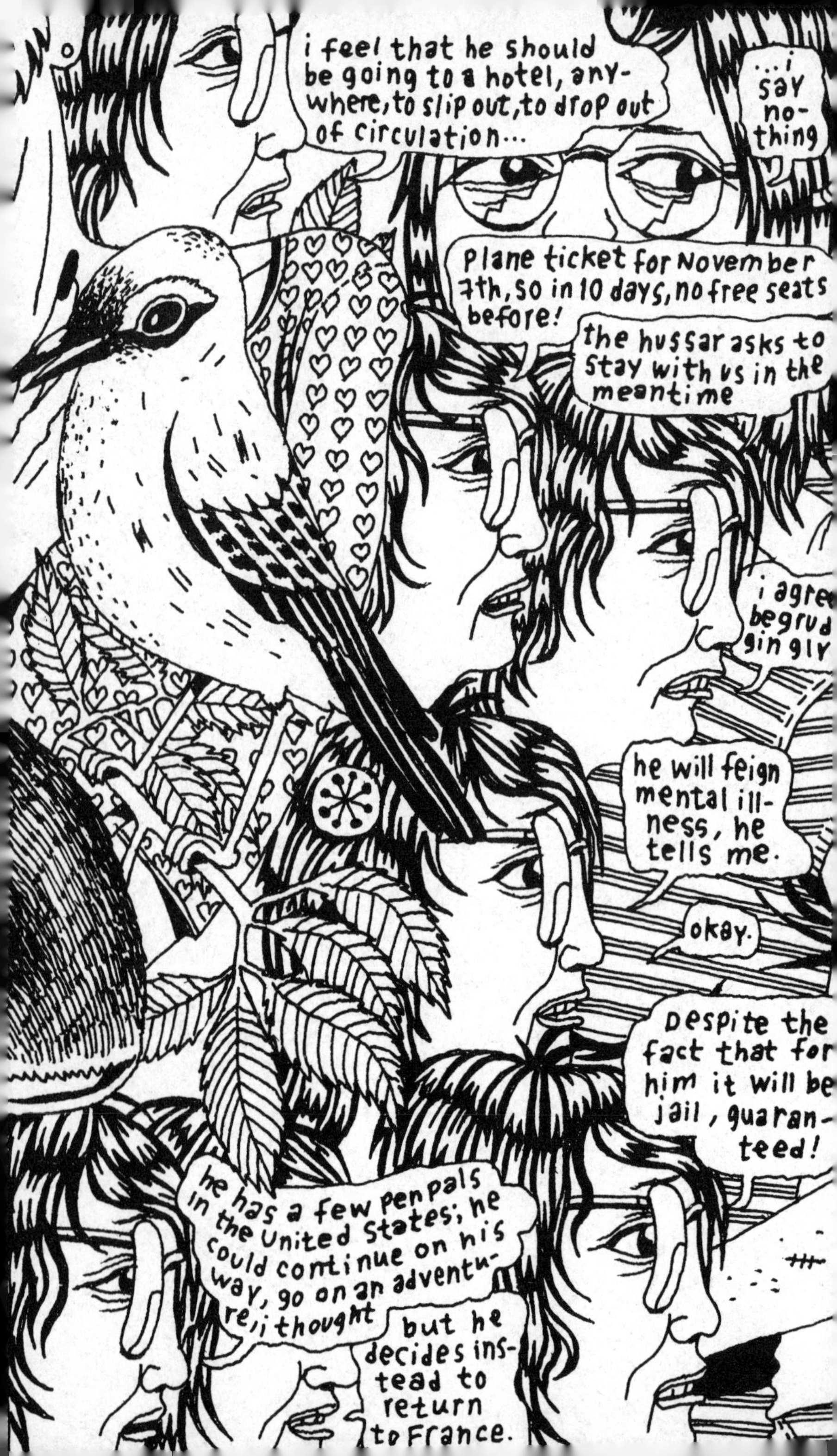
i feel that he should be going to a hotel, anywhere, to slip out, to drop out of circulation...
...i say nothing
plane ticket for November 7th, so in 10 days, no free seats before!
the hussar asks to stay with us in the meantime
i agree begrudgingly
he will feign mental illness, he tells me.
okay.
Despite the fact that for him it will be jail, guaranteed!
he has a few pen pals in the United States; he could continue on his way, go on an adventure, i thought
but he decides instead to return to France.

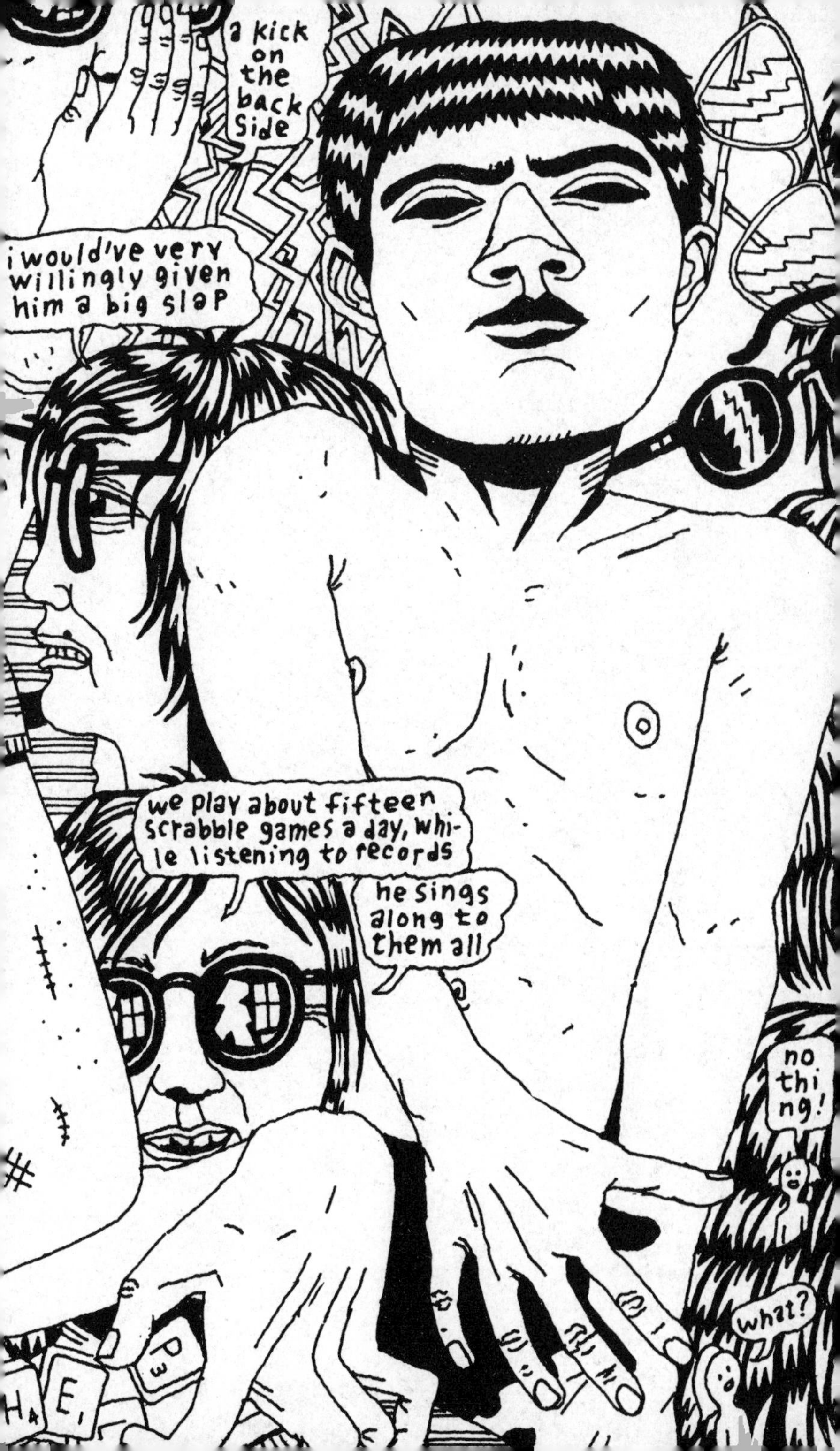
a kick on the back side
i would've very willingly given him a big slap
we play about fifteen scrabble games a day, while listening to records
he sings along to them all
no thing!
what?

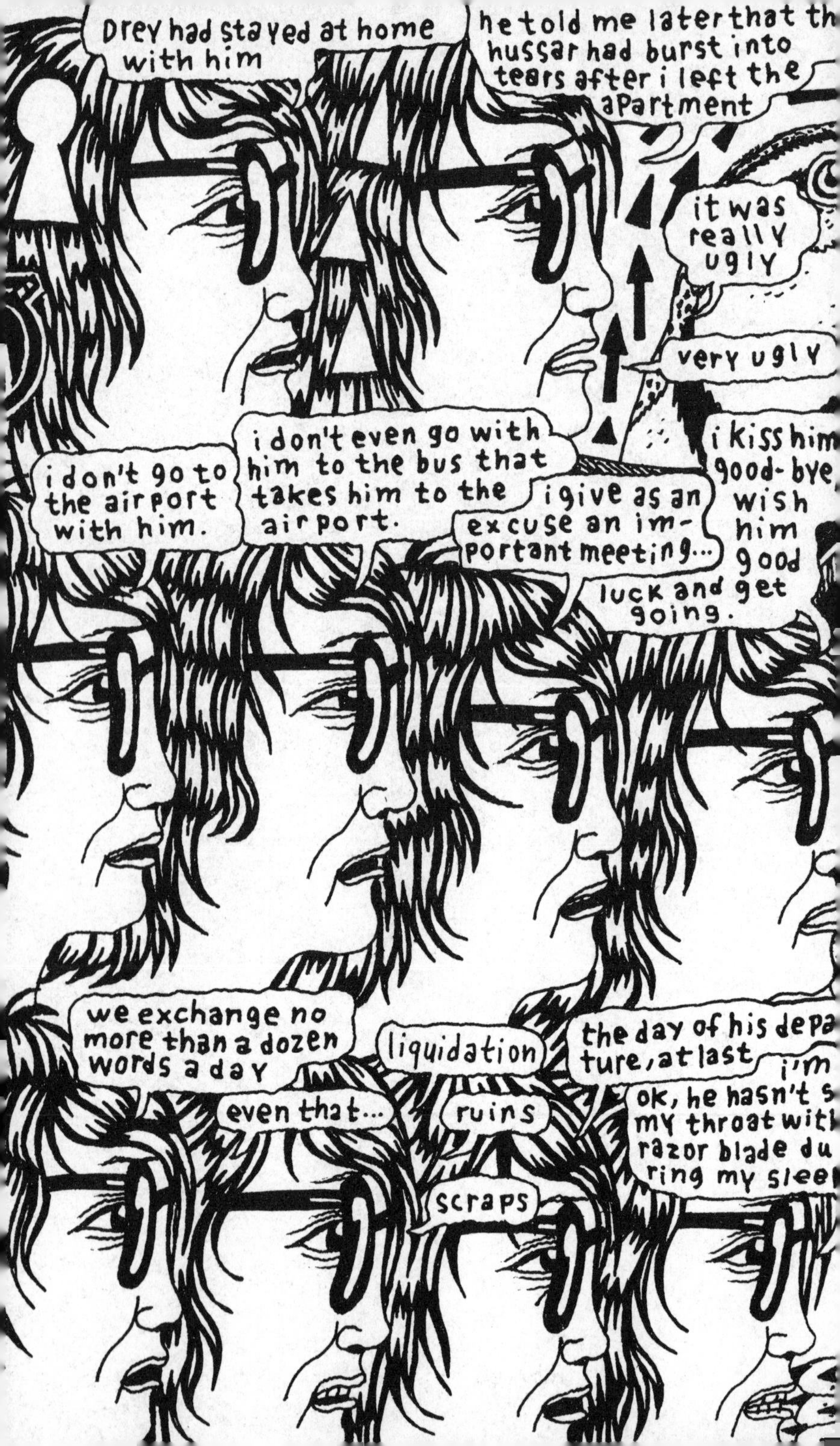
Drey had stayed at home with him
he told me later that th
hussar had burst into tears after i left the apartment
it was really ugly
very ugly
i don't go to the airport with him.
i don't even go with him to the bus that takes him to the airport.
i give as an excuse an important meeting...
i kiss him good-bye, wish him good luck and get going.
we exchange no more than a dozen words a day
even that...
liquidation
ruins
scraps
the day of his depa ture, at last
i'm ok, he hasn't s my throat with razor blade du ring my slee

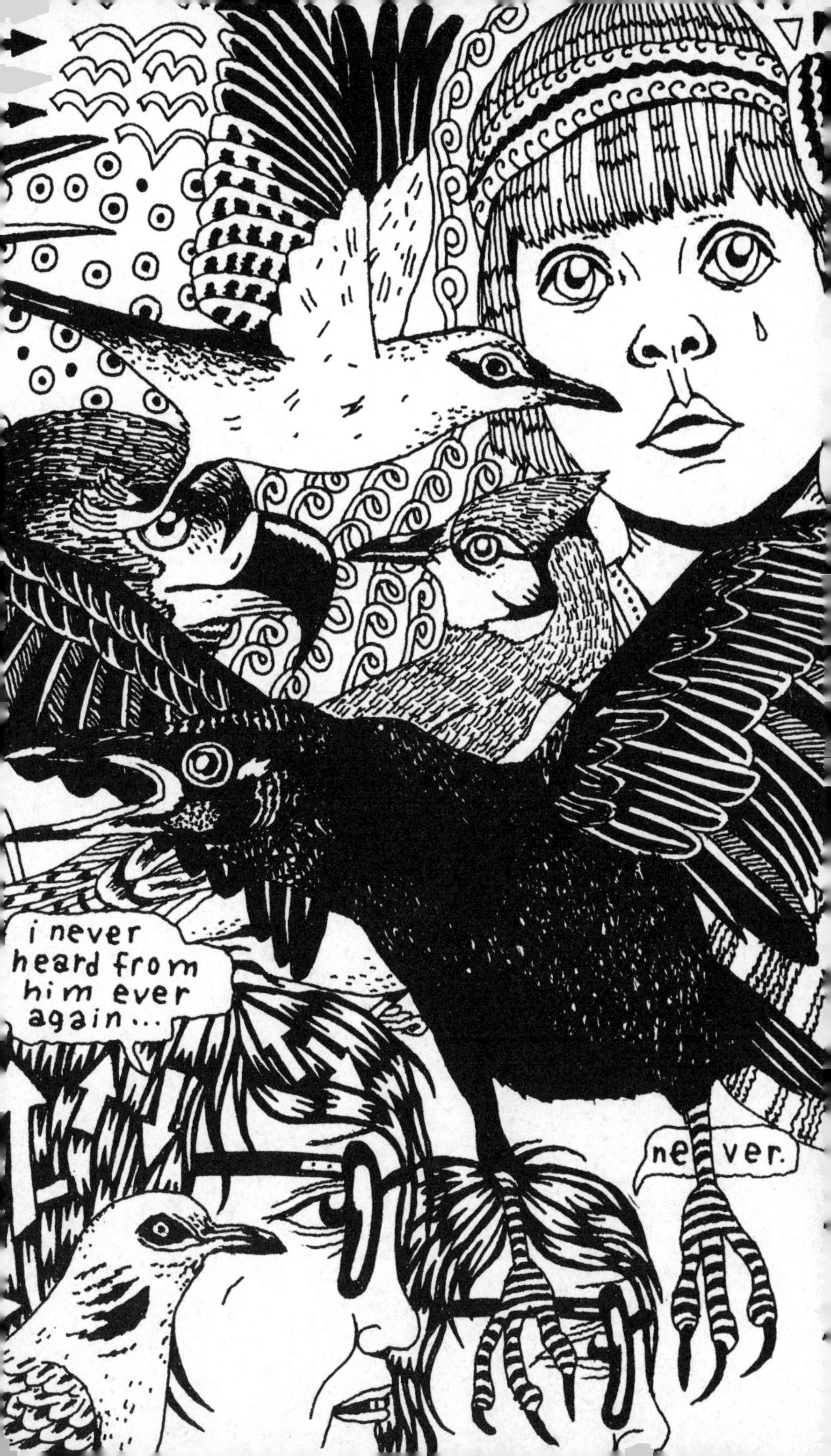
i never heard from him ever again...
never.

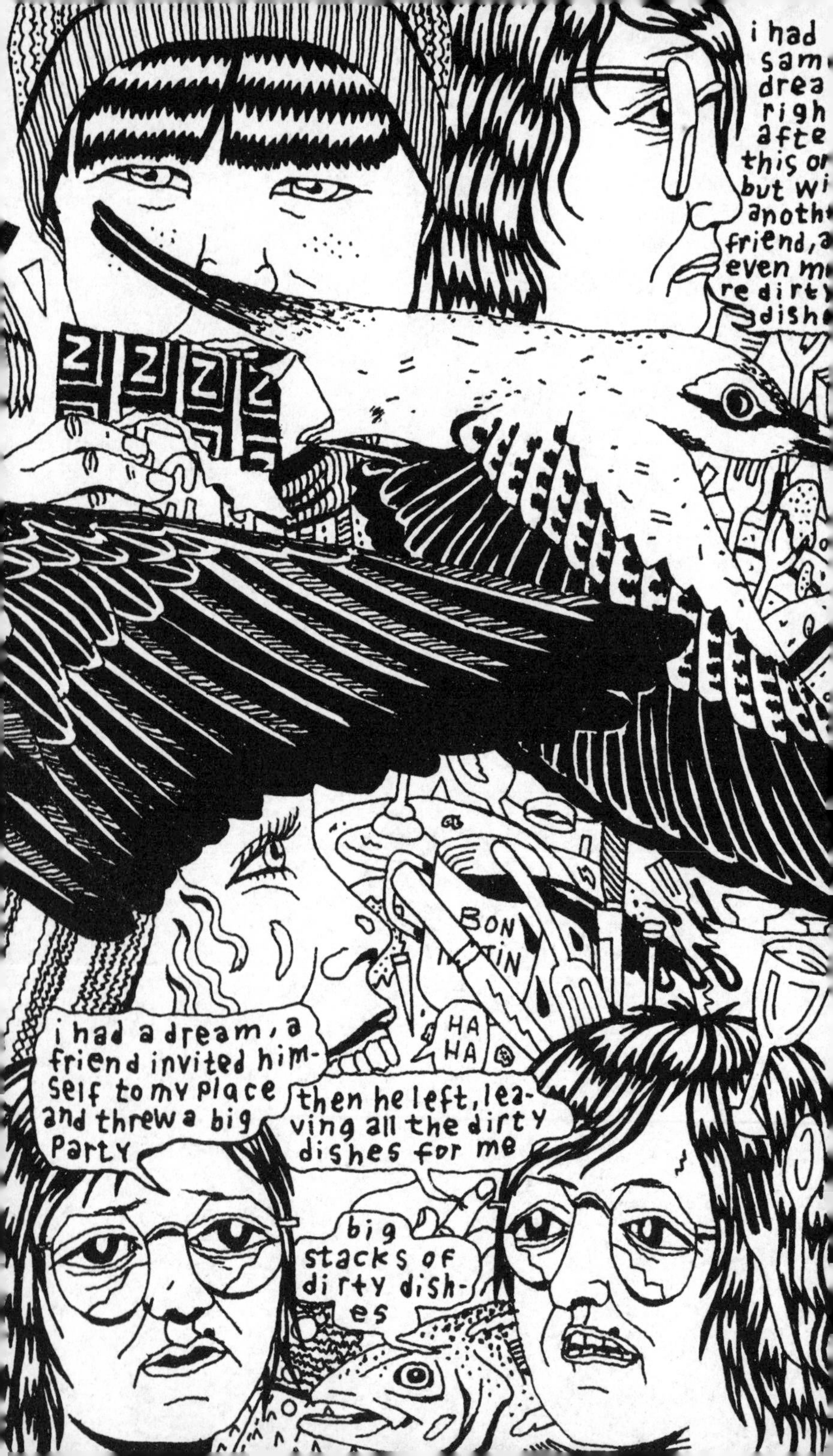

i had sam
drea
righ
afte
this or
but wi
anoth
friend, a
even mo
re dirty
dishe
ZZZZ
BON
HA HA
i had a dream, a friend invited himself to my place and threw a big party
then he left, leaving all the dirty dishes for me
big stacks of dirty dishes

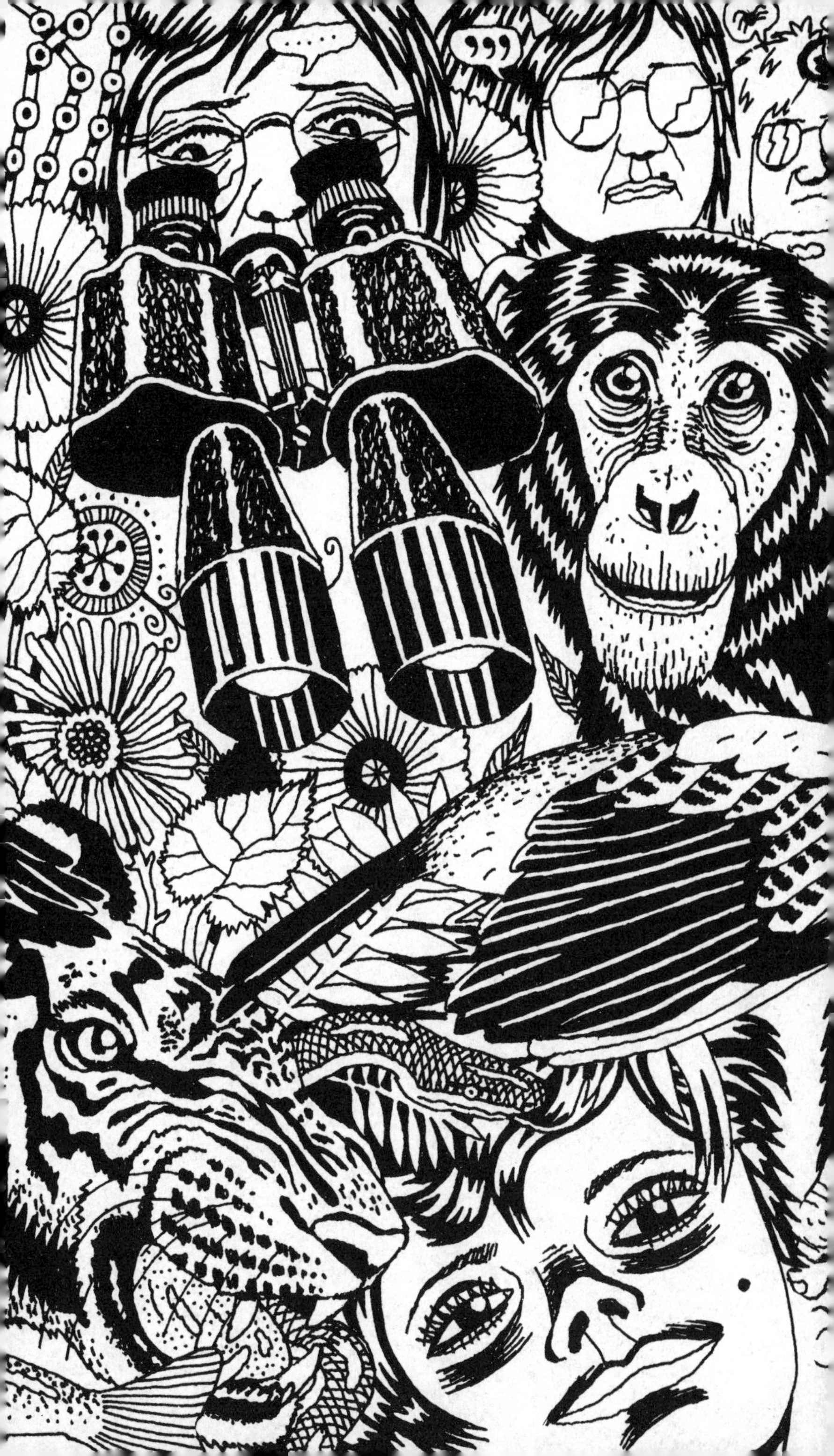

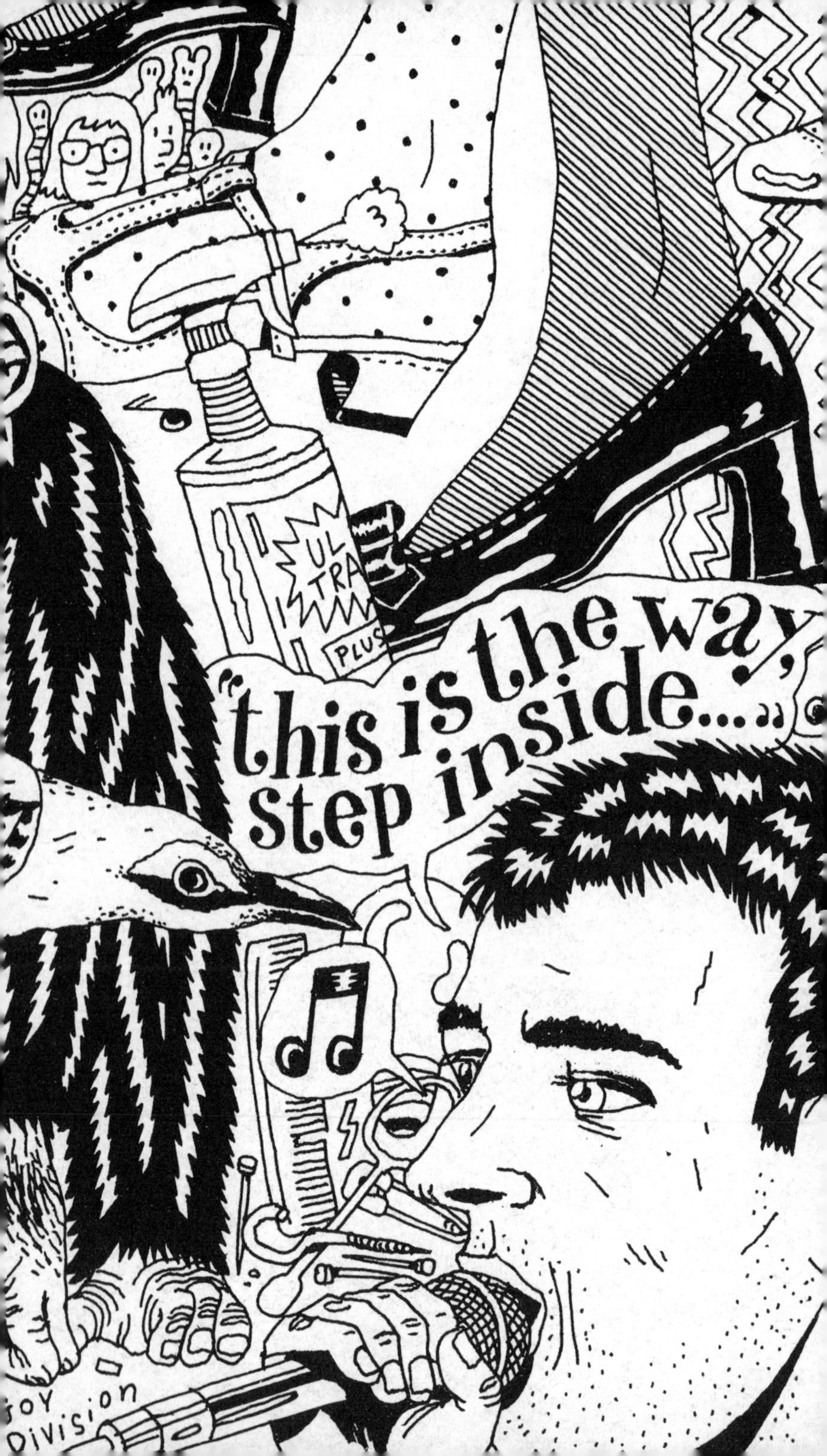
ULTRA
PLUS
"this is the way, step inside..."
JOY DIVISION

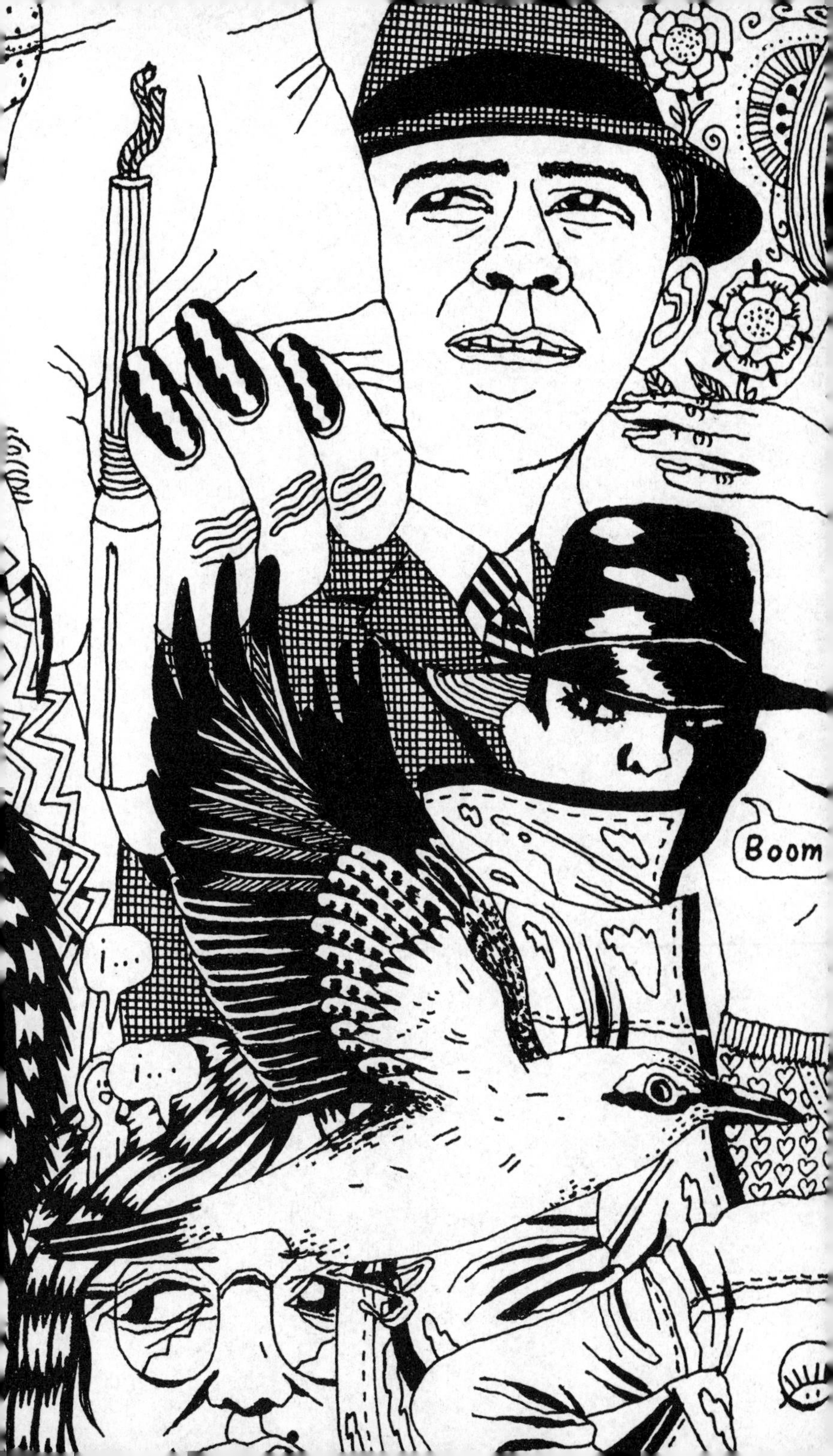
Boom
i...
i...

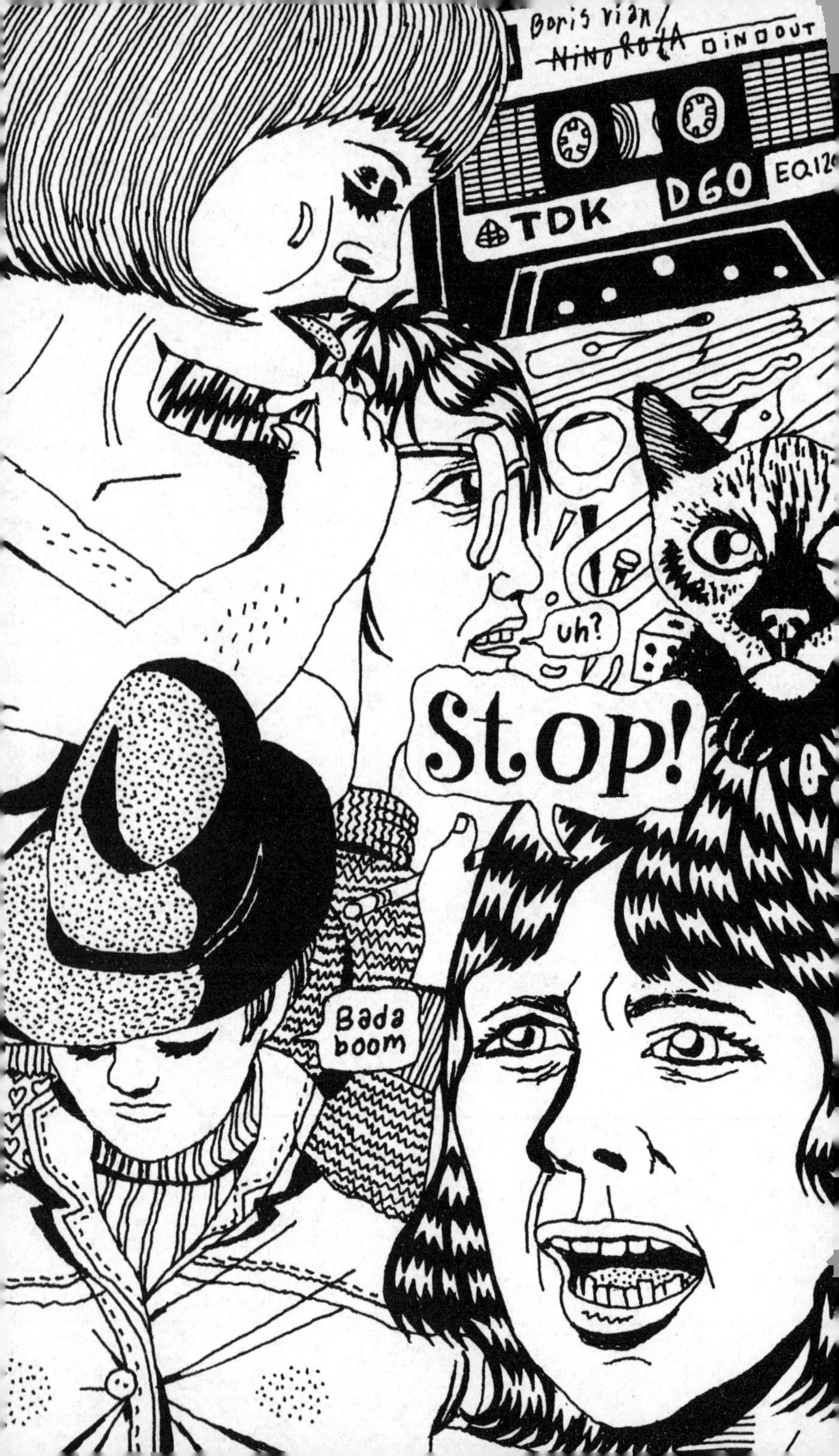
Boris vian /
NiNo RoTA
IN OUT
TDK
D60
uh?
Stop!
Bada boom

curtain

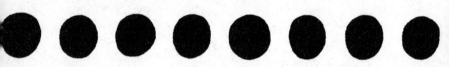

• drawnandquarterly.com juliedoucet.net • ISBN 978-1-77046-498-8 • First edition: March 2022; Second Printing: June 2022 • Printed in China • 10 9 8 7 6 5 4 3 2 • Cataloguing data available from Library and Archives Canada • Published in the USA by Drawn & Quarterly, a client publisher of Farrar, Straus and Giroux; Published in Canada by Drawn & Quarterly, a client publisher of Raincoast Books; Published in the United Kingdom by Drawn & Quarterly, a client publisher of Publishers Group UK • Drawn & Quarterly acknowledges

Canada

the support of the Government of Canada and the Canada Council for the Arts for our publishing program • Drawn & Quarterly reconnaît l'aide financière du gouvernement du Québec par l'entremise de la Société de développement des entreprises culturelles (SODEC) pour nos activités d'édition. Gouvernement du Québec—Programme de crédit d'impôt pour l'édition de livres—Gestion

Québec

SODEC. La création de cette oeuvre a été rendue possible grâce à l'appui financier du Conseil des arts du Québec.